THE UNIVERSITY OF
WINCHESTER

Martial Rose Library
Tel: 01962 827306

To be returned on or before the day marked above, subject to recall.

Becon

Teach   ng

D1332917

UNIVERSITY OF
WINCHESTER

KA 0430303 2

SAGE was founded in 1965 by Sara Miller McCune to support the dissemination of usable knowledge by publishing innovative and high-quality research and teaching content. Today, we publish more than 750 journals, including those of more than 300 learned societies, more than 800 new books per year, and a growing range of library products including archives, data, case studies, reports, conference highlights, and video. SAGE remains majority-owned by our founder, and after Sara's lifetime will become owned by a charitable trust that secures our continued independence.

Los Angeles | London | Washington DC | New Delhi | Singapore

Becoming a
Teacher of Reading

Margaret Perkins

UNIVERSITY OF WINCHESTER
LIBRARY

Los Angeles | London | New Delhi
Singapore | Washington DC

Los Angeles | London | New Delhi
Singapore | Washington DC

SAGE Publications Ltd
1 Oliver's Yard
55 City Road
London EC1Y 1SP

SAGE Publications Inc.
2455 Teller Road
Thousand Oaks, California 91320

SAGE Publications India Pvt Ltd
B 1/I 1 Mohan Cooperative Industrial Area
Mathura Road
New Delhi 110 044

SAGE Publications Asia-Pacific Pte Ltd
3 Church Street
#10-04 Samsung Hub
Singapore 049483

Editor: James Clark
Assistant editor: Rachael Plant
Production editor: Tom Bedford
Copyeditor: Rose James
Proofreader: Salia Nessa
Indexer: David Rudeforth
Marketing manager: Lorna Patkai
Cover design: Naomi Robinson
Typeset by: C&M Digitals (P) Ltd, Chennai, India
Printed and bound by CPI Group (UK) Ltd,
Croydon, CR0 4YY

© Margaret Perkins 2015

First published 2015

Apart from any fair dealing for the purposes of research or
private study, or criticism or review, as permitted under the
Copyright, Designs and Patents Act, 1988, this publication
may be reproduced, stored or transmitted in any form, or by
any means, only with the prior permission in writing of the
publishers, or in the case of reprographic reproduction, in
accordance with the terms of licences issued by the Copyright
Licensing Agency. Enquiries concerning reproduction outside
those terms should be sent to the publishers.

Library of Congress Control Number: 2014948707

British Library Cataloguing in Publication data

A catalogue record for this book is available from
the British Library

UNIVERSITY OF WINCHESTER

04303052   372.4
            PER

ISBN 978-1-4462-7313-5
ISBN 978-1-4462-7314-2 (pbk)

At SAGE we take sustainability seriously. Most of our products are printed in the UK using FSC papers and boards.
When we print overseas we ensure sustainable papers are used as measured by the Egmont grading system.
We undertake an annual audit to monitor our sustainability.

For my mother, Peggy Jackson, who taught hundreds of children to read, including me.

CONTENTS

ABOUT THE AUTHOR

Margaret Perkins has been working in initial teacher education for many years with undergraduates, postgraduates and those on employment-based routes in different provider institutions. She is an experienced primary teacher and has gone back into school to teach for periods varying between a day and a year since entering higher education. She is now managing the primary School Direct Programme at the University of Reading. This is a large programme which works with trainees in schools located in more than eight different authorities. She also teaches English specialists on the undergraduate course and loves the excuse to read lots of different books and talk about them!

ACKNOWLEDGEMENTS

Author acknowledgements

This book is the product of many years of teaching English to intending primary teachers. I am grateful both to all those trainees who have had to sit through my lectures and workshops and to all those colleagues with whom I have worked. All of you have been an inspiration to me and discussions with you have refined and challenged my thinking. You have been a support when it has sometimes felt as though the world is against us. I apologise to anyone whose work I have inadvertently used without acknowledgement. Please contact me and I will put it right. Any fault is mine entirely.

I would also like to thank my friend and colleague, Liz How. She gave me her time by talking through ideas and reading and commenting on drafts as a critical friend and I am so grateful for that.

Thank you also to my family, Jonathan, Hannah and Ben, who have put up with much during the writing process.

Soli Deo Gloria.

Publisher acknowledgements

SAGE would like to thank the following reviewers whose comments at the early stages of this project helped to shape the book:

Jane Briggs, University of Brighton

Jane Carter, University of the West of England

Val Chamberlain, Edge Hill University

Ruth Harrison-Palmer, University of Cumbria

Helen Hendry, Bishop Grosseteste University

Thanks also to Christina Schiveree and Doug Buehl for kindly allowing us to use extracts from their reading blogs.

PREFACE

Reading, teaching and learning

For me, the three elements in the subheading are some of the most exciting things in the world, and to put them together in one book is almost too much.

Reading is such a wonderful thing to be able to do. It offers experiences, emotions, relationships and expressions which are either new and challenging or familiar and comforting. Why do I read? I cannot answer that question in any better way than to use the words of Wendy Lesser (2014: 4):

> The kind of pleasure you can get from reading is like no other in the world ... Because reading is such an individual act, the pleasures we derive ... will not be identical. That is as it should be. Reading can result in boredom or transcendence, rage or enthusiasm, depression or hilarity, empathy or contempt, depending on who you are and what the book is and how your life is shaping up at the moment you encounter it. This effect will be particular to each person, and it will change over time, just as the person changes over time – and the richer and more complicated the book is, the more this will be true.

What a privilege it is to be able to introduce children to experiences like that. Being a teacher of reading allows me to have those experiences on an almost daily basis, to watch children and students discover the joys and sorrows of reading and to learn from texts and other readers more about myself and the world.

For me, the heart of reading, teaching and learning is relationship; relationship between reader and text, teacher and learner, reader and reader. These are relationships which are scary and exhilarating but also exciting and supportive. Becoming a teacher of reading is about discovering more of those relationships and introducing others to them.

I think that there is hardly any topic in the field of education which has received so much attention as the teaching of reading. When I began as a young teacher many years ago, who would have dreamt that there would be government policy on how to teach children to read? Being a teacher of reading is one of the most political acts anybody can do. Even a brief review of the history of the teaching of reading reveals changes in emphasis: flash cards to teach sight vocabulary, the whole-language approach and 'real books', language experience with lots of words on tiny cards, the first, fast approach of systematic synthetic phonics. Primary teachers have accommodated the whims of politicians and academics and carried on teaching children to read. The best teachers of reading are those who make decisions about pedagogy and resources according to their professional knowledge and experience and match that to the needs of the children with whom they are currently working. They take what is the best on offer and filter out that which does not work for them at that moment in time. If I have learned anything over the years, it is that one approach does not suit all children.

It is my hope that trainees and teachers who read this book will feel empowered to make those decisions and will gain an understanding of what it is we are teaching when we teach reading. Teachers of reading are under great pressure to comply; the accountability that comes with external forms of assessment and particular definitions of reading is invidious and forces teachers to conform. I hope that within the pages of this book they will find some ideas to enrich the reading curriculum and the confidence to implement them.

I chose the title of this book very carefully. It is not a collection of tips and ideas for teaching children how to read. It is about becoming the sort of teacher who has a deep understanding of what they are teaching and wants to enthuse and inspire children to become readers. Teaching reading is not about following a system; it is about making informed decisions. Those decisions are influenced by the experience of being a reader, critical reflection on research and policy, talking with those who are more experienced, and above all, from knowing children. I hope this book will help you do all those things and so become an enthusiastic and inspirational teacher of reading.

CHAPTER 1

KNOWING ABOUT THE READING PROCESS

Chapter objectives

When you have read this chapter you should have:

- considered your own reading behaviours and how you make sense of a text
- appreciated what different theoretical perspectives can offer to the classroom practice of teachers of reading
- developed an understanding of the theories underpinning practice
- begun to develop the skill of listening to children read analytically.

Introduction

In order to become an effective teacher of reading it is important to be absolutely clear about what it is that we are teaching, and to ask ourselves the questions,

'What is reading?' and 'What happens when we read?'. The answers to these questions are not as straightforward as you might first imagine and many books, learned papers and carefully constructed research projects have been devised in order to find out the answers. There are several aspects to both of these questions. First we need to consider *what* we can find out about the reading process and *how* we can find it out. In recent years, the development of neuroscience as a discipline has enabled researchers to look at what is physically happening in the brain when we read. Other researchers look at what readers actually say when they read aloud, arguing that analysis of the errors made will give some insight into the thought processes. Psychologists look at experimental designs which show either the development of skills over time or the causes of reading success, or more often, of reading failure. Yet other researchers consider the social, cultural and historical expectations on readers and how this impacts on reading behaviours or what readers actually do.

All of these approaches can offer interesting insights into the reading process and how people can best be helped to become readers. This chapter puts forward perspectives on the reading process from a variety of different theoretical viewpoints and considers them from the point of view of an intending teacher of reading. It is important to understand these approaches but even more important to understand how they can help the professional decision making of a teacher. As we will go on to consider in the next chapter, being a teacher is about being able to consider, reflect on and make judgements about policy and research in order to make informed decision about pedagogy. This chapter aims to give teachers of reading an informed basis for those pedagogical decisions about the teaching of reading that they make many hundreds of times each day.

At the outset, it is important to know that each perspective has something to offer the teacher of reading but none can give the whole story. There is much that we do know about the reading process but there is much more that we do not know and it is as important to ask the questions as it is to provide clear answers. Many answers are not clear but lead on to more questions.

Reflecting on your own reading

As a reader, there will often be times when you need to read a text which you find challenging. Remembering those times, it is useful to consider what it is that makes a text challenging to read. Sometimes it is because there are words you have never seen before and do not know how to pronounce, or it may be that you do not understand what the text is about or it may even be that you would prefer to be doing something completely different at the time! The following activity will help to understand what is happening when you read.

Reflective activity

Read the following text (Milsom, 1969:114) and try to work out what it means:

In the essentially non-feudal world of the thirteenth century and later, the assize affords what may be described as a possessory protection for heirs. The demandant in mort d'ancestor is indeed an heir claiming as such, but not, as in a writ of right, basing his claim upon the seisin of a remote ancestor: it was one of his parents, or their or his brother or sister who has died. The question for the assize comprises three points: had this relative been seised on the day that he died; had he died within a limitation period; was the demandant his nearest heir? If yes to all these, the demandant was put in seisin. The principle was later extended to relations more remote by the writs known as aiel, besaiel and cosinage.

I am sure there are no words in that passage which you are not able to read out loud. Some of them might cause you to pause and think a while but for the most part you are able, I imagine, to decode that text fairly well. I wonder how you managed to comprehend it? Most of the words are fairly simple and I imagine that you have an idea of what they mean. Some words, however, will be outside your experience. I do not know what 'seisin' means and so what it means to be 'seised'. I do not know if it has any connection to the word I do know – 'seized'. The word 'affords' in the second line is also rather confusing; in my vocabulary the word 'afford' is something I use when I am going shopping and considering if I should buy something. That does not seem to relate to the way the word is used here and so confuses my meaning-making of the whole text.

As I was reading that text for most of the time the focus of my thinking was on how to make sense of it. The decoding element, for the most part, was subconscious. I was asking all the questions I suggested above and more, and was desperately trying to make connections between what was in the text and what I already know. Finally, I think I have the general gist of what the text is about but could not be very detailed and specific about it. The text was challenging for me to read because it was outside my sphere of experience and knowledge and so I did not have the strategies to make sense of it. Occasionally, what I did know actually hindered my sense-making processes. I could decode it but not understand it.

Making sense of the text

Goodman (1969) believed that the way to understand the reading process is to look at what readers actually do when they read, and so argued that examining the errors or 'miscues' children make when reading aloud will offer a 'window' to their thinking processes. Through this he identified three main sources of information that are drawn on when attempting to make sense of a written text. These are:

- Semantic knowledge. If we know the topic of the text, we can draw on our experience and understanding to make sense of what we are reading. We can also use the illustrations and the context of the text to help us understand.
- Syntactic knowledge. This means that, as fluent users of spoken language, we use our knowledge of the patterns and structures of language to predict and work out what comes next. We might not know grammatical terminology but we know what sounds right and have an empathy with the rhythms of natural language. This, so it is argued, is why it is easier to read texts written in longer natural sentences than short simple sentences.
- Graphophonic knowledge. In order to read at any level, we need to have an understanding of the relationship between the marks on the page and the sounds of spoken English.

Goodman claimed that as we read a text we draw on all of these areas of knowledge in varying degrees, according to the text being read, in order to understand. The reading process could therefore be described as a 'problem-solving activity' or as Goodman (1967) said, a 'psycholinguistic guessing game'.

Another proponent of this psycholinguistic view of the reading process is Frank Smith. He (1971) argued that meaning is the driving force in our development of reading. As readers, our first priority is to make sense of the text and so we will use all cues in order to do this. He claimed that fluent readers predominantly use context in order to make meaning.

The key issues of this view of the reading process are that there is essentially no difference between the way in which experienced and beginner readers approach texts, and that learning written language is a similar process to learning spoken language. There is a continuum with spoken language at one end and written language at the other and we move along that continuum in a sense-making process. Reading is constructive; it is the reader who constructs both the text and the meaning so what the reader brings to the text is as important as what lies in the text itself.

For Smith reading is not something that is taught but something that is learned and it is learned because of membership of a literate society. Readers draw on what they already know and make predictions about what the text says. He argued that readers give minimal attention to the visual information of the words on the page (Smith, 1973: 190) and do not use the alphabetic nature of print to decode or sound out unknown words. This was highly controversial, even at the time; reading is seen not as a linear process but a problem-solving one.

It is from these views of reading that the term 'whole language' came, seeing the process of learning to read as best happening through the experience of using whole texts for authentic purposes. The isolation of skills was seen as a way of making life harder for the learner. Smith (1978) identified two essential requirements for learning to read: interesting materials that make sense to the reader and an adult who can guide the learner through the process. This led to an emphasis on the texts that are given to early readers; they should use natural language rather than be written solely for the purpose of teaching using words which can easily be decoded. Waterland (1988) described these as 'free-range' books as opposed to the 'battery books' of many reading schemes.

The 'whole-language approach' was hugely popular amongst teachers and had much impact on pedagogy, although, as is usually the case, not all teachers adopted the approach in its purest form. During this time (the 1980s and 1990s) the teaching of reading became highly political and there was great debate in the media. The key turning point was the publication in 1990 of Martin Turner's claim that a perceived fall in reading standards could be directly attributed to 'whole-language'. Ofsted (1996), reporting on the teaching of reading in central London schools, claimed that practice in schools did not include the systematic teaching of phonics. Were these criticisms justifiable? The psycholinguistic approach to reading, or the whole-language approach, put strong emphasis on the motivation of the reader and the response of the reader to the text and so it is difficult to make a direct link between that and quantifiably measured reading standards. I will say more about the response of the reader to the text in Chapter 3, but the emphasis that Goodman, Smith and others put on the value of meaningful literacy experiences is an important one and should not be marginalised in any consideration of the reading process.

Many cognitive psychologists, however, criticised the psycholinguistic approach for its descriptions of what happens when we read, claiming that they were not based on verifiable data. Our understanding of the reading process develops over time as more and more research is done; as we consider new evidence it is important not to throw the baby out with the bathwater but to consider carefully what can be added to our pedagogical knowledge. Harrison (2004: 35) wrote:

the evidence suggests that for fluent readers the visual processing of text is both fairly complete and very fast, and that, most of the time, engaging in hypothesis-testing behaviour seems to play a minimal role in word recognition.

Rayner and Pollatsek (1989) argued that the reading process follows mainly a 'bottom-up' model but brings in 'top-down' processes when necessary. Technology allows us to record eye movements more accurately and to know where a reader is fixating. It would appear that fluent readers fixate nearly all words and access the meaning of the word that is being fixated before moving on to the next word. This happens, of course, extremely rapidly and the length of the fixation depends on the relative frequency of the word. This appears to contradict the views of Smith and Goodman and places the focus back on individual words rather than whole texts.

Reflective activity

Think back to your own journey towards becoming a reader. Who taught you? How did you learn? What did you read in those early days?

Can you relate your story to anything of the psycholinguistic approach that has been described so far? It is likely that some things will ring bells but other things will not apply to your experience. Many people will say that they did learn from books that were not part of real schemes but still had regular phonic lessons. Others will have followed a reading scheme but had lots of opportunities to play at literacy, for example in the role-play area.

Reading the words

Think back to the activity at the start of this chapter. Whatever issues you identified, you will have spent some time reading the words which together formed the whole text. How did you go about doing that? Look carefully at this page in the book you are reading and consider what it contains. You will notice that it is full of words which are comprised of letters; there are 26 letters and the words on the page are made up of those letters put together in various combinations. Those 26 letters are known as the alphabet and so our system of print in English is alphabetic – it consists of the letters of the alphabet. The written language or the orthography of English is alphabetic. This is not the case for all languages. You are probably aware that other written systems, for example that of China or Japan, are not alphabetic but for now we will focus on the English alphabetic system.

The 26 letters of the alphabet are used to represent the sounds of spoken English. Immediately you will realise that this makes for complications as there are more sounds in spoken English than there are letters, but we will return to this in Chapters 6 and 7. The English language is not transparent: there is no straightforward correspondence between the letters and sounds and so processes are followed to make

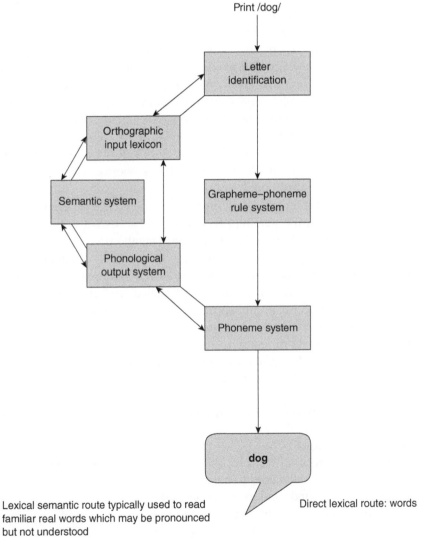

Figure 1.1   Dual-route cascade model of word recognition

Source: adapted from Coltheart et al. (2001)

sense of the complexity of the written word. Cognitive–psychological approaches to the reading process believe that the starting point for readers are those individual letters; readers relate those to the sounds of spoken language, blend the sounds together to make words and so come to the meaning. This is in direct contrast to the starting point of the psycholinguistic approach described above.

Psychologists (Coltheart et al., 2001) refer to what is described as the 'dual-route cascade model' of reading; this identifies two routes or processes that we follow in order to work out what a word says.

The direct lexical route means that we focus on the letters and use our knowledge to relate those letter shapes to the sounds of spoken language. We put those sounds together and come up with another sound unit which gives us a phonological identity of the word; this means we can pronounce the word because we have access to the orthographic representation. However, in order to understand the word we need to relate it to our bank of known words and understand what it refers to by using the semantic system. The second route is the 'non-lexical' one where we use our phonic knowledge to translate a string of letters into a spoken, or pronounced word. This is when children 'sound out' words. The word may be enunciated but not necessarily understood.

These routes are not in competition; they complement each other and the route that the brain follows in the reading process depends on what is being read and how it relates to previous knowledge. Flynn and Stainthorp (2006) consider this a useful theoretical framework for investigating the processes children need to develop in order to become skilled word-readers. It is important to remember though that this model comes from analysis of skilled readers, and that beginner readers may not have access to all aspects of knowledge assumed in this model. The teacher of reading needs to evaluate the model and see if and how those 'knowledges' can be taught or learned.

Consider how the model relates to pedagogy. It is clear that for it to work in practice, children need to know certain things:

- the relationship between the written letter shapes and the sounds of spoken language
- a bank of known words
- the experience of relating word to objects, events, feelings etc. and the understanding of the symbolic nature of language
- the ability to hear sounds and to see visual patterns
- the motivation and interest to engage in the process, for example realising that the written symbols have an interest or a purpose.

These are the required areas of knowledge which underpin much pedagogy of reading and they can be simplified into two broad aspects of reading: decoding and comprehension. The two are interdependent and neither can work alone. If readers cannot decode a text independently they will never be able to understand it and I am sure you have had the experience of being able to decode a text without understanding its meaning at all. I hope that is not your experience as you are reading this! This relationship between decoding and comprehension is often expressed in the following way:

Reading Comprehension = Decoding × Language Comprehension

Behaviour as a reader is determined by our ability in both of those components. We can be very good at comprehending but not so good at decoding; we can decode almost perfectly but not understand much; we can decode and understand or we can do neither. Both decoding and comprehension work on a continuum and readers can be placed at different places on both of those. This is demonstrated in the 'Simple View of Reading' (Gough and Tumner, 1986). Decoding is 'efficient, context-free word recognition' and comprehension is 'the ability to access word meanings and produce sentence and discourse interpretations' (Cain, 2010: 214). Notice that in this model reading comprehension requires that both decoding and language comprehension are present; reading does not occur when one is not present. In practical terms, this means that the very young child who reads along with an adult and enjoys a story is not reading and neither is the student who reads a challenging academic article but does not understand a word! This contrasts with other models of reading which will be discussed later in the chapter.

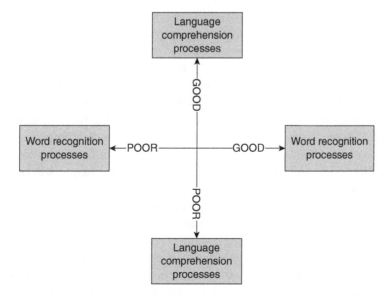

Figure 1.2 The simple view of reading

Source: DfES (2006a: 53)

The simple view of reading provides a useful framework for teachers to identify where children are on the continuum of both aspects of reading and as such provide appropriate interventions. In Chapter 12 we will discuss these further.

Staged models of reading

It is clear that becoming a reader does not all happen at once but that efficient word-reading is both fast and automatic. There has been much theoretical work on creating staged models of reading development which identify the different stages that readers go through as they become readers. The important question is: do all readers go through the same stages of development? You will have seen that the models of reading described above use the behaviours of skilled readers to construct the model; staged models argue that there are real qualitative differences between beginner and experienced readers. These differences are in the processes that are used rather than the control readers have over the processes. Stage models see word identification as the key to comprehension, and so knowledge of orthography (written symbols) is more important than knowledge of syntax (grammar) or semantics (meaning).

There are many stage models of reading development but we are going to focus on just two: Ehri and Adams. Ehri (1999) was intrigued by the way in which experienced readers can just look at a word and know its meaning without any need to decode it and asked how beginner readers developed that ability. Her research is her attempt to find the answer to these questions. For Ehri, the term 'sight word-reading' was crucial and she defined that as the process of accessing words in memory. It is important to remember that the term 'sight word-reading' does not relate to flash card teaching or the learning of words by their shape.

The key to sight word-reading, so Ehri believed, was a process she described as 'connection forming'. These connections link the written form of the word to the sound and meaning and the connections are stored in the reader's word memory or lexicon. Different types of connection take precedence at different stages of reading development, thus the notion of a staged theory. Ehri identified four phases through which readers go as they become skilled readers and these stages will be discussed in greater detail in Chapter 4.

So far we have seen that models of reading acquisition have placed an emphasis on autonomous processing through connection-making and that context does not have such a great effect on word recognition. You may also have noticed that the theorists we have discussed so far talk about *word* reading. Stanovich (1995) broadened out this idea when he said that the main purpose of reading is comprehension, although word recognition is central to this. Stanovich argues that the process whereby a word activates the lexical memory, as described above, is the first process and following this comes the second process of comprehension of the text. However, because this is dependent on the first process it is a 'constrained reasoning'; the reasoning is constrained by the ability to recognise the word quickly.

You may remember that Smith, the psycholinguist, argued that fluent readers pay little attention to the visual features of text and how that has been contradicted by recent research. Research by Juel (1991) showed that in fact skilled readers can only predict accurately from the context about 25 per cent of words and these words tend to be very high-frequency function words such as 'is' or 'the'. Only about 10 per cent of content words (those which carry the meaning such as nouns, adjectives and verbs) are predictable and so need to be decoded. This means that rather than seeing the reader as constructing the meaning of a text, the text itself limits the meaning (Perfetti and McCutcheon, 1987).

Adams (1990), after reviewing much of the current research on the reading process, argued that through their exposure to words, children build up a network of relationships between letters and sounds. As they sound out words, so they focus on the order of individual letters in words. For Adams children cannot learn to read until they can recognise individual letters. However, for Adams it is vitally important that this 'bottom-up' learning is done in a context which gives understanding of the forms and functions of text. She says.

> Phonological awareness, letter recognition facility, familiarity with spelling patterns, spelling-sound relations, and individual words must be developed in concert with real reading and real writing and with deliberate reflection on the forms, functions and meanings of texts. (Adams, 1990: 422)

In Adams' words we are beginning to see a view that both perspectives have something to offer the teacher of reading, and the work of Bussis et al. (1985) can make further contribution to this.

This research looked at 26 children in different classes in America and found that the children read in one of two different ways. Some children read for speed or momentum and others read for accuracy. Consider how you would go about assembling a bookcase: some people would lay out all the pieces carefully and read through the instructions; others would just dive straight in and start putting different bits together, keeping in mind the final product of a bookcase. The difference in reading styles of children is a little bit like that. Neither approach is perfect: children reading for speed would misread a word and that would make them go off on a tangent, reading something very different from what was actually on the page. Those reading for accuracy would read word-by-word with little expression or fluency and so would often fail to appreciate the story at all. In order to be an effective reader, there needs to be a balance of both approaches.

The idea of different approaches to reading was developed by Barrs (in Dombey et al., 1998) who identified the 'big shapes' and the 'little shapes'. Big shapes are things like syntax, semantics and also knowledge of the type of text that is being read. Little shapes are letters, sounds, spelling and punctuation. Barrs described reading as 'a multi-level process in which the reader attends to both the big shapes and the small shapes, confirming at each of these levels hypotheses that have been set up at the other' (Dombey and Moustafa, 1998: 2).

This definition draws together several of the ideas that have already been proposed. The use of the word 'hypotheses' immediately relates back to the psycholinguistic notion of a 'guessing game', but in Barr's model the guessing is much more explicitly informed. It is almost like a jigsaw where the little shapes fit inside the big shapes; the merging of the shapes is always easier when there is a clear picture of the whole. Think back to Adams' view that it is important to place the teaching of phonics and alphabet skills within authentic reading experiences.

Review and reflect

I hope that you are now beginning to understand that there is no single model that fully explains reading processes. Both of these theoretical positions discussed so far have something to offer the teacher of reading and both have weaknesses as well as strengths. Consider all that you have observed in schools which might be described as the teaching of reading and try to place each activity within a theoretical framework, justifying your position. It might be helpful to create something like Table 1.1:

Table 1.1

Classroom activity	Theoretical perspective	Justification
Reading a story out loud to the class	Psycholinguistic	Giving the children the opportunity to hear written language and to become attuned to its rhythms
Building a collection of words with the long vowel phoneme /ow/	Cognitive psychological	Part of systematic phonic teaching of grapheme–phoneme correspondences to develop skill of decoding

The purpose of this activity is not just to attach a theoretical label to classroom practice but to help you, as teachers of reading, to understand why certain pedagogies are useful and how they contribute to the teaching of reading. If teaching is to be recognised and valued as a profession, all teachers need to be able to explain why they carry out certain practices in their classrooms and how those activities are supported by research.

More than words

You may have noticed in the discussion so far that the role of the text has played an important role within each theoretical perspective and each of them views the text slightly differently. For the psycholinguist the text is crucial as it supports the problem-solving meaning-making role of the reader. As each reader makes sense of a text and responds as an individual so the text is constructed in a way which holds meaning for that reader. Knowledge and understanding of the big shape of not only the single text but also the whole genre is vital to that reading process.

In the cognitive psychological perspective the text is more of a static entity and it is the reader's task to access the meaning hidden within the text. This is done by decoding each word and coming to an understanding of the words before putting the words together to see the text as a whole. Cognitive psychologists talk about 'word-reading' rather than text-reading and much of what they discuss is related to the 'small shapes'. In fact, at the start of the twenty-first century, it is government policy that synthetic phonics should be taught as the first strategy to be used when attempting to read an unknown word. We will return to that in later chapters but I mention it now to make the point that word-reading through phonics is the current dominant pedagogical strategy.

Davis (2013) argues against this current policy and disputes the claim that phonics alone can be used to teach reading. All phonic schemes claim to teach grapheme-phoneme correspondences (GPCs) and the skills of blending for reading and segmenting for writing. Miskin (1999) says, 'The synthetic approach teaches children to blend phonemes ... into words for reading.'

Davis questions the use of the terms 'sound' and 'phoneme' as synonyms of each other, arguing that linguistically the phoneme is a more abstract concept. In phonic teaching it is usually said that a phoneme is the smallest unit of sound that can affect a change in meaning but that is not always the case. When my children were young they were used to having a 'bath' (long vowel sound) with Mummy but a 'bath' (short vowel sound) with Daddy. The sound was changed but the meaning stayed exactly the same and was understood completely by my children. In Davis's terms the ideas expressed by the word 'transcend the acoustic characteristics of the sounds we hear when people speak' (2013: 21). Thus, Davis argues, the use of the term 'word' is problematic. We can blend sounds together and make another composite sound but this is not necessarily a word because the meaning of a word is not necessarily found in its pronunciation. Several examples are given when the sound of a word is exactly the same but the meanings are very different, for example, mints and mince, paws and pause, nun and none. The meaning cannot be understood without reference to a context. The implication of Davis's argument is that a reader frequently needs to know the meaning of a word before they know how to pronounce it. We will return to this argument in Chapters 5 and 6 but for now it is enough to say that in attempting to define the reading process it is necessary to go beyond the word.

Reflective activity

Read the first verse of the poem 'Jabberwocky' by Lewis Carroll.

Twas brillig, and the slithy toves

Did gyre and gimble in the wabe;

All mimsy were the borogoves,

And the mome raths outgrabe.

After reading reflect on your understanding of the poem by considering the following questions:

- What do you think this text is about? Explain to somebody else or draw a picture of what it means to you.
- What helped you to understand?
- How did you know how to pronounce each word?
- What difference did reading the poem aloud make to how much you understood it?

Compare your answers with those of a friend and discuss the similarities and differences. What does this tell you about the reading process?

Sociocultural perspective

It may well be that when you compared responses to the activity above with a friend there were some differences in what you came up with. What sort of differences were they? Which one of you was correct? You might feel rather indignant at that last question, feeling that there was no correct response because it is such an individualistic thing. You would, of course, be right but children are not always given the luxury of giving individualistic responses, particularly in formal assessment tasks. Why do you think this is?

So far in this chapter we have broadened out our considerations from the letter to the word and then to the text. The sociocultural perspective widens the lens even more to focus on the community within which the reading is taking place. Moll (2000) defines culture as a set of practices which are adopted by a group of people and in this theoretical framework the attention moves from the individual reader to the social and cultural context. The culture in which each of us operates is so completely a part of us that it is challenging to step aside and attempt to recognise what it is that shapes our thinking and our behaviour. This is what we are going to try and do in relation to the way reading is viewed and practised.

Those researchers approaching the study of the reading process from a sociocultural perspective tend to adopt a multidisciplinary approach, drawing on the fields of anthropology, sociology and sociolinguistics. Reports of research tend to be ethnographic accounts or 'thick descriptions' (Geertz, 1973) of individual or group reading behaviours (for example, Solsken 1993; Au 1997; Gregory and Williams, 2000). The implications of this perspective for the teacher of reading is that learning to read becomes more of a process of acculturation rather than just about learning a set of skills.

Bruner (1996) used the ideas of 'subjectivity' and 'intersubjectivity' to explore this issue. 'Subjectivity' is our personal take on a situation or event and 'intersubjectivity' is the way in which we know the minds of other members of our community. Children learn to become readers in almost an apprenticeship model; it is through being members of a community that is located in a social, cultural and historical place that they learn what reading is used for, how it is valued and what it can offer them. Children learn what it means to be a reader by seeing readers within their own cultural context. This will impact on their motivation and emotional responses to reading and also on the intellectual and academic demands that reading places on them. Research by the Booktrust (Gleed, 2013) showed that a significant minority of adults had negative attitudes to reading: 56 per cent of 18–30-year-olds preferred the Internet and social media to reading books and 64 per cent of them thought the Internet will replace books in the next 20 years. An interesting aspect of this research was that the higher the socio-economic group that someone was in, the more likely they were to read. There was also a significant link between reading history; those whose parents encouraged them to read as a child are more likely to read as an adult and those who enjoyed reading at school were more likely to read more as an adult than those who didn't. What an important role the teacher of reading has! Hall (2003: 135) says: 'As literacy educators we are hugely interested in improving our learners' human capacity to use that symbol system. But we must recognise that symbol system as constructed historically and culturally'.

Language, both spoken and written, is the means by which meaning is constructed and shaped and that meaning is determined by the culture within which it is formed. The work of Vygotsky (1978) foregrounded this view and it is developed further in the work of Bruner. Bruner (1996) argued that mind and thought are shaped by culture, and indeed, could not exist without it. The implication of this is that the focus on the individual found in both the cognitive psychological and the psycholinguistic perspectives is superseded by the view that learning is a social process. How does that work when we relate it to the process of learning to read? When I read a book I am using a symbolic system which has developed and been refined over many many years and I am encountering ideas which similarly have been formulated, defined and recorded over many years. I am entering into the ways of thinking of others. The American author, Joyce Carol Oates, once said, 'Reading is the sole means by which we slip, involuntarily, often helplessly, into another's skin, another's voice, another's soul'.

In this way, children assimilate the reading behaviours and attitudes of those around them as they grow up. Through a sort of apprenticeship model of learning, children come to appreciate what reading is for and what it can offer them. They experience reading through other people – reading to them, reading with them or just reading. They become part of what has been described as a 'community of practice'.

The issue is that for some children the literacy they find, and in which they are assessed, in school is different from that which they have encountered at home. It may be that this is an explanation for the findings of the Booktrust research. Cole (1990) supported this view when he argued that some children have difficulties with reading at school, not because of the acquisition of cognitive skills but because of the nature of the tasks and activities they are required to do in the classroom. For Freebody and Freiberg (2001) it was an even stronger issue, for they argued that 'school literacies' have come to define what we mean by 'literacy'. The work of Au (1997) defined the classroom as a culture and a context for learning and, as such, a community of practice. This means that within the classroom there are reading behaviours and attitudes which are particular to that classroom or school. In order to be an effective reader within that classroom, children need to adopt the values and behaviours of that cultural context. The essential consequence of this argument is that there are many different definitions of reading and ways of being a reader.

The next chapter will look at the work of Shirley Brice Heath (1983) and Eve Gregory (1996) in more detail but for now it is enough to say that both pieces of research found evidence to support Freebody and Freiberg's view. They found that reading in school, despite being in many ways more limiting, was the expected and so validated reading. Freebody and Freiberg go on to criticise those adopting a cognitive psychological perspective (such as Adams discussed earlier) for being prescriptive about reading behaviours rather than starting from where the children are. Duke (2000) found that there were significant differences in both the reading environments and the experiences offered to children between different socio-economic groups. She carried out a quantitative analysis of American schools and found that not only were the resources less plentiful in low socio-economic status classrooms but also pupils were given less rich opportunities for reading. The research by the Booktrust cited above bears this out in an English context, finding that children in lower socio-economic circumstances are less likely to see either the value or the pleasure of reading books.

Moll (2000) coined the term 'funds of knowledge' to identify the underlying knowledge of everyday activities in the home. In articulating these he argues that the gap between home and school may be narrowed as schools and teachers become more aware of the skill and knowledge base of children from different cultural and social backgrounds. He argues that if classroom activities are devised which draw on these 'funds of knowledge' pupils will be more empowered. Au (1997) adopted these principles in developing a project with elementary schools in low-income communities in Hawaii. Adopting familiar practices, Au aimed to increase the sense of ownership of reading so that pupils saw that reading could be an important part of their everyday lives. The consequence of this would be that pupils would be empowered to reach higher levels of reading because the reading behaviours they encounter in school are similar to those they encounter at home.

Mark wanted to be a lorry driver like his dad and was marking time at school until he could do this. At the age of 11 his reading was way below age expectations. Using the Highway Code and the regulations for transport of freight Mark became a fluent reader. It was because the reading behaviours he was now experiencing in school paralleled those he saw his dad engaging in at home and at work that he saw reading as a relevant and necessary skill, and so reached higher levels than when he was following numerous intervention schemes and reading texts which were at his reading level but below his interest level.

Consideration of the sociopolitical perspective gives teachers of reading a greater awareness of the value of beginner readers knowing the purposes that reading can hold for them personally and its relevance to their lives and experiences. It is apparent that at the start of the twenty-first century this theoretical perspective does not hold much significance. However, the importance of authentic activities and the centrality of meaning remain crucial to the development of readers.

 ## Reflective activity

Talk to as many people as you can who are part of the community of a local school. You might like to talk with parents, teaching assistants, lunchtime supervisors and children. Ask them about the sort of reading they do. It might be helpful to ask them to list everything they have read in the past 24 hours. Don't forget to include all sorts of texts and not just printed books.

(Continued)

(Continued)

Look at your list and consider the type of texts that are being read, the types of reading and the contexts in which reading takes place.

Now think about all the reading that pupils are asked to do during one day in the class where you are currently based. Again consider each reading activity in relation to the type of text, the type of reading and the context of the reading. Identify the similarities and differences.

How could the reading activities in school be modified to reflect more closely the reading of the community?

Sociopolitical perspective

There is no doubt that the written language plays an important part in the way decisions are made in the world today. Communication takes place digitally and through print and as news is transmitted and values and beliefs conveyed, this communication can be nuanced by the means of communication. Since the very beginnings of literacy this debate has raged; there were those who thought that if people were able to read they could be controlled more easily because those holding power could control what was read by the people. There were others who argued that enabling all people to read would be a liberating force as they would encounter different perspectives and opinions.

 # Reflective activity

List all the sources of news that you can think of – television channels, newspapers, tweets, blogs and websites. When there is a major news item emerging where would you instinctively go to find out information? Which source of information would you consider to be the most 'reliable'? Is this because you trust that source to be telling the 'truth'? Look at all those sources and try and articulate what particular perspective each might put on a news story. How do you know this? How would you discern that perspective?

Reflections such as those above soon make it apparent that reading is much more than decoding the symbols on the page into sound, more than using existing knowledge to make meaning of a text and more than reading texts which are socially and culturally authentic. Reading, and particularly learning to read, is a highly political activity. That might seem a very strange thing to say, especially when you try and relate it to a typical primary classroom but let's consider that point a little further.

Powell et al. (2001: 780) said that teachers of reading can either teach reading as a series of skills and codes or they can teach it 'as if the words matter'. A sociopolitical perspective on the reading process argues that no text is neutral but carries a significance that is dependent on a particular perception of reality and of what is important. Learning to read involves learning that texts have power and exercise that power over knowledge, belief, attitudes and values. The words matter because of the values they convey. I am writing this on the day after the London Marathon. Mo Farah, an Olympic and world champion for track events, ran the marathon for the first time ever and came eighth. In my mind, that was a great achievement. One newspaper, however, reported that his 'debut in the race proved a step too far as he trailed home in eighth place' (Mail Online, 2014). The words used in that short remark serve to impose a particular negative judgement of the race and can make the reader view Farah's achievement as a failure. The words chosen by the writer of that article mattered a lot in the influence put to bear on the reader's understanding of the situation.

Effective readers are consciously aware of this impact of the text and the term 'critical literacy' is used for the way in which readers make this explicit. Morgan et al. (1996: 9) said that:

> Critical literacy is concerned with enabling us to take particular texts and explore the ways in which these texts are implicated in making the world the way it is; in helping us to keep the world the way it is; and in coercing us to see the world in certain ways rather than others.

In other theoretical perspectives the relationship between the reader and the text is implied or constructed in the way in which reading is defined, and this was discussed earlier in the chapter. This relationship is crucial within the sociopolitical perspective for it is this which determines the nature of the reading act. Bloome (1993) explores the social relationship that is set up between the author of the text and the reader. Let us try and understand that by considering the relationship I, as the author of this text, and you, as the reader, have. In order to do this there are certain aspects of this text which need to be looked at more closely.

Reflective activity

- Look at the language I have chosen to use – the pronouns, the tense, the choice of vocabulary, the tone and the style of writing. How would you describe this? Is the text including you or excluding you?

(Continued)

(Continued)

- What sort of identity am I establishing for myself? If you do not know me, what assumptions could you make about me? What clues are there about that?
- What sort of identity am I establishing for you as a reader? Are there any clues about the sort of person this text seems to be written for?

I would love to know the answers you give to those questions but I hope that in answering them you are beginning to see that the author of a text constructs a particular relationship between the text, the writer and the reader. That relationship can be challenged and changed by different readers. One reader might find this text simply written and clear but another might find it simplistic and patronising. The role I create for the reader may be changed by the reader's interpretation of particular linguistic and stylistic features.

In this chapter I have written about four different theoretical perspectives on the reading process. Do you, as the reader, have any idea which of those perspectives is closest to my own views? If you think you know, what are the clues in the text that lead you to believe that? Would another reader agree with you? This text is also being written within a particular social and political context where there are many different views expressed on the teaching of reading. Consider this sentence from earlier on in this chapter:

> If teaching is to be recognised and valued as a profession, all teachers need to be able to explain why they carry out certain practices in their classrooms and how those activities are supported by research.

How am I positioning myself within the current political situation in relation to the teaching of reading? Consider the choice of words I made and how those words relate to each other; reflect on the structure of the sentence and so the emphasis placed on the first word of the sentence; look at the verbs and the tenses used and think how those portray a perspective on the present reality.

Reading in that way is critical reading; it is reading with an awareness that texts are constructed within a context and from a particular perspective. It is an awareness that language can, and usually is, used to manipulate attitudes, beliefs and feelings. Effective readers, argues the sociopolitical view, are those who understand that texts can construct certain effects. It is apparent, however, that many readers do not read in such a way. Have you ever heard somebody say to you, 'It must be true – I read it in a book'? Readers such as this are disempowered in a modern democratic world. It is not the ability to read that is empowering but the ways in which reading is used (Scribner and Cole, 1981). Within a sociopolitical perspective reading is as much about learning to decode or to comprehend as about learning about identities and values. This has implications for classroom practice which will be returned to in Chapter 4.

Conclusion

Why has this book begun with a consideration of these four theoretical perspectives? Why is it important for teachers of reading to know about this?

I believe it is important because teachers of reading need to know exactly what it is they are teaching and the impact that the way they teach reading will have on children's lives as readers. Print is a devised system and so has to be taught. It has evolved and come under many influences over the years and readers need to be aware of how and where these changes arise. The very act of reading defines the relationship between the text and its author and also between the ideas and values embedded within the text. Reading is not a neutral act and so cannot be taught in a neutral way. Teachers of reading need to know what it is they are teaching and what reading can offer children both as inheritors of culture and creators of meaning.

In order to be effective teachers of reading, teachers also need to be conscious of what reading means to them and how they perceive and use reading in their own lives. This is the focus of the next chapter.

The key messages of this chapter are:

- the reading process is very complex and multilayered
- understanding the reading process can be approached from a variety of different perspectives and each offers a particular viewpoint
- the teaching of reading is a value-laden activity and teachers need to be aware of their own positioning within the value systems
- teachers of reading need to understand the theoretical underpinning of their pedagogical choices and so be able to justify those choices
- political decisions on policy do not always stem from an awareness of all theoretical positions.

Further reading

Hall, K. (2003) *Listening to Stephen Read; Multiple Perspectives on Literacy*. Buckingham: Open University Press.

In this book Hall gave a transcript of a child's reading to several different reading 'experts', who each approach reading in a different way. She uses their analyses to provide a commentary on the different theoretical perspectives on reading. In contextualising theory, she makes it much easier to understand.

Clay, M.M. (1991) *Becoming Literate: The Construction of Inner Control.* Auckland: Heinemann.
This is an old book but a classic and important for a deep understanding of the reading process. Clay draws on her observations of children to construct a theory of reading in which children build on past experiences to become readers.

Cain, K. (2010) *Reading Development and Difficulties.* Chichester: Blackwell.
This book lies firmly within the cognitive psychology approach but aims to provide an overview of reading for those wishing to study it.

CHAPTER 2

BEING A READER

Chapter objectives

When you have read this chapter you should have:

- understood the purposes behind reflecting on practice
- practised reflecting on your own teaching and identifying learning points from your reflection
- created your own autobiography as a reader
- identified different ways of being a reader
- reflected on what it means to read for pleasure and have some classroom strategies to help children to do this.

Introduction

The previous chapter considered several different ways of looking at the reading process and saw how, depending on the discipline or theoretical perspective which influences your point of view, reading can be described in many different ways. It was also noted that reading is a highly political topic and has been used by governments in many countries over many decades as the measure of the success of current educational policies. The growth in theoretical understanding of the reading process and the implementation of new national policies can be confusing for practitioners, especially beginner teachers who are looking for 'the way' to teach reading. If you were to ask experienced teachers about what informs their day-to-day decisions in the classroom, I expect a common response would be that it is their experience of the journeys of many different children towards reading. It is knowing what reading means to children and how you, as a teacher, can broaden their understanding of and experience of reading that will make an effective teacher of reading. This knowledge comes about from reflecting on children's responses and attitudes towards reading but also from reflecting on your own view of reading – of knowing what reading means to you and your life and what your understanding of reading is.

This is the focus of this chapter. We will consider what it means to be a reader and will come to see that there are many different kinds of reader in the world. In reflecting on our own experiences of reading and on the experiences of a range of children we will see there are many varieties of readers and reading, and this variety will be found in each and every classroom in each and every primary school. What are the implications of this for the teacher of reading? This chapter considers the impact of recognising different types of reader on our provision both in terms of resources and pedagogy.

Finally, the chapter considers the whole notion of reading for pleasure. That phrase has many connotations and some of those are not helpful for all children. We examine what it means to actually read for pleasure and how we, as teachers of reading, can create authentic, relevant and pleasurable reading experiences for the children in our classes.

Reflecting on practice

I hope that you will have appreciated from the introduction to the chapter that much of this chapter will involve thinking deeply and seriously about both the children we have taught and known and about ourselves. In doing this, we will be 'reflecting on practice'. This process is a common one in professional development, including teacher education, and I have no doubt that many readers of this book who are training to become teachers will be required to write a 'reflective journal' or something very like it. For some this is a challenging task: what do we mean by reflection?

Paterson and Chapman (2013) argue that through reflection we can learn from experience and also develop detailed schema for our professional practice. You will remember from your study of child development that a schema (Atherton and Nutbrown, 2013) is the framework by which we organise thoughts, understandings and behaviours and the relationships among them. As developing teachers this enables us to come to a deeper understanding of our growing pedagogical skills and the theory that underpins them. When you are training you will observe many teachers and they will each have slightly different practices; you will also be given many excellent ideas for classroom practice by your tutors and mentors. It is reflection that enables you to assimilate all this information and to personalise all that you are learning. It was Dewey (1933) who first said that reflection enables us to move from routine to informed practice; you will not become an effective teacher if you just copy what you see or are told; it is important to make it your own. Larrivee (2000: 293) said:

> unless teachers develop the practice of critical reflection, they stay trapped in unexamined judgments, interpretations, assumptions, and expectations. Approaching teaching as a reflective practitioner involves fusing personal beliefs and values into a professional identity.

Reflective practice, therefore, enables us to link theory to practice and so understand the 'why' of what we are doing; it helps us to improve our practice by forming an evidence base of what works best and what doesn't work so well, and it helps us to understand what is happening and so strengthen that vital skill for teachers of thinking on our feet. As Rolfe et al.'s (2001) model of reflection suggests, it enables us to answer three important questions:

- What?
- So what?
- What next?

One of the most influential thinkers on the development of reflective practice was Schön (1983) who distinguished between 'reflection-in-action' and reflection-on-action'. The first is what happens when you are in the classroom and monitoring what is going on; as you develop the skill of 'reading' what is happening, so you modify what you say and do and your expectations of the pupils. That is a challenging skill to learn. It is helped by 'reflection-on-action' or reflection after the event. This is what you do when you evaluate a lesson you have taught or observed or think carefully about a response a child made to an activity or a question. It also helps the development of our teaching skills when we reflect on our own experiences as learners, or in relation to the subject of this chapter, our behaviour as readers.

Pollard et al. (2014) stress the importance of teachers making informed judgements about their actions. They argue that teaching is such a complex and multifaceted activity that teachers need to have a solid basis for their actions. I am sure that however limited or extensive your teaching experience may be, you will agree with this. Amongst many others, Pollard makes two important points about reflection. First, it is not a solitary activity; collaboration and co-operation are key features of effective teaching and discussing and reflecting on practice with colleagues enhances learning and development. Second, reflection is an ongoing process; it never comes to an end. There are always opportunities to develop understanding and to enhance practice and the best teachers are continually reflecting on their practice and learning from their reflection.

Reflection on self: the beginning of autobiography

Ghaye's (2010) book *Teaching and Learning through Reflective Practice* (see Further Reading at the end of this chapter), recommends beginning the process of reflection with a series of reflective questions. He suggests using these to identify a topic for reflection, but as this book is all about the teaching of reading and this chapter in particular is about being a reader, I am going to use the questions suggested by Ghaye (2010: 3) to reflect on what it means to me to be a reader.

First, he suggests I reflect on my passions. What do I love to do? What do I care about?

I love reading and I love talking about books. When I am in a bookshop I will feel despair that there is so much to read and not enough time to read. Sometimes when I read a novel I will become completely engrossed and will read all the time until it is finished. I have to limit the times I can do this and often have to stop myself from starting to read a book. As a consequence, I will dip into anything to read and skim books to find key words or phrases that speak to me at the moment. I read extracts and reviews of books and try, but usually fail, to remember to read them in the future. I read websites and follow through links – frequently getting distracted and ending up at a point far from my intended destination. I read magazines, newspapers, notice boards and hoardings. If there are words I will read them. If the words are in a language I do not know I love trying to puzzle out what they say and am frustrated when I do not know the alphabet in which they are written.

As a teacher of reading, I am passionate about sharing my love of reading with others. I do not understand people who gain little pleasure from the printed word. My weakness is that I read quickly and I have had to teach myself to focus on the details, particularly to look carefully at the pictures in picture books. I am grateful to friends and colleagues who have taught me to do this.

Second, Ghaye suggests I focus on my proficiencies. What am I good at? What are my strengths?

I am good at finding good books to read; I read reviews and newspaper articles and am aware of what is going on. I am good at reading quickly to find out the basic message of what something is about but bad at reading slowly to appreciate the detail, be it of plot, character or style of language.

As a teacher of reading I am good at sharing my love of books with my pupils – be they children or trainee teachers. I have taught lots of children to read in my career and have used a huge variety of teaching strategies to address their interests and learning styles.

Finally, he suggests I focus on my priorities. What is important to me? What do I spend most time on? My priority is to enjoy reading, to be able to make informed choices about what I read and to be able to understand beyond the literal meaning of the text. As a teacher of reading, it is my priority to enable children and trainee teachers to read beyond the text and to appreciate why texts are written and the underlying values and message.

What do answering these questions tell me about myself as a reader and as a teacher of reading? Do they show me a starting point for reflection with a view to improving my practice?

First, I can see that I have a strong emphasis on the printed word and do not really give much time to reading on screen, particularly for pleasure. I have an e-reader and a tablet but do not naturally turn to these to read. I miss the feel, smell and tactile nature of reading a book. Second, I need to take time to look at how authors have made choices of language structure and vocabulary in order to convey meaning and create effects. From this I could then go on to set myself challenges for future reading and conversations about reading with colleagues.

 ## Reflective activity

Why don't you ask yourself the same questions now? Think about yourself as a reader and ask yourself:

- What are my passions?
- What are my proficiencies?
- What are my priorities?

The answers to these questions will help you to construct your own reading auto-biography later.

Autobiography

The bookshops are full of celebrity autobiographies, especially at Christmas time. These are books about people's lives, written from their own personal perspective. They can be both entertaining and illuminating. The word 'autobiography' comes from the Greek and literally means a written account of life by self. This can be a useful way of reflecting on the significant features of my life and as the writing develops it will often reveal issues and thoughts that can surprise. As such, autobiography has been used as a research tool and, in the context of this book, it can help reveal the sort of reader you are.

Lejeune (1989: xxi) said that 'every person has within himself a rough draft, perpetually reshaped, of the story of his life'. My husband bought me, as a present, a voucher for a 'Reading Spa' at an independent bookshop. As part of this experience I will spend 60 minutes talking with a member of staff about my reading autobiography, sharing my likes and dislikes, and they will then recommend books I might like to read (and purchase). I have spent many hours thinking about what I am going to say. If I am honest, I want to convey an impression of myself as a 'good reader'; I probably will not admit to the fat gold embossed novels I read on holiday. Yet I am aware of a tension – if I only talk about books that I think I 'should' like, they might not recommend to me books I really will like and the experience will not be as useful. I am a good example of Harnett's view that 'culture frames our language, shaping our interactions with others and the meanings which we want to convey' (2010: 167).

My memories, influenced by the experience which provoked me to remember, construct a story of my past which is just one version of that past; other memories might construct another version. Bruner (1990: 100) describes 'self' as 'a concept created by reflection, a concept constructed much as we construct other concepts'. As I relate my reading autobiography I am constructing a concept of myself as a reader. However, the idea that we make narratives or stories of our experiences of the world means that our narratives are not always reliable as accurate records of the truth but do reveal our perception of ourselves and, as Bruner found, often form a justification of our constructed reality. Think back to my account of myself as a reader – the narrative I construct of that is determined by the sort of reader I want people to think I am, and that is determined both by the listeners or readers and by my perceptions of those listeners. Life is complex and multilayered.

Why is it important to consider these issues as we reflect on the process of becoming a teacher of reading? It is because my experiences of reading have made me into the sort of reader I am and so into the sort of teacher of reading I am. The experiences, responses and emotions evoked within me by my reading experiences are a part of me and so part of what reading means to me. I want to share those with my pupils and help them to have the same positive experiences I have had and to avoid the negative experiences I have had. There is a difficulty with this, however. Not all my pupils will be the same sort of reader as I am. Mark saw no reason to read at all; he wanted to be a truck driver and reading fiction played no part in his view of the sort of person he was and the life he wanted to lead. When introduced to The Highway Code and the rules and regulations about transport his attitude changed and he eagerly read texts which to me were dry and boring. As a teacher, I cannot and must not assume that all children will approach reading in the same way as I do.

Pennac (1994) describes how we can present to people the 'gift of reading' and argues forcefully that the books must be allowed to speak for themselves: 'Once the fear of not understanding has been conquered, the notions of effort and of pleasure work powerfully in each other's favour' (1994: 134). This is what happened to Mark; he saw the purpose of reading those challenging texts and so worked hard to read and make sense of them. It was the relationship between the text and Mark's life interests which created the pleasure in reading.

As a teacher of reading, if I am able to recognise what texts inspire effort and so create the pleasure of reading for me, I will be able to understand both the relationship and the process and so help my pupils to become readers. As Pennac says, 'books are not written so that ... young people may comment on them, but so that, *if their heart is in it,* they may read them' (1994: 136).

A large element of being a teacher of reading is to inspire children in their hearts to read, and in order to do this as a teacher you need to understand where your heart is in relation to the texts which are read. Recognising my own profile as a reader is a good starting point to recognising the many different sorts of reader there will be in every class I teach.

Reading autobiographies

No books in the barn! My father was adamant about this rule. My job was to carry milk, to lug brimming pails full of warm frothy milk down the barn driveway to the milkhouse, slosh the contents into the cooler, and then return to be on call until the next milking machine was ready to be emptied. But it was these constant waits I could barely stand, and it was too tempting to sequester a comfortable spot on the ground-feed bags to catch a couple of quick pages in 'Kidnapped' or 'The Three Musketeers' before resuming the evening's routine. Of course, a person can easily lose oneself within a few pages, only to be yanked back to the pungent smells and wintry warmth of Wisconsin by the insistent hollering of my father: 'Where are you? There's milk to carry!'. (www.weac.org/news_and_publications/education_news/2000-2001/read_auto.aspx, accessed 23 January 2014)

The first book I fell in love with however, was certainly one to remember. This book is the one most romanticized in my memory because the years I spent reading it left me with the biggest impact. The Two Princesses of Bamarre by Gail Carson Levine was the first book I read over, and over, and over, and just when you thought I'd be sick of it, I read it again. (http://abookaday365.wordpress.com/2013/01/23/my-reading-autobiography-a-reflection-on-reading/, accessed 24 January 2014)

These two brief extracts are examples of how a book can evoke memories and feelings. Note how prevalent the emotions are in these accounts; it is the feelings generated by reading that enable readers to engage and want to continue to engage. What does it mean, as the last writer wrote, to 'fall in love with a book'? Have you ever had that experience? Does it matter?

Spufford (2002: 21–2) says that 'the words we take into ourselves help to shape us.' He continues

> They help form the questions we think are worth asking; they shift around the boundaries of the sayable inside us, and the related borders of what's acceptable; their potent images, calling on more in us than the responses we will ourselves to have, dart new bridges into being between our conscious and unconscious minds, between what we know we know, and the knowledge we cannot examine by thinking. They build and stretch and build again the chambers of our imagination.

If this is truly the case, how important it is to be aware of the books that have shaped us both as people and as teachers, for only then can we introduce children to the books that will shape them. We can, as Pennac says, talk about the books: how they are constructed and the linguistic features they contain, the images and themes that are part of them, their characterisation and plot development or their significance within a particular period of time. We can discuss what other people, our peers, teachers or critics, think of a book but unless a book interacts with us in the way Spufford describes above, it will never touch our hearts and imaginations or shape us as people. Through recalling the books that have impacted on our hearts and lives, we can introduce children to books which will do the same for them.

 Reflective activity

Construct your own reading autobiography addressing the questions listed below:

- When and how did you learn to read? Who had the most influence on your development as a reader? What books did you read – at home and at school? Was it a positive or negative experience?
- How did you develop as a reader as you got older? Was there a time when you read just one type of book or just one author? Did you ever stop reading?

(Continued)

(Continued)

- Do you read for pleasure now? What sort of things do you read? What are your favourite books?
- What influence has reading had on your life so far? How important is it to you?

You can create your reading autobiography in whatever way feels easiest to you. Some ideas are:

- Write a reflective account – make it almost a stream of consciousness – don't worry about spelling or grammar but just let your thoughts flow.
- Stick images of the covers of significant books on sheets of paper and annotate these, writing around the margin, to say why they are significant to you.
- Draw a road or a river, starting from your earliest memory to the last book you read. Draw or note significant events on that journey, including the books you remember.
- Take one or two key books which have been really significant to you and explore how and why they impacted on your life, trying to identify links between them.
- Make a video diary – talking about what reading has and does mean to you.

Reflection

As teachers of reading, what can we learn from this activity and how can we learn it? First, look at the books or texts that you have identified. Is there anything in common between them? Do they share a similar theme, style of writing, type of plot or period when they were written? Second, consider the times in your life that you recorded as significant to your development as a reader. What else was going on in your life at that time? What role was reading playing for you? Lastly, try and identify the emotions that were invoked by the books. Were they comforting, challenging, scary, escapist, familiar, strange, exciting or restful?

 ## Reflective activity

Draw a large gingerbread man shape on a piece of paper – that is you as a reader. Think about all the ideas generated both by your reading autobiography and the reflection on it and fill the shape with words or phrases coming from them. This is a description of you as a reader.

Children as readers

If we are to become effective teachers of reading, it is important not only to know what sort of readers we are, but also to know what reading means to the children in our classes. There is much research which can give us some generic insights into this.

I was teaching the reception class in a West Midlands school when Ed started his schooling. He was the eldest of three children and both he and his mother were excited about this big step in his development. Ed was a lively boy but did not engage willingly in free or structured play activities; he wanted to be with me, the teacher, all the time. Initially, I found this strange as he was not a timid or shy child. I began to understand however, when his mother came to ask me at the end of Ed's third day in school, when I was going to start to teach Ed to read. During those three days I had read to the class many many times; I had talked about books with them; I had begun to look at some letter–sound relationships and had even sent home picture books for the children to share with somebody. To Ed and his mother this was not what they considered 'learning to read'. They wanted a tin of small flash cards to learn, a 'reading book' containing those words and with a number on the front so they knew how good a reader Ed was, and a daily opportunity for Ed to read a book aloud to me as his teacher. Ed had come to school – this was where he was going to learn to read and he was waiting to be taught. It was the job of the teacher to do this and anything he had done before had nothing to do with it.

Bromley (1996), in her descriptions of literacy learning in her classroom, echoes the idea that prior values and ideas about reading influence the experience of learning to read in school. She described how Momahl, fluent in Urdu and not yet fluent in English, had learned traditional English nursery rhymes at home and recognised the characters. This meant that when sharing *Each Peach Pear Plum* with a first language English speaker who did not know the nursery rhyme characters, she supported her. Each child came to reading with different experiences and knowledge; in recognising these, the teacher was creating a community of reading in the classroom where there was mutual support.

The seminal work by Heath (1983) also makes this point. She describes three communities from which children came. In the white working-class community named Roadville, children were given books both for enjoyment and learning. These books consisted of labelled pictures, alphabets or nursery rhymes. Adults read these to the children, asking them to label objects and recognise words. The adults themselves seldom read for sheer enjoyment but used texts as a source of information; the written word therefore was considered a source of authority. In the black working-class community called Trackton, there were no special books for the children but literacy was seen as central to life and the practice of religion. Adults read aloud to each other and texts were commentated on and elaborated. Reading was necessary for everyday aspects of life, such as shopping, but it was the spoken word which gave a richness and depth to understanding and community cohesion.

When they went to school, the children from both of these communities began fairly well but did not develop because their experiences and understandings of the role and purpose of reading did not match that of the schools. It was children from the 'mainstream', whose experiences most closely matched the orientation towards reading that was found in school, who made the most significant progress. Heath argues that this is because they learned, 'the rules for talking about and responding to books' (1983: 262) and so came to know that what is contained in books is a written decontextualised representation of an event or artefact. This was the behaviour expected of readers in school and was of second nature to those from the mainstream community but strange to those from Trackton and Roadville.

The work of Heath seems to indicate that the reading behaviours in schools are different to those that many children have experienced in their homes and communities. The work of Gregory and Williams (2000) develops this point. Looking at the process of learning to read in the Spitalfields area of London, they claimed to challenge four myths about learning to read:

1. That poor achievement is equated with economic poverty. Gregory and Williams recount many examples of rich and varied literacy skills embedded in the lives of children.
2. That a certain type of parenting is needed to ensure early reading success. Many children were successful readers but had never enjoyed the 'bedtime story' experience so valued and did not have access to quality children's books.
3. That there is no match between the language and learning styles of the home and those expected in school. The research showed the skill of children in transferring skills and understandings and adapting to different expectations.
4. That there is a 'correct method' of teaching reading. Children in Gregory and Williams' research had learned to read in many different ways and in many different contexts. The key factor identified was the clear and definite passion in teachers for teaching about learning.

These researches may be challenging because they expose the deeply embedded assumptions with which we approach the teaching of reading. When you are next spending some time in a school, put them to the test. Are their findings transferable to the context in which you are teaching reading?

Reflective activity

- Talk to a sample of the children in your class about the reading they do out of school. You may like to create reading autobiographies with them. Find out about the reading they do at home, in clubs, societies, other school centres, informally. Remember to include all sorts of reading – not just printed books.
- Ask one or two children how they learned to read. Who helped them to read? What sort of things did they use to help them to learn to read? What was the first thing they can remember reading by themselves?
- Ask if the children can read in any language other than English? How did they learn to read in that language? In which language did they learn to read first? Which is the most difficult to read and why? In which language would they choose to read for fun?
- What has this activity told you about the sorts of readers the children in your class are?
- What does that mean for how you teach reading?
- How will you need to change your pedagogy and resources?

The National Literacy Trust carried out a survey in 2012 of the reading behaviours of children and young people and the results are challenging for teachers of reading. Read the report to find out detailed information but in summary the survey showed that levels of reading enjoyment have stayed the same since 2005; fewer children and young people read daily outside of school; technology is having a huge impact on reading behaviours; more children and young people think that reading is not 'cool' and would be embarrassed to be seen reading by their friends (Clark, 2013). In addition, the research showed a clear relationship between enjoyment of reading and attainment in reading. Those who achieve below the expected level for their age read less, read less frequently and do not enjoy reading. You might not be surprised by those findings but careful consideration needs to be given to the implications of the findings for teachers of reading. Can children be helped to become readers if they do not enjoy reading and do not read for pleasure?

Reading for pleasure

The programme of study for English in the 2014 National Curriculum for England says that, 'reading widely and often opens up a treasure-house of wonder and joy for curious minds' (DfE, 2013a: 14). We are highly unlikely to argue with that but how do teachers of reading evoke that curiosity which leads to the pleasure of reading? In trying to answer this question we need first to consider what government policy in recent years has said about the whole idea of reading for pleasure.

In 2003 the document *Excellence and Enjoyment: A Strategy for Primary Schools* (DfES, 2003) was published. The document stated that schools, while continuing to raise standards, should not be 'afraid to combine that with making learning fun' (DfES, 2003: 4). Unfortunately this seemed to have little impact as only a year later Ofsted (2004) commented that few schools were 'successfully engaging the interest of those who, though competent readers, did not read for pleasure'. Again in 2005 in its review of inspection evidence between 2000 and 2005, Ofsted said, 'Some teachers tell inspectors that teaching reading has lost its fun' (2005: 26). The idea that reading should be enjoyable continued to be emphasised by the Chief Inspector of Schools, David Bell (2005), and by a parliamentary inquiry into the teaching of reading which concluded that, 'Whatever method is used … we are convinced that inspiring an enduring enjoyment of reading should be a key objective' (House of Commons Education and Skills Committee, 2005).

However, there was little official recognition that this lack of enjoyment of reading stemmed from a strict emphasis on skills-based learning and the way in which the National Literacy Strategy (NLS) had led to a rigid implementation of defined pedagogy. There is no doubt that this strong emphasis on decoding skills had led to a rise in achievement in this aspect of reading.

International comparisons give an interesting picture of the progress of pupils in England towards becoming readers. The Progress in International Reading Literacy Study (PIRLS) is a large international survey which looks at pupils in about 40 different countries in relation to attainment in reading and attitudes towards reading. The survey was first conducted in 2001 and has since been carried out in 2006 and 2011. The next survey is due in 2016. The National Foundation for Educational Research has published a detailed analysis of the 2011 results for England and compared them to previous surveys. If you are interested in knowing more detail, it is worth looking at www.nfer.ac.uk/publications/PRTZ01/.

In 2001 England was ranked third overall, in 2006 fifteenth and in 2011 tenth in reading attainment. This is an interesting profile and needs to be placed in the context of what was asked in the survey and what was happening at the time both in terms of national policy towards the teaching of reading, and what was actually happening in classrooms. In relation to attitudes to reading, however, results in England have been more or less constant over time and in this aspect pupils in England tend to demonstrate poor attitudes to reading. In other words, they know how to read but do not enjoy doing so.

One has to be careful when reacting to large international surveys such as PIRLS. Hilton has criticised it (2006, 2007) both in terms of its methodology and also its cultural bias: 'I also point to the larger issue of subtle cultural hegemony involved in this kind of international survey where richer nations apparently do much better in what is claimed to be a context-free measurement' (2007: 987).

You might like to consider this criticism in the light of Gregory and Williams' work, which was discussed earlier in this chapter. Although the British government has taken the PIRLS results very seriously and used them to implement policies which seek to drive attainment even higher by emulating those countries whose pupils achieve more highly than those in England, it has to be asked if it is possible to get an accurate statistical representation of reading for pleasure.

Dictionary definitions of 'pleasure' describe it as a 'feeling of happy satisfaction and enjoyment', 'a source of enjoyment and delight' or 'something which is worth seeking out'. I am not sure how I would begin to measure that quantifiably, and yet there is no doubt that it is a significant element in being a reader. In 2003 five children's authors (Chris Powling, Bernard Ashley, Philip Pullman, Anne Fine and Jamila Gavin) published a booklet, *Meetings with the Minister*, lamenting the way in which the pedagogy of the teaching of reading was destroying the enjoyment of books. Philip Pullman said:

> The purpose of what I do as a writer is to delight. I hope that the children who read me will do so because they enjoy it (Powling et al., 2003: 9).

Way back in 1998, Brian Cox edited a collection of thoughts on reading written by the great and the good. Those who, for the most part, were enthusiastic and ardent readers emphasised the importance of reading for pleasure. Roy Hattersley wrote, 'Reading was meant to make us glad – and ought not to be described and discussed as if it were, like good manners and clean shoes, essential to the prospect of employment and the hope of promotion' (Hattersley, 1998: 50). The author Doris Lessing wrote, 'books, literature, libraries should be seen as treasure-houses of opportunity and pleasure, full of surprises and paths leading to whole worlds of delight, and never a sort of agenda or requirement of the adult world' (Lessing, 1998: 49).

Lessing's words are echoed in the introduction to the 2014 National Curriculum and reading for pleasure is beginning to come back onto the agenda. In 2010 Ofsted identified 12 schools who were successful in teaching children to read by the age of six (Ofsted, 2010). Ofsted drew out five characteristics of best practice from these case studies but the word 'enjoyment' did not appear in any of them. In 2011 Ofsted published a report entitled *Excellence in English* (Ofsted, 2011a) and here gave a high profile to reading for pleasure, advocating an innovative and creative curriculum which matches the pupils' needs and interests. This teaches us that government emphases and policies come and go but as teachers of reading, we need to hold firm to the essential purpose of reading, which is to gain information but also to give pleasure and enjoyment. This is what we need to demonstrate to the children whom we are teaching. How do we do that?

Reading for pleasure in the classroom

There are many ways of ensuring that classrooms offer opportunities for children to experience all that reading has to offer and these will be considered later in this chapter. The reflections you have already made on yourself as a reader will very likely have shown you that what is enjoyable to you may not be enjoyable to other people. Just the other day, I was enthusing to my husband about a book I was reading and talking about how the author created what, for me, was the essential meaning of the book. He looked at me in a rather perplexed way, commenting that it seemed a lot of fuss about not much! What to me was a source of much enjoyment and pleasure, to him was not worth bothering with. This difference in viewpoint will be repeated many times in classrooms and, as teachers of reading, it is important that we recognise this and avoid the false assumption that what brings us pleasure will be the same for every child in our class. However, it is also important to remember that it is part of our responsibility to introduce new sources of pleasure in reading to our pupils through both the texts we offer, the opportunities and experiences we create and by sharing our own excitement about reading. How is this done?

Reflective activity

When you spend some time in a primary school, consider how that school enables pupils to read for pleasure. You can discover this in several ways:

- Read the school's policy on the teaching of reading; see how often reading for pleasure is mentioned and what it says about it.
- Walk around the school and look at how reading is portrayed throughout the school. Consider wall displays, books and texts, the time given to reading and the emphasis given to reading in assemblies and other school events.
- Look carefully at the classroom in which you are working. How are books displayed? Are books read aloud to the children frequently? Are there opportunities for children to browse and read independently? What sort of texts are used in the classroom?

(Continued)

(Continued)

- Talk to the teacher or the literacy co-ordinator. What school-wide book events are held during the year? Is there a school library? Are there links with a local library or bookshop? Do authors visit? How do teachers keep up to date with recent publications?
- Talk to some children. Do they enjoy reading? What book are they currently reading? How did they choose that book? Do they read different books at home? Do they talk about their reading and who do they talk to?

The answer to these questions and observations will begin to give you an idea of the place of reading within the school and what the school thinks it is teaching when it teaches reading. Could you summarise this in a short paragraph? When you have done that, consider what is missing and reflect on what could be done to enhance the teaching of reading and what you will do as a teacher responsible for helping children to become readers.

Whole-school strategies

There are many things which can be done within the whole-school community to raise the profile of reading and there are many sources of ideas. One useful source is a website by a previous children's laureate, Michael Rosen, sponsored by Pearson, called Reading Revolution (www.readingrevolution.co.uk). The mission of this site is stated as to make every school into a 'book loving school' where 'books are prioritised and enjoyed'. The site contains a lot of ideas, some of which are incorporated in the rest of this chapter. They, and others, will be developed further in Chapter 5, 'Providing a reading environment'.

The school library

A school library should be a place which is vibrant and exciting and draws people in to explore books and reading. It should be situated at the heart of the school and not in a dark unused classroom or in a corridor. It should be somewhere which introduces children (and staff) to new books and authors and invites them to read and browse. Books will be displayed with the front cover showing so that they are attractive and colourful. The whole library should be bright and cheerful with continually changing displays of different genres, authors and texts in different modes. The library should be well organised and signed so that readers can easily find what they want. The library should be comfortable to use, with cushions, bean bags, chairs and tables, not looking like a classroom. The library should be a place that is constantly in use; children reading and looking for information, adults reading to and with children, children and adults talking about books and what they have read, children and adults browsing and reading independently.

Making books accessible

There are lots of ways in which quality reading materials can be made accessible to children, teachers and parents:

- Book clubs – I belong to a group which meets once a month to talk about a book which we have all read. Sometimes I love the book I read and sometimes I hate it, but I enjoy being introduced to books which I would not have normally chosen to read by myself. Groups like this can happen in schools: children meeting at a lunchtime or after school, teachers using staff meetings to share children's books that they have enjoyed, parents meeting in the school to share books that their children enjoy or even just to talk about what they enjoy reading.

- Book swaps – place large boxes of books in the entrance to the school. Parents and teachers can put in books they have read and choose one which somebody else has enjoyed. In another box children can do exactly the same thing. It does not matter what 'level' these books are at (this idea of 'levels' will be discussed more in the next chapter); the purpose of these book swap boxes is to encourage children and adults to read for pleasure in whatever way they want to.

- Bookshops – there are many organisations which will come to schools and set up a display for a day or two, encouraging children to buy books. As a parent, I can remember feeling under enormous pressure to buy a book from these sales when often I would prefer to buy other books. Look carefully at these book sale promotions and if you have a good local bookshop then ask them if they will come to sell books instead. Incorporate it with a parents' evening, school fête or special occasion. Try and ensure that the book sale has as wide a range as possible; of prices, of publishers and authors, of titles and of types of reading materials.

- Reading events – hold sponsored reads, author visits, book-making workshops. In fact, look for every opportunity to incorporate reading into the life of the school. Make reading the 'cool' thing to do and ensure that all these activities do not mention ability to decode, attainment in reading or require children to write or do anything to follow-up their reading. They are for enjoyment and pleasure with the purpose of wanting the children to read even more and understand how good reading can be.

- Reading display – create displays throughout the school which entice children into reading. You could make a focus on one particular author and have lots of pictures and snippets of information about her/his life. Focus on one or two books, giving comments by the author on them and short extracts, finishing on a cliffhanger but telling the children where they can find the book to read it for themselves. Other themes could be books about school, funny books, 'baddies' in books, ways of finding out about something, poetry, and so on. Collect photographs of famous and not-so-famous people reading and display them around the school.

- Reading assemblies – once a month a school assembly could be all about reading. Teachers could take it in turns to talk about books that they have enjoyed reading, different classes could tell the rest of the school about the book they have been listening to, the local librarian or bookseller could come and tell about new publications, extracts from films of books could be shown, stories and poems could be performed by children or staff!

- Time for reading – it is often said that we spend so much time and effort on teaching children how to read but rarely give them much time to read in school. Over the years there have been many initiatives to support this: Everybody Reading In Class (ERIC) and Drop Everything And Read (DEAR) are just two examples. All that has to happen is that for anything between 5 and 15 minutes everybody in the school reads, including all adults and any visitors to the school. Adults read whatever they happen to be reading at the moment and a selection of reading materials can be supplied for visitors. Why is this a good thing? It shows children that reading is something worth giving time to, it is not something which is fitted in when 'work' is finished but something which is prioritised.

Classroom strategies

All of the activities outlined above as whole-school strategies can be very easily adapted to use in individual classrooms. Do not feel that because a school is not willing to adopt a strong policy you are not able to do anything in your classroom. Of course, it is best if ideas permeate throughout the school but it may be that the enthusiasm and excitement generated in your classroom will spread throughout the school in time! In addition to those things described above, there are two really important things which you need to ensure are happening within your classroom in order to create a climate of reading for pleasure.

- Reading aloud to children. There should be a planned regular time when you read aloud to children and this should happen whatever the age of child you are teaching. This will be discussed in a later chapter as a teaching strategy but for now it is important that you appreciate how crucial it is. By reading aloud to children you are broadening their knowledge of children's books and authors, enticing them in to reading for themselves and showing them what is waiting for them out there in the big world of children's books. You are also demonstrating to them the rhythms and patterns of language, modelling good reading and showing the power of language.

- Talking about books and reading. Again we will discuss this later as a teaching strategy but it is important that there is talk, talk and more talk about reading. In my book club I am often amazed that other people see things in a completely different way from me and in hearing their views and perspectives my own are challenged and I re-think and either justify or change my own views. Not every child will like or interpret books in the same way; that is good, but they need to be shown how to justify and explain why they think or feel in the way they do and what it was in the book that caused that reaction in them. It is through talking about books that readers who read critically, responsively, intelligently and with pleasure are created.

In reflecting on encouraging reading for pleasure in your classroom, it is important to realise that this is not just for a warm fuzzy feeling about books and the enjoyment they offer. There is increasing evidence that reading for pleasure increases attainment. Sullivan and Brown (2013) discovered that children who read for pleasure made more progress between the ages of 10 and 16 in mathematics, vocabulary and spelling than those children who read infrequently. Reading for pleasure was a more significant factor in cognitive development than the level of education of parents. However, cognitive development is not the only aspect and Cliff Hodges (2010: 66) argued that reading literature, among other things, allows the reader to 'reflect on themselves as human beings as they shuttle back and forth between literature and life', thus offering support for social, emotional and creative development.

Conclusion

This chapter began by reflecting on myself as a reader and coming to an understanding of what sort of reader I am and how pleasurable reading is to me. It was recognised that readers are all individual with different ways of approaching books and responding to them. In acknowledging this, teachers can begin to identify ways in which they can support the children in their classrooms to become readers, not just to know how to read.

It may well be that some teachers do not enjoy reading and do not consider themselves to be readers. How then can they help children to become readers and read for pleasure? There are two points to be made in relation to this. First, it is important not to have too narrow a concept of what being a reader means. Recognition of the reading that takes place during the normal course of a life will usually show that we all read a variety of texts, on screen, in the environment as well as in print. These are all valid and important reading experiences and no less significant than other types of reading. Second, we need to acknowledge that reading for pleasure is not restricted to reading fiction; it might be non-fiction or any sort of multimodal texts such as film, computer games or websites. All these make similar demands on the reader in response and comprehension, although the decoding skills might be different.

The key messages that this chapter offers to the reader who is becoming a teacher of reading are:

- recognise the sort of reader you are and what pleasure reading gives to you
- acknowledge different types of readers and the different ways in which reading gives pleasure to them
- identify the many different types of texts there are to read in the world and the different reading behaviours needed by each type of text
- consider a range of strategies that you can adopt in your school and classroom to give children access to the pleasure of reading.

All these messages can be summed up by ensuring that your classroom both is and offers up to children the 'treasure-house of wonder and joy' that is reading.

Further reading

Clark, C. and Rumbold, K. (2006) *Reading for Pleasure: A Research Overview.* London: National Literacy Trust.

Lockwood, M. (2008) *Promoting Reading for Pleasure in the Primary School.* London: Sage.

Reading for pleasure has an important place in the National Curriculum and should be at the core of all teaching of reading. The first of these books helps an understanding of why this should be so and the second gives some practical ideas for making it work in school.

Ghaye, T. (2010) *Teaching and Learning through Reflective Practice: A Practical Guide for Positive Action,* 2nd edn. London: David Fulton.

Pollard, A., with Anderson, J., Maddock, M., Swaffield, S., Wairn, J. and Warwick, P. (2014) *Reflective Teaching in Schools,* 4th edn. London: Continuum.

Outstanding teachers are, in their very nature, critically reflective and these two books help to unpick what that really means and how it works out in practice.

CHAPTER 3

WHAT DO WE READ?

Chapter objectives

At the end of this chapter you should:

- appreciate the importance of a secure and current knowledge of children's books
- know how to keep up to date with knowledge of children's books
- have read and thought about key texts and made a personal response
- understand the broad range of texts and how the text type affects the reading process.

Introduction

In this first section of the book which looks at the subject knowledge required by teachers of reading, we have so far looked at the different theoretical perspectives on the reading process. It became apparent that reading is a very complex process and priorities in teaching will be determined by the theoretical perspective adopted by the teacher of reading. It also became clear that teachers' understanding of reading is influenced by their own experiences and behaviours. The second chapter looked at teachers themselves as readers and acknowledged the many different types of texts and the different ways there are of reading different texts.

The role of the text has become a key element in our discussion of reading and the teaching of reading. It is crucial to acknowledge that any consideration of the teaching of reading must include consideration of the texts that are being read and this is the focus of this chapter. We begin by looking at research which demonstrates how important it is that teachers of reading have a strong knowledge of children's books. The chapter then goes on to consider what it means to have that knowledge – what there is to know about children's books and how teachers can develop that knowledge. The chapter will then broaden out to look at different types of texts and how they affect the reading process and reading behaviours.

Teachers of reading knowing about children's books

At the end of the last chapter we discussed the importance of reading for pleasure and how it is beginning to come back into the foreground after many years out in the wilderness. Some strategies were suggested for ensuring that reading is a pleasurable experience for the children in your class. However, you might well have realised that in order to effectively create those experiences, you, as the teacher, need to have a secure knowledge of children's books and ensure that that knowledge is continually developing. Without pleasure in the reading experience, the teaching of reading can become just 'nutritious technical cabbage' without the joy of the 'list of desserts' (Dombey et al., 1998: 129–30).

The National Curriculum 2013 places reading for pleasure at the heart of the programmes of study. In the programmes of study for Key Stage 1 it states that 'pupils should be taught to develop pleasure in reading, motivation to read' (DfE, 2013a: 4 and 18) and in Key Stage 2 teachers are required to teach pupils to develop 'positive attitudes to reading and understanding what they read' (DfE, 2013a: 25 and 33). This gives teachers of reading the opportunity, indeed the requirement, to use whole texts in a way which encourages children to read and respond in readerly ways. They need, however, to know about books which enable that sort of reading to take place.

The work of Cremin et al. (2008b) looked at primary teachers' knowledge of children's books. They found that teachers relied on a limited set of books to use in their classrooms and that many of these were books they themselves had known as children. Teachers were asked to name six authors, poets and picturebook makers, and those named were within a very narrow range of well-known authors.

Teachers only seemed to know those books which were to be found within classrooms already and often the same authors were named within all categories. This is an issue of concern if part of being a teacher of reading involves introducing children to the world of books and broadening their repertoire and experiences. The teachers in this sample did not have a strong or diverse enough knowledge of children's books to enable them to comply with the requirements of the 2014 National Curriculum to teach every pupil to develop enjoyment of reading. This requires a broad knowledge of what is available.

The clear implication for intending teachers of reading is the importance of knowing a wide range of children's books, being able to discern quality texts and knowing what they can offer to children. However, research by Applegate and Applegate (2004) carried out with trainee teachers had similar findings to that of Cremin et al., working with experienced teachers some years later; knowledge of children's books was very limited. Applegate and Applegate described the situation in a rather powerful way:

> We began to think of the problem in somewhat biblical proportions, recalling the story of the Apostle Peter who, when asked for money by a beggar who had been crippled from birth, replied by stating that he could not give what he did not have (Acts 3:5). We began to refer to the 'Peter Effect' as the condition characterizing those teachers who are charged with conveying to their students an enthusiasm for reading that they do not have. (2004: 556)

 ## Reflective activity

Consider your own knowledge of and attitudes towards children's books. The Applegate and Applegate research with trainee teachers included the following questions:

- What reading did you do this past summer? Are there any titles or authors you can recall? In general, what did you read for recreation?
- Who is your favourite author? What, in particular, do you like about this author?

The Cremin et al. research asked teachers to:

- List six 'good' children's writers
- Name six 'good' poets
- Name six picture fiction creators

How did you fare in answering those questions? It may well be that you are now feeling a little unsure of your own knowledge of children's books! Don't worry – later in this chapter some sources of information and ways of discovering the latest 'good' texts will be discussed. First, we will explore why this is considered to be so important. Do you have to be an enthusiastic reader to be an effective teacher of reading? Why can't you enthuse children about reading using a small number of classic and well-loved texts?

Knowing about children's books

In subsequent chapters we will consider several strategies that teachers use for teaching children how to become readers. Two of those are reading aloud to children and talking with children about books. Through these means children are introduced to everything that texts, of all different kinds, can offer them. If these activities are to be really meaningful, however, it is important that teachers themselves have a deep understanding and appreciation of the books. Michael Morpurgo (2012) argues that children are able to see when teachers are not sincere about what they are saying, and so, 'To use books simply as a teacher's tool is unlikely to convince many children that books are for them, particularly those that are failing already, many of whom will be boys'.

Books are not just a teaching tool but offer entry into other worlds and minds. If teachers are to open these doors for children, it is their professional responsibility to know what lies behind them and to have experienced what is offered for themselves. A limited knowledge of texts means a limited offering of experiences for children. Many teachers or parents will tell you that fashions often occur in the reading experiences of children; a series of books will catch the imagination of a particular age group and everybody will read and re-read every book in the series. Many of you reading this will have grown up with Harry, Ron and Hermione and the Harry Potter phenomenon will have been part of your childhood. Those books were the gateway to reading for many children who read those long books, carried along by their popularity. As a teacher, you would probably have read the Harry Potter books yourself and so been able to engage in dialogue with your pupils about them, but the next stage is to use that enthusiasm to introduce them to other texts and broaden their reading repertoire. Do you know what texts you might suggest a keen Harry Potter fan to read next? If the reader was into fantasy, they might like the Percy Jackson series by Rick Riordon, *Seraphina* by Rachel Hartman, *The Spiderwick Chronicles* by Tony DiTerlizzi and Holly Black or the *Artemis Fowl* series by Eoin Colfer. Have you, as a teacher of reading, read books that you could recommend to a child in your class and so fully exploit the enthusiasm that was generated by the fashion of Harry Potter?

In being able to make appropriate recommendations for reading to children, the teacher of reading is acting in the role of, what Aidan Chambers describes as 'the enabling adult' (1991). This is the person who determines the selection of books that are available in the classroom, makes time for reading and encourages children's responses to reading. This is an important element of the teaching of reading. In the first chapter, the centrality of the text in the reading process was established and it was seen how what is read has a huge impact on the process of becoming a reader. Reading impacts on cognitive, social and emotional development. It might be thought to go without saying that in order for this influence to be at its most effective the text needs to be powerful enough to make an impact; it needs to engage with the readers at all those levels. In Chapter 7 we will explore further about how this can happen.

However, not only do books need to engage children at an emotional and imaginative level, they also need to support them in the process of making sense of the text. It is this second point which determines the quality of a text for beginner readers, and it is the knowledge of this which is essential for teachers of reading. When choosing books to use in class, teachers have to decide if a text is:

- worthy in relation to the quality of its writing and 'literariness'
- has suitable content for the children
- provides adequate and appropriate support for an early or developing reader
- relates to the children's interests and enthusiasms.

All these decisions require considerable depth of knowledge on the part of a teacher, and we are now going to take each point in turn and examine in detail the criteria on which choices can be made.

Identifying 'quality' texts

I remember that for my daughter's third birthday, a friend gave her a paperback copy of the complete original version of *The Wind in the Willows*. I was astounded that anybody should consider that a suitable book for a three-year-old and bemused as to why it had been chosen. I guessed that it was a book my friend had read as a child and knew to be a 'classic' text and one which every respectable child should possess. There is much elitism around the world of books and it is easy to feel intimidated when expressing opinions about books. Goodwin (2008) distinguishes between literary appreciation and personal enjoyment and that is an important distinction to make. I am very able to appreciate the literary merits of *The Lord of the Rings*, but I have to admit that I do not enjoy it and have not been able to finish reading even the first book.

How then do we define a 'quality' text? Margaret Meek (1988) claimed that some of the most important lessons children need to learn about reading are taught by the texts themselves. Quality texts are those which teach readers about how texts work and lead them through a sense-making process, allowing them to interact and respond to the text. Her point can be easily understood when one compares the rich language of texts by authors such as Anthony Browne and David McKee among others with the language of texts written with only words which can be phonically decoded. Barthes (1993) described texts as being either 'readerly' or 'writerly'. The latter are those which demand much of the reader, who is as much a part of the creation of the text as the author. In many such texts the illustrations and the words relate to each other in such a way that the reader fills the gaps in order to create their own meaning. Iser (1978) talked about the gaps in texts where readers are required to build bridges; in such texts reading becomes an active process in which the reader has to participate fully in the meaning-making process and bring to bear all they have learned about language, the world and how people operate with and within it. Different readers will create different meanings.

An example of a text for young children which draws the reader in is *Don't Let the Pigeon Drive the Bus* by Mo Willems (2003). If possible, have a copy of this book in front of you while you read the next few paragraphs. The cover shows the large figure of a pigeon and coming from somewhere off the page is a speech bubble which contains the title of the book. The next double-page spread shows the pigeon, eyes closed with a dreamy expression on his face and a large thought bubble showing different images of the pigeon driving the bus. What does the reader understand and whose side are we on? We see a pigeon longing to do something and an unknown figure is stopping him. What is our role as the reader in this?

Over the page, the title page shows the bus driver. A large speech bubble comes out of his mouth and he explains who he is and involves the reader by asking him to watch the bus for a while. He reminds the reader of just one thing and again the title of the book is printed. The reader is now part of the story and what happens next is up to him. Willems is making very explicit what theorists such as Iser, Barthes and Meek have been discussing. In order to make complete sense of the story the reader has to take an active part and fill in the gaps. On the next page the bus driver exits to the left and on the far right we see the head of the pigeon peeping in. The physical pages of the book have become the stage for the drama that is about to be played out with the reader as a key player. The pigeon positions himself centre stage and engages in a string of persuasive language, trying to make the reader give him permission to drive the bus. He directly addresses the reader and within the text there are natural breaks for the reader (or listener in the case of very young children) to make a response. This is not explicit but assumed by the nature of the role given to the reader and the language used within the text.

Some children I have shared this book with have wanted to allow the pigeon to drive the bus and have been literally bouncing with excitement at the thought of him driving the big red truck at the end! Others have become very 'adult' and 'responsible' and strictly forbid the pigeon to ride the bus.

In Margaret Meeks's terms, what has this text taught the young reader about reading? It has taught that:

- reading is an active interaction between the words, the illustrations and the reader
- there can be many different interpretations of a text
- readers bring their experiences of life to help them understand what a book is about
- readers identify with characters in books.

Contrast this with the reader from a well-known scheme. On the left-hand page of the double-page spread are pictures of the characters, each labelled underneath. On the right-hand page is a small coloured picture of a troll sitting on a bridge facing a small goat wearing a hat. The text says:

'Let me cross!' said Billy the Kid. 'Let me get a fat red plum.'

'No,' said the big bad troll.

The words which are not phonically decodable are printed in red.

There are 'gaps' in this text but they are the sort of gaps which require a certain amount of knowledge: if this knowledge is not there the reader has to make sense of the text only from the limited information given. The young child is unlikely to make the link of the name of the goat with the notorious outlaw Billy the Kid, known both for his charm and his propensity to shoot people. The very young child might not even know that a young goat is known as a kid. The reader learns that he can either decode this book or he can't: if he possesses certain knowledge the story will make more sense to him than if he doesn't. The role of the reader is to access the text.

Teachers of reading need to know about what texts offer to readers and to make the appropriate choices about what they want children to learn or practise at that time. Both these texts have something to offer but teachers need to know what that is and to be aware of the limitations and opportunities of each text. *Billy the Kid* (Munton and Miskin, 2006) is a more useful text for practising decoding skills and *Don't Let the Pigeon Drive the Bus* is a more useful text for exploring what it means to be a reader.

Identifying 'suitable' texts

Goodwin (2008: 7) gives the synopsis of a well-known book for young children:

Peter, whose father has been killed whilst taking part in a robbery, is determined to get involved in similar criminal activity despite the pleas of his mother. The story starts as the lad sets out with the deliberate intention of stealing from an elderly neighbour. He breaks into the old man's property and steals some food. The rest of the story recounts the consequences of Peter's delinquency.

If you were given that synopsis, would you choose that story for a very young child? I doubt it, and yet *Peter Rabbit* is commonly considered a classic book for young children. What makes a book suitable or unsuitable? Who decides? I know parents who worried about their pre-teen children reading Harry Potter – were they right to worry? Can books do harm to children?

Reflective activity

Go to your local library and browse through the children's section. Are there any books which you would not choose to give to children?

Read the opening pages of *The Graveyard Book* by Neil Gaiman. It includes the following,

> The man Jack paused on the landing. With his left hand he pulled a large white handkerchief from the pocket of his black coat, and with it he wiped off the knife and his gloved right hand which had been holding it; then he put the handkerchief away. The hunt was almost over. He had left the woman in her bed, the man on the bedroom floor, the older child in her brightly coloured bedroom, surrounded by toys and half-finished models. That left only the little one, a baby barely a toddler, to take care of. One more and his task would be done. (2008: 3–4)

What age child would you suggest read that book?

What are the criteria on which you made your decisions?

Every text, even the simplest, is full of the values of the writer and many texts are written with those values explicitly foregrounded. Others are more subtle and the values are not so obvious to the inexperienced reader. Historically, for some people the universal development of literacy was seen as a means of transmitting particular values and belief systems. Tucker (1981) writes of the 'cognitive dissonance' experienced by children when what they see in literature does not match with their experiences of life. Life no longer makes sense to them and so they need to, in Piagetian terms, accommodate the new knowledge.

Hollindale (1988) identifies different levels of ideology which can operate within texts. An ideology is the set of beliefs held by a particular individual or group. These are:

- implicit ideology – those which are deeply embedded within the text and are often 'taken-for-granted' and sometimes unrecognised but usually unproblematised by the writer.
- the ideology of the dominant culture of the time – a text which unquestioningly reflects the ideas and values of the time and place.
- Explicit ideology – where a text deliberately seeks to convey a particular value system. An example of this is *The Conquerors* by David McKee (2004). The army of a powerful country takes over the world by invading, fighting and subduing all other countries. Eventually only one tiny country remains and so an invading force is sent to conquer. No resistance is offered and so the invading soldiers lodge with families and share with them in their daily work and play. The invading soldiers learn the stories and songs, the food, the customs and the lifestyle of the new country. On returning home, the General finds his lifestyle has become like that of the small country. Who had conquered whom?

For inexperienced readers, it can be challenging to identify the underlying ideology of a text. We rarely articulate our own values and assume that they are shared by the majority. Talking about the text and playing with a text, by making changes to it, is a way of making underlying values explicit. Stephens (1992) argues about the importance of teaching children strategies to enable them to be aware of implicit value systems in texts and of how authors 'manipulate' readers. This is clearly an important skill of effective readers and a crucial skill in a modern democratic society. However, Chambers argues that 'a requirement of fulfilled readership is a willingness to give oneself up to the book. Mature readers have learned how to do this: how to lay aside their own prejudices and take on the prejudices of the text' (1985: 36–7).

Lowe (2007) in her detailed account of the development of her two children as readers, discusses this dilemma. Her children loved to have read to them the Narnia books by C.S. Lewis, and yet for Lowe the underlying ideology of these books contradicted the value system which she, as a parent, held and wished to convey to her children. She writes:

> I continued to read and reread the series when they were requested despite all my ideological disagreements. The children gained from the series ... Although, for the duration of the story Lewis's ideology could be accepted, I was also capable of pointing it out on occasions ... it was the covert ideology that temporarily influenced the children rather than the overt one ... Ultimately it was the family ideology that influenced the children, not that of the authors they read, however often and with whatever passion. (2007: 117–18)

Learning how to read critically, or against the text, is an important part of becoming a reader. Teachers of reading can help children do this through activities that

UNIVERSITY OF WINCHESTER
LIBRARY

involve talk and manipulation of texts. More of this will be discussed in Chapter 8. However, if teachers of reading are to help children to read in this way, it is important that they are able to do so themselves. I hope that as you are reading this book, you are relating what I say to your own experiences of reading and of sharing books with children. Look for hints in how I write about my own underpinning ideology, as I suggested you do in the first chapter, and consider your own position and how it relates to mine.

In making judgements about the suitability or otherwise of books, the teacher of reading is entering an unclear world where there are no right answers. The teacher needs to know the children for whom the book is chosen, the parents/carers and their value systems and ideals, the social and cultural environment of the school and its community and their own ideology. While the choice of book has to be a very personal one, influenced by the context and purpose of its use, there are some key principles surrounding that choice process:

- As the teacher, know the book well. Never use a book with children that you have not read and thought about before – preferably several times.
- Always mediate any 'controversial' book with the children – talk about it – what it means and why the author might be writing about that topic or in that way.
- Do not court controversy for the sake of it, consider how the book supports the development of children as effective critical readers.

Identifying texts that support the young reader

Previous discussions have already hinted at some key elements within a book which can provide scaffolding for the young reader. Quality texts will engage children and draw them into the story or narration. Suitable texts will challenge readers and cause them to reflect on viewpoints and ideologies. Yet readers at the beginning of their journey will need texts which support them and allow them to practise all those skills of becoming a reader safely. What sort of texts do that?

We have already referred to the work by Meek (1988) *How Texts Teach what Readers Learn* and have seen how texts support the reader. Look at this useful book and you will see how Meek demonstrates how the classic children's book *Rosie's Walk* teaches children how texts work and guides the reader through the text. Because of the relationship between the illustrations the reader feels in control and knows more than Rosie herself does. The meaning of the text is much more than what the words alone convey and so the young reader begins to learn about irony.

Smith (2008) takes Meek's arguments a step further, saying that it is not just the good texts which teach powerful lessons but that all texts do; it is just that the less good texts teach less useful lessons. Smith analyses two texts – one from a well-established reading scheme and one by the author Lauren Child. Smith identifies the lessons taught by the reading scheme book:

- reading is achievable. A phonically consistent limited vocabulary which allows a beginner reader to decode a text alone gives a strong sense of personal achievement and confidence. This is a good thing
- the way in which conventional texts are laid out
- the importance of the narrative voice and of narrative direction. There is an absent third-person narrator who drives the story along in one direction.

Smith agrees that these are important lessons for readers to learn but asks if they are enough. She argues that early reading experiences establish the 'habits of thinking we will use as readers all through our reading lives' (2008: 36). Her analysis of *My Uncle is a Hunkle, Says Clarice Bean* by Lauren Child yields more reading lessons offered by quality texts. Smith identifies these as:

- that reading is an active process
- that readers bring all they can to the reading process
- that readers read against the grain
- that readers need to be flexible.

Bear those points in mind as we look closely at a text to identify the lessons it will teach readers and how it will support them in the reading process. The text is *The Yes* by Sarah Bee. For a really detailed analysis of this book which will explore in real depth how it works, read an entry on the blog 'Did you ever stop to think and forget to start again?'. This is a blog where comments on children's literature are posted – you can find it here: http://didyoueverstoptothink.wordpress.com/2014/03/01/interplay-in-the-yes-by-sarah-bee-and-satoshi-kitamura/.

The cover of the book shows a large orange creature with no distinguishable features except for an open mouth and three legs. The creature is standing on a hill, with trees in the distance and the green grass covered with leaves. The centre of the figure is filled with the bold letters 'the Yes'. The use of lower case for 'the' and the larger font for 'Yes' with a capital 'Y' gives a clear indication of the positivity of this book. It is all about 'Yes'.

The story begins with the Yes curled up in a dark nest surrounded by plants. It is safe and secluded – the only sight of the world is through a small round 'window' at the top. The Yes looks comfortable and settled. On the next page, however, we are out in the world. The Yes is there – but much smaller and heading off on a journey. It is taking him to the next page and the reader needs to turn the page to see where he is going. The text provides the explanation:

... the Yes had a Where to go to.

As the journey progresses, the Yes moves from left to right, taking the reader's eyes in the direction required for reading English. The pictures show the danger of the Where – it is full of Nos and they cover the Where in darkness – not full and cosy like the nest but spiky and threatening. The meaning is conveyed not only through the print but also through the illustrations. The journey of the Yes through the Where parallels the reader's journey through the text. Sometimes the print itself changes – it becomes smaller or larger, bolder or fainter, and words leap out of lines to position themselves elsewhere on the page.

The penultimate double-page spread is a superb example of this. A hill rises from the bottom left-hand corner to the top right-hand corner. At the bottom of the hill are the Nos, black and scratchy. As the hill climbs the Nos get smaller and fainter and there are no Nos on the right-hand page. On that page is the Yes. On the left-hand page the print reflects what is happening, not only in the words chosen but in the font and positioning. It starts off large and black with the word 'up' written even larger and bolder and jumping up the page. The words which describe the disappearance of the Nos get smaller and fainter and descend down the page. On the right-hand side are the words, 'There was only the Yes.' – the final affirmation.

How does this book support the beginner reader?

- The interplay between the print and the illustration is powerful; they work together to tell the story and so the inexperienced reader has lots of clues to help the meaning-making process.
- The language is simple and yet reflects the patterns and rhythms of everyday language.
- There is repetition and rhyme.
- The journey of the story reflects the physical journey of reading the book.
- The text is simple yet full of emotion and readers can relate to it at many levels.
- The anonymity of the figures used means they can be made into anything which relates to each reader and yet the emotion is universal.
- The words chosen play about with familiar language in a way that draws children in; it is not difficult but playful.
- The layout reflects the meaning and makes demands, while at the same time giving hints to a reader of how the book is to be read.

There are many books which enable children to develop these good habits of reading, and it is the task of the teacher of reading to ensure that these are available for the readers in the classroom. In order to do this, a teacher needs to be able to see the lessons that texts teach readers. As Smith says, 'Books produced by creative people for creative purposes are likely to encourage creative thinking. Books that tease, charm and challenge will produce readers that are alert and responsive' (2008: 41).

Identifying books that relate to children's interests and enthusiasms

So far, we have only discussed fictional texts yet it is evident that there are many more different types of text which we read. It is important that we recognise this and do not limit children's reading experiences to fiction. For some children this may be an excluding factor to the pleasure of reading. When my copy of *The Yes* arrived in the post, I read it once and was so excited I wanted to share it with everyone. I read it to my husband and showed him why I thought it was so good; he listened in a rather bemused way and said he did not know what all the fuss was about. He never reads fiction and yet spends hours poring over model railway, photography and gardening magazines. Teachers of reading need to know about all types of text and make them available in the classroom.

My husband may not like it but he is typical as a male reader in his preference for non-fiction texts. Smith (2004) looked at six young successful readers and found that their reading of non-fiction concerned with stereotypical male interests (for example football, space, dinosaurs) validated them as readers among their peers because of the knowledge gained on each subject and so reading became a socially acceptable activity for them. This contrasts with the experience of many boys (Gilbert and Gilbert, 1998).

The National Literacy Framework (DfEE, 1998) identified six different types of non-fiction texts: discussion, explanatory, procedural, non-chronological reports, persuasive and discursive. For each text type specific characteristics were given in relation to the language used and the structure of the text. In many classrooms today children are still learning these characteristics and yet when we consider the many types of text – both on paper and on screen – we can see that life is not as simply defined as the National Literacy Framework would have had us believe.

Let us look at one book which informs us about polar bears: *Ice Bear* by Nicola Davies (2005). This is certainly a non-fiction book and yet both the language used and the illustrations have a poetic and magical quality to them. The first thing one notices about this book is that it is written in the first person from the perspective of the Inuit. The first words are, 'Our people...', which immediately creates a sense of identity and empathy. There is a sense of ownership of the polar bear, 'A polar bear, made for our frozen world!' and this leads to a pride and identification both with the bear and the landscape. The reader is drawn in and sometimes the position of the reader and the text is directly addressed, 'A single paw would fill this page and shred the paper with claws'. Some words are written in upper case for emphasis – 'ALONE' – and others are written in a larger and bolder font – 'Play!'. Sometimes the language used is sheer poetry:

Giants flowing in the whiteness, tumbling, beautiful as snowflakes ...

None of this matches the expected characteristics of an information text. There is an index at the back and on most pages there is a sentence written in a smaller font weaving across the bottom of the page, giving the relevant facts. Below the index, the reader is reminded to read both types of of font in order to find out information. This is a book which conveys lots of information but in a particular way. What sort of child would you introduce this to? Might it serve as a bridge between non-fiction and fiction for some readers?

Another non-fiction book which does not follow the traditional conventions of non-fiction information texts is *Archie's War* by Marcia Williams. This takes the form of a scrapbook created by Archie Albright, aged ten years, created to tell his personal story of the First World War. The book starts with a note stuck in at the end of the war by fifteen-year-old Archie and the following pages are full of drawings, annotations, things stuck in, speech bubbles and pictures. Together they tell the story of how the war affected Alfie and his family. In order to make sense of this text the reader has to put together information from a variety of sources and create the story for themselves. There is no one way to read the text and each re-reading reveals different elements and information.

 Reflective activity

If possible, take one of these books and share them with a child. Look at the book together, talking about it, but letting the child take the lead. Watch and listen carefully and consider the decisions that the child makes about which bit to read first, how long to look at the pages without speaking, what the book is about and how it relates to their life.

Compare the child's reading with your own reading of the text and try and fit both into the theoretical perspectives on reading discussed in the first chapter.

What does that tell you about the relationship between the text and the reading process?

Identifying multimodal texts

Books are not the only thing that children (or adults) read. In many classrooms you will find comics, magazines and graphic novels, although Clark (2012) found that children's reading of comics is declining quite rapidly and even classic comics are now published only online (www.dandy.com). The teacher of reading needs to provide texts which will engage children and entice them into the reading experience. This can be a challenge for teachers and it is important that they know what it is that excites children. We have already seen that this is not always what teachers might expect. Technology has had a huge impact on not only what we read but also how we read. Rose (2011) describes this situation: 'a new type of narrative is emerging, one that's told through many media at once in a way that's nonlinear, participatory and above all, immersive'. *Archie's War* is an example of a non-linear text in which the reader immerses themself to find a way through and to make meaning.

Graphic novels tell stories using both images and words. When I was young there was a clearly held belief that when you were beginning to read you read books with lots of pictures and few words, and as you became more competent, the words became smaller and more numerous and the pictures disappeared. That is certainly not the case today. Graphic novels are often similar to comics in their format and the way in which image and word work together sequentially, using both speech and thought bubbles. It could be argued that the difference lies in the literary merit attributed to graphic novels which is often not given to comics. Many publishers have brought out graphic novel versions of popular books, for example the *Alex Rider* series by Anthony Horowitz, and Gareth Hinds has created graphic novel versions of some Shakespeare plays.

Graphic novels can take many forms and the only way to become familiar with them and the demands they place on the reader is to read some for yourself. Start with the *Robot City* series by Paul Collicutt (www.robotcity.co.uk) and then read *The Invention of Hugo Cabret* by Brian Selznick. This combines the conventional use of print and the use of image and is a challenging read. The website about the book (www.theinventionofhugocabret.com/about_hugo_intro.htm) says of it, '*The Invention of Hugo Cabret* is not exactly a novel, and it's not quite a picture book, and it's not really a graphic novel, or a flip book, or a movie, but a combination of all these things.'

There are many picture books which have no words or very few words and they provide yet another reading experience. Do not assume that these are an easier read; they can be very challenging. Look at *Clown* by Quentin Blake or *The Red Tree* by Shaun Tan.

In considering the texts we provide in the classroom it is important to ensure that we include texts which will appeal to children. As David Booth (2006: 33) says:

> The new literacies, as they have been labelled, are concerned with multi-modal texts, such as comics, magazines, newspapers, the internet, email, graphics, video and sound. Together, these 'texts' fill the lives of our students and meaning accrues as students combine the messages from the different media into their own construct of the world. We adults need to acknowledge our children's literacy lives with comics and graphic novels ... and open their ... lives to all of the different texts they will want and need in their immediate and future lives.

Identifying digital texts

Strictly speaking, digital texts are multimodal texts, but for the purposes of this chapter I want to distinguish between multimodal texts on paper and those on screen. The reading experiences of many children now take place on screen and digital texts dominate, certainly in many homes. How do those reading experiences relate to our understanding of the reading process and what implications are there for teachers of reading?

There has been much research on the reading experiences of young children in the home compared to the experiences they have in the classroom and this will be considered in greater depth in the next chapter. The focus of this chapter is the text and how the nature of the texts experienced in the home impacts on the perception and development of reading. We have all seen and smiled at images of very young children stroking the pages of books because they think that is the way to move to the next page. Even very young children today experience a huge variety of media which involve interaction with print. Arrow and Finch (2013) found that teachers were, on the whole, unaware of the variety of practices children engaged in at home and concluded that teachers need to ensure that digital texts are part of a multimedia reading experience in school. Earlier, Levy (2009) had found that young children at home were able to make meaning from print on a computer screen, although not to decode it. However, when they began to be taught how to read in school they lost confidence, both in their ability to make sense of print and also to use computers in school. Arrow and Finch argue that there is a strong disconnection between what children know about digital communication and the expectations teachers have.

Simpson et al. (2013) observed in detail the processes children go through when reading for information using a tablet. They identified many actions with which we are all familiar: typing a key word into a search engine, clicking on a hyperlink after selecting a page from the list offered, reading the screen, copying and pasting text into a document they have created. Such reading experiences are non-linear, multimodal and multidirectional and the reading process becomes even more complex. They argue that the profile of touch needs to be raised within consideration of the reading process.

Kucirkova et al. (2013) looked at parents and young children sharing texts using a tablet. It was the sort of book-sharing experience that has happened between adults and children for many years and which has been studied many times – but in this case the text used was digital and created by the readers. They were using an app which enabled them to use text, images and sound to create a personal story. The researchers, echoing Simpson et al., found that the physicality of the experience distinguished it from other book-sharing times and created a personal shared space of story.

What are the implications of these pieces of research for the teacher of reading? It is evident that decoding the alphabetic code is still an essential part of reading and needs to be taught. But it also appears evident that the reading process is becoming more complex and different skills and understandings need to be included in our teaching. For now, it is enough to say that it is evident that the text impacts on the way in which we read and that in classrooms teachers need to provide a wide range of different texts in order both to introduce children to new authors and types of text and also to draw on their own prior experiences of texts of all sorts.

How do we get to know children's books?

The world of children's books is enormous and huge numbers of new books are published each year. Some of these are superb but some are best left on the shelf. How do teachers of reading find out about the best? There are key sources of information and ways of finding out and some of those are outlined below.

Booktrust (www.booktrust.org)

This is an independent charity which claims to 'change lives through reading'. The website is a huge source of information about all things to do with books and reading and can be used to track down books or to look for recommendations.

Seven Stories (www.sevenstories.org.uk)

Seven Stories is the national centre for children's books. It is where original manuscripts and collections are housed, telling the story of children's books from the 1930s to the present. It states its mission is to 'champion children's books as an essential part of our childhood, our national heritage and our culture'.

Centre for Language in Primary Education (www.clpe.org.uk)

CLPE is a resource centre which provides courses for teachers and has a collection of books and resources to be used by teachers. It claims to 'emphasise the importance of books and literature in enabling children to become confident, happy and enthusiastic readers and writers, with all the benefits this brings'.

National Literacy Trust (www.literacytrust.org.uk)

The National Literacy Trust organises campaigns and carries out research in order to fulfil its aim of transforming lives through literacy and improving public understanding of the vital importance of literacy.

United Kingdom Literacy Association (www.ukla.org)

UKLA's website says that the charity:

> has as its sole object *the advancement of education in literacy*. UKLA is concerned
> with literacy education in school and out-of-school settings in all phases of education
> and members include classroom teachers, teaching assistants, school literacy
> co-ordinators, LEA literacy consultants, teacher educators, researchers, inspectors,
> advisors, publishers and librarians.

Books for Keeps (www.booksforkeeps.co.uk)

This is an online children's books magazine which reviews children's books, interviews authors and illustrators and writes about key issues in the world of children's books. It claims to 'hold a mirror up to the children's book world and reflect back its output, issues and preoccupations with intelligence, scholarship and wit'.

School Library Association (www.sla.org.uk)

The School Library Association provides support for everyone involved with school libraries and aims to promote quality reading opportunities for everybody. Don't think it is just for librarians; there is much to offer teachers, including a project called 'Building an Outstanding Reading School'.

These resources are just some of the many sources of information about children's books available to teachers to help them to develop their own knowledge of children's books. One way of getting to know new books is to look at the many prizes that are given to children's books. Awards such as *The Blue Peter Book Awards*, the *Caldecott Medal* and the *Red House Children's Book Award* can signpost to teachers new and respected children's books. One of the oldest is the *Kate Greenaway Medal* which is given to an outstanding book for children or young people in relation to its illustration. There is a shadowing site (www.carnegiegreenaway.org.uk) which gives teachers and children the opportunity to read, discuss and decide their own winner from each year's shortlist.

Shadowing is a wonderful opportunity to have a real focus on children's books between the announcement of the shortlist in March each year to the announcement of the winner in June. The website provides a huge range of supportive resources and ideas and research carried out by Cremin and Swann (2012) found that, as well as increasing opportunities for reading for pleasure in schools, the experience of shadowing introduced them to new authors and challenged them to read more widely.

Conclusion

This chapter began by emphasising the importance of the teacher of reading's knowledge about children's books. Findings from research indicated that this impacts on their effectiveness as teachers of reading and how they can best help children to become readers. The chapter then went on to discuss children's books, looking at the basis on which teachers choose which books to have and use within their classrooms. The issues of quality, suitability, appeal to children and variety of modes and genres were discussed and examples given of different types of text.

The essential messages of this chapter to the teacher of reading are:

- become familiar with children's books by reading them and becoming familiar with newly published books
- recognise that part of your role as a teacher of reading is to introduce children to a wide range of new and challenging texts
- have clear criteria for making judgements about the books you will make available in your classroom and know what each book can offer
- understand the different reading demands that different texts make on the reader
- know the resources available to you as a teacher of reading and make active use of them.

Further reading

Goodwin, P. (2008) *Understanding Children's Books: A Guide for Education Professionals*. London: Sage.
This book is exactly what it says in the title and will give you, as the author states, 'an introduction to the pleasures and power of writing and illustration for children', and 'information about children's books for anyone who shares books with children' (2008: 1).

Gamble, N. and Yates, S. (2013) *Exploring Children's Literature*, 3rd edn. London: Sage.
This is a useful resource and goes into the issues introduced in this chapter in more depth. It would be useful for those who want to take their study a bit further.

Waugh, D., Neaum, S. and Waugh, R. (2013) *Children's Literature in the Primary School*. London: Learning Matters.
This is an immensely practical book which shows how a knowledge of children's books can be used to inform classroom practice.

CHAPTER 4

HOW DO CHILDREN DEVELOP AS READERS?

Chapter objectives

At the end of this chapter you should:

- understand how the knowledge, skills and understandings held by very young children are learned
- recognise the social and cultural nature of reading
- be informed of different models of reading development
- be able to identify and reflect on the reading behaviours of young children.

Introduction

So far, in this first section of the book which focuses on subject knowledge, we have concentrated on what it is that teachers of reading need to know about children and reading. In this last chapter of the first section, we turn our attention to children.

What do they need to know about reading in order to become effective readers and how do they learn that? What do they already know and how have they learned it? We begin at the very beginning by considering the knowledge, skills and understanding required to enter the world of reading.

Knowing about print

One of the most basic things necessary in order to become a reader is an understanding of the nature of print. Written language is a strange thing and behaves in strange ways. As readers we know that those marks on the page are linked to words that are spoken and ideas that are thought. Moreover, we understand that the relationship between the written marks and the words is constant. The written marks always represent the same words; whoever reads them, they always say the same thing and whenever they are read, they always say the same thing.

How do children learn that? There are several ways, and the extent of the knowledge children have is determined by the extent of the experiences they have had. It is wrong to assume that children come to reading as blank canvases and that everything they know about print is what they are taught.

Reflective activity

Go for a walk around your local environment. You do not need to go far but go around roads which include houses, shops and some traffic. Note the key examples of print that you see around you and identify the purpose of the print. For example, a street sign is to tell people the name of the road so that they can find their way; a poster in a shop window is to advertise what is reduced on a particular day and to persuade people to come in and buy.

I am sure that as you started to record all the examples you saw, you very soon began to realise how many there were and did not record all of them. Children grow up surrounded by print, hardly a second passes when print is not a key element of their life. However, what is more important is that they grow up surrounded by people using that print.

Much research has claimed that these early encounters with print in the environment are the early stages of reading and that children who encounter these 'roots' of literacy (Goodman, 1986) have an advantage when they come to be formally taught how to read. Smith (1976) argued that as soon as children are aware of environmental print they are 'reading' and Burke (1982) believed that print awareness takes place very early on for most children. This takes us back to the question of the definition of reading as discussed in the first chapter. When does reading happen? Frith (1986) identified three stages in developing literacy which we will consider in more depth later in the chapter but her first stage – the logographic – is relevant when considering the nature of very early reading. According to Frith, the logographic stage is highly visual and children recognise words as whole units. This means that they do not pay much attention to individual letters or their order within words.

There is another viewpoint which argues that this recognition of whole words within a social and cultural context is not real reading at all and does not lead on to accurate word reading. Gough et al. (1992) would claim that the first stage of real reading is when letters are recognised and children know the relationships between sounds and letters. Masonheimer et al. (1984) gave 'non-reading' children familiar labels which had been changed, for example OcDonald's or Xepsi. In all other aspects the labels were the same as those with which the children were very famil-iar. Most 'non-readers' could find nothing wrong but the 'readers' began to try and sound out the changed label. Masonheimer et al. argued from this that before 'real reading' could take place children needed letter knowledge and phonological skills. In responding to this research finding, the key question which needs to be asked by teachers of reading is, 'What is meant by "real reading"?', and this is crucial to any discussion of children's knowledge of reading.

Cronin et al. (1999) took the research a stage further, wanting to see if knowing the logos in the environment gave children an advantage when it came to learning to read words. They found that children who could recognise the words within the logo learned to read them more quickly when they were presented outside the logo in a different font and colour and that the children tended to access them as whole units rather than sounding them out. Cronin et al. argue that familiarity with print within the environment means that children can learn some words without the use of phon-ics. This places the emphasis on reading as being able to understand the meaning of the text within the context in which it is presented. This is certainly an important aspect of early reading behaviour, and the ability to do this serves as a key foundation for the development of more sophisticated reading skills and understandings.

It is important to acknowledge that in talking about 'word-reading', as much of this research is, the emphasis is on the decoding aspect of reading rather than a broader perspective which takes into account the context and the meaning. Some might argue that recognising OcDonald's or Xepsi in a shopping mall serves the required purpose, but others could argue that precise decoding is required to ensure a 'fake' is not purchased. The importance of purpose and of the reading activity is again emphasised. More recent work by Neumann et al. (2013) showed that children whose attention was drawn to environmental print out-performed a control group which was taught only phonics, on letter-sound knowledge, letter writing, print concepts and print motivation. They argue that the contextual nature of environmental print gives children an understanding of the nature and purpose of reading. As Hall (1987: 1) said, 'Children, from birth, are witnesses to both the existence of print and the relationship between print and people'.

The basic knowledge and understanding which children need in order to become readers is that print conveys ideas and serves important functions in the life of most people. As children see print in use so they come to appreciate those functions and to see what reading can offer them. The knowledge that print conveys meaning is an important prerequisite for 'real' reading.

Knowing about texts

Much of what we know about how texts work is taken-for-granted knowledge and we do not appreciate that this has been learned. No child is born with an inbuilt understanding of how texts work; indeed, different texts work in different ways.

Reflective activity

Pick up a picture book that you might use with young children and try to look at it with new eyes. For the moment, forget about the decoding aspect of reading but consider all you know about how to approach that book in order to read it.

You know that the cover will tell you the title and the names of the author and the illustrator. You know that if you turn to the outside back cover you will find a short paragraph telling you what the book is about and that sometimes there will be comments from different people telling you what they thought of the book. More fundamentally, you know which is the front and which is the back of the book. As you open the book you are likely to automatically turn several pages over quite quickly, paying little attention to them, knowing when the story starts. You will have passed the title page with the dedication, publishers and bibliographic detail. How did you know that these pages are not an important part of the story? When you get to the start of the story, you know the difference between the print and the illustrations and know that they give you different sorts of information and need to be read in different ways. You know that you start reading the print from the top; you read from left to right and when you finish reading one line you move to the left-hand side of the line below. You know that you turn the pages from right to left.

There is a huge amount of assumed knowledge and that is only in relation to a traditional picturebook. Do the same exercise with a traditional non-fiction text, a website, an ebook, a recipe, the instructions in a flat-pack, a newspaper, a comic, a graphic novel or a manga. You will probably find that you approach each of those texts in different ways and for some of them, with which you are not so familiar, you may not completely appreciate how they are read. I remember the first time I read a manga I had no idea that they were read from top to bottom and from right to left and initially was very confused as I tried to make sense of the text.

Clay (1991) talked about the 'concepts of print' which young children hold and emphasised how important it is that teachers of reading know the concepts that their pupils hold. Do not assume that all young children, looking at a picture book, would have the same knowledge that you have, as illustrated by the activity above. Some will be used to reading texts in a non-alphabetic script and others will have shared texts which are read from bottom to top or right to left. Their social and cultural experiences of reading will be very different from those they encounter in school and so they will need to learn many new skills.

 ## Reflective activity

Share a picture book with a very young child (perhaps aged about three years old). Allow the child to take control of the book and as you look at the book ask certain questions to see what they understand about how books work. Looking at the cover, ask what the book is about. Ask the child to turn to the page where the story starts. Ask what the first pages are about. When you get to the first page, ask the child to tell you which is the bit you read. Then ask them how many words are on the page.

The child's responses to these questions will give you some indication of their understanding of how books work. How often do we talk about reading 'words' with young children when many of them are unable to distinguish word units on a page of print?

Knowing about texts is more complex than might first be imagined and there is much assumed knowledge which readers possess. This is usually not made explicit because most learn it through experiences. However, not all children do and for them that knowledge needs to be made explicit. Remember that we have mainly focused on traditional books here and there are many more kinds of text. Those of us who are slightly older may find we do not have the required knowledge of how some texts work in order to make full meaning of them. This was my experience on first reading a manga and I am just beginning to fully exploit the meaning potential when I read my Twitter feed.

Knowing about language

Young children come to school with a range of language skills and experiences. Within one class many different varieties of language can be used and some children are adept at switching from one to another. Many children are skilled in many different languages and can change from one to another according to whom they are speaking. Some can speak one language and understand another. All this knowledge and experience of registers, varieties and languages enrich children's understanding of how language is used and the potential for communication that it has to offer.

Most texts which children encounter in school will be written in Standard English and for some children that might be a hindrance to their personal meaning making. In talking about books with young children, teachers of reading are not only introducing them to new vocabulary but also to the patterns and rhythms of Standard English. Fletcher and Reese (2005) found that when talking about books with children adults talk in more complex ways than when playing with them.

I am going to illustrate that point by using an extract from *Actual Minds, Possible Worlds* by Bruner (1986: 159). He says,

> I have tried to make the case that the function of literature as art is to open us to dilemmas, to the hypothetical, to the range of possible worlds that a text can refer to. I have used the term 'to subjunctivize' to render the world less fixed, less banal, more susceptible to recreation. Literature subjunctivizes, makes strange, renders the obvious less so, the unknowable less so as well, matters of value more open to reason and intuition. Literature in this spirit, is an instrument of freedom, lightness, imagination and yes, reason.

Try and put that into your own words, imagining that you are explaining what Bruner is saying to somebody else. My guess is that you find that rather challenging. You can probably decode all the words, most of the words you know as you will have seen them before and yet to work out what Bruner is actually saying about literature is challenging. That is because the way in which language is written is very different from spoken language; this applies even when both are Standard English. Just think how much more challenging it makes it when you do not speak Standard English.

What would help you to understand this text? There are three ways which I find best to help me make meaning from a challenging text. The first is to embed it into a context which I know well. So instead of thinking about literature in general I would apply what Bruner is saying to a text I have recently read and reflect on what that experience was like for me. Second, I would talk about it with somebody else, sharing understandings and trying out ideas. Third, I would look some words up in a dictionary!

Having tried all these strategies, I would then come up with my own meaning: for me Bruner is saying that when we read a text we go beyond what is stated in the actual text to create our own 'virtual worlds' based on what we understand the author to be saying, on our relationship with any characters in the text and our own previous experiences and expectations. The word 'subjunctivize', as far as I can tell, is Bruner's own but links to the 'subjunctive' which the dictionary tells me refers to something that is not necessarily real. That relates to the meaning I have created.

In order to make meaning of that text, the reader needs to know how language works and how Bruner is using and appropriating language to convey his intended meaning. A few days ago I was sharing the book *Don't Let the Pigeon Drive the Bus* (discussed in the previous chapter) with a bright three-year-old. We read it through once and he joined in eagerly, shouting out loudly 'NO!' when the pigeon asked if he could drive the bus. On finishing the book, Jamie immediately wanted to re-read it and this time he shouted out 'YES!' when the pigeon asked. He had realised how the author was using language to create the story and involve the reader and also how he, as the reader, could use his involvement to subvert the story.

Texts use language to convey meaning and readers need to know how language is used to fully exploit the text and create their own meaning.

Knowing about the purposes of reading

We have already hinted at the importance of this in the process of becoming a reader. It is a rare person who will invest a lot of time, energy and hard work in something which to them appears pointless. Learning to read is hard work and children need to see that it will be both useful and pleasurable for them. It is not enough to tell them they need to be able to read in order to do well in school or to get a good job when they grow up; it is not likely that such delayed gratification will give much motivation!

In Chapter 2 reading for pleasure was discussed and it was established that reading needs to be an enjoyable experience for children. In Chapter 3 it was seen how the nature and subject matter of the text can impact on children's understanding, and in this chapter this will be related to children's understandings of the reading process.

I once went into an infant school to talk with the children about what they were reading. It was evident that they were reading very different texts at home from the texts they were reading at school. At home they read longer novels connected to television programmes; they read comics and magazines and one boy regularly read newspaper reports of football matches. When I asked them about the texts they were reading at school they told me the colour of the sticker that was on it, what colour sticker they would move on to and struggled to tell me the title of the book, let alone the author. For them, the purpose of reading in school was to progress onto a 'harder' book. Rachael Levy (2011) found the same issue in her research into how school practice defines reading for children. She uses a very useful analogy of learning to play the piano. When can you be said to be able to play the piano – when you have passed grade one or grade eight, when you have given your first recital or can play at home to relax, when you can make out a tune with your right hand or can sight read a concerto? Levy's research showed how the discourse of the school shaped children's perceptions of themselves as readers and of what reading is and what it means to be a reader. Teachers of reading need to be aware of the impact of their practice on these perceptions.

There is much work to show how the use of popular culture within the curriculum can increase motivation and engagement (Dyson, 2002; Marsh, 2000). Research by Marsh et al. (2005) also implied that it had a positive impact on children's progress in speaking and listening. Merchant (2010) however has argued that digital literacies are difficult to integrate into the norm of school literacy practices because their means of communication are so different. The types of reading required in gameplay challenge the traditional reading that is practised and assessed in school. Digital practices tend to be used in classrooms to serve old views of reading rather than being allowed to create and innovate. In a later paper he proposes that changes in technology should not be seen as a means or reason for changing only pedagogical practice but that broader and more challenging changes in definitions of reading should lead to innovative uses of technology. As he says, 'The real transformation may rest on how we can re-imagine meaningful interactions in which pupils and teachers have the wider access to the ideational and relational resources that new technology can enable' (2010: 145).

The point of this is to show that children are reading all sorts of texts in all sorts of ways outside the classroom and this reading is deeply embedded in play, digital or otherwise. They also see adults reading all sorts of different texts – digital and otherwise – and observe reading as an integral part of everyday life to a greater or lesser extent. Teachers of reading should try and make the reading opportunities on offer within classrooms as authentic as possible to reflect the purpose and pleasure of real life reading. In this way children will learn why it is important to read. Lennox (2012), writing from an Australian perspective, claims that an emphasis on skills alone will not help children to become real readers:

> Effective teaching avoids a narrow image of early literacy as the acquisition of a set of discrete skills. Performance on isolated skills does not necessarily result in ability or the disposition to use reading and writing in meaningful ways in the real world. (2012: 33)

Reflective activity

Keep a record of everything that you read in a 'normal' period of 24 hours. Look through the list and try to categorise those reading experiences. What was the purpose of the reading? How did you read?

I would imagine that you read a huge variety of different types of text and that you read them in different ways. Some you gave a lot of close attention to because it mattered that you understood exactly what was written; others you skimmed to just get the gist of what was said and others you just glanced at and might wonder if what you did could really be described as reading.

Next, keep a record of everything that one child reads during a school day and categorise those reading experiences.

Compare the two lists. What do the differences and similarities tell you about reading that is relevant and engaging for children?

In the next section of the book consideration will be given to how we teach children to read, but here it is enough to say that a consideration of what children need to know to become readers is a clear indication of what they need to learn or be taught. In summary, it is evident that children need to encounter a variety of all types of text in all possible modes; they need to be in an environment which allows them to read authentically in situations where reading is embedded and they need opportunities to talk about books, to respond, to problem solve and to create.

Children's development as readers

Having considered what it is that children need to know in order to become readers, we now go on to discover the development of reading, that is, how they come to know those things. As with any type of development, development as a reader is not linear and does not happen in a smooth rising trajectory. It is difficult to talk about development as a reader without referring to development as a writer and so frequently in this section we will be talking about literacy development. It is important to retain a holistic view and not to see any description of stages of development as a tick list through which children must proceed. We are going to consider just three models of reading development, although there are many more.

Uta Frith

Uta Frith is a developmental psychologist working in the field of neuroscience with a particular interest in autism. Her description of the stages that children go through when they are learning to read is one of the most useful and is still applicable today even though it was first published in 1985. Frith proposed three stages but argued that reading needs to be considered holistically.

The first stage is the *logographic*. In this stage children recognise words as a whole. They do not give much attention to the smaller units of letters and their order within the structure of a word but basically recognise whole words through their visual pattern. They remember particular key characteristics of the written word, for example, as mentioned above, many children recognise the golden arches of the 'M' in McDonald's. It is often the first letter in a word that is recognised and children often 'know' the initial letter of their name and recognise it in other words they see in the environment or in books. Frith would describe this first stage as 'pre-literate', as children are learning or have learned the symbolic nature of print, that is they know what print represents but they do not know what each element of the print signifies. This can lead to 'misreading' when a child is focusing on the visual image of the whole rather than the details of the individual letters. For example, it is easy to confuse the words 'horse' and 'house'; visually they are very similar but the meanings are very different and confusion can significantly change understanding of a text!

Frith's model of development is a model of literacy development and so puts development of reading and writing together. She argues that in this early logographic phase it is reading which dominates and most influences development. Children are experiencing print in the environment and through their encounters with books and other print texts, and their learning about how print works comes from that. At this stage, you may have noticed very young children playing at writing; their mark-making visually resembles 'grown-up' writing but contains no details of letters or recognisable words.

The second stage within Frith's model is the *alphabetic* stage and as its name suggests, during this stage children become more aware of how words are made up. They will hear different sounds within spoken words and begin to relate them to the letter shapes they see in written words. In reading, this often means a slowing down of the process because of the greater attention and thought given to the details of the letters; it can also mean an increase in mispronunciation of words because children do not yet know all the different relationships between sound and letter and use the most common. Children's increasing knowledge of the relationship between letters and sounds means that they will now attempt to decode unfamiliar or new words when they read and also attempt to write them down.

The third and final stage in Frith's model is the *orthographic* stage and by now children are practically independent readers. Their 'mental lexicon' of words, that is the collection of words known and recognised by sight, has grown and their knowledge of the relationship between letters and sounds is such that they are able to read many unfamiliar words by sight. Frith argues that at this stage morphemic knowledge also increases in significance, that is the units of words that influence meaning impact on word recognition. For example, children will recognise prefixes and suffixes and know how they affect both the decoding and the meaning of words.

Frith's model, as has already been said, needs to be considered holistically; the implication is that reading development happens not in a linear fashion but in a qualitative way. Children build on each stage, developing and enhancing their knowledge as they increase their reading skills and not dismissing prior strategies but building on them. There is an assumption in Frith's model that teaching needs to take place; children need to be taught about the relationship between letters and sounds and how these sounds work together to make words. Ramus (2004) criticises this model because he claims it assumes particular teaching strategies, based on explicit phonic instruction; he argues that there is strong evidence that many children become fluent readers without ever having any teaching in phonics at all. I remember one child in an urban school where I taught, arriving at the age of four, able to decode fluently. The reception class teacher was puzzled at how he was able to do this without phonic knowledge! He needed teaching in comprehension, not decoding. Ramus would argue that children like him move directly from the logographic to the orthographic stage. He says:

> the necessary cognitive resources brought by the child to the task of learning to read would seem to include fully functional phonological (and therefore auditory), lexical and visual systems. The input necessary for learning to occur includes massive exposure to written words, presented together with their phonological forms (at least at the beginning). Explicit instruction of letter sounds and grapheme-phoneme correspondences would seem to be a facilitating factor for most children, in that it does allow to bootstrap the formation of the orthographic lexicon: without it, the child has to rely for a very long time on the simultaneous presentation of written and verbal forms to acquire new words; with it, it is possible to read aloud, understand and therefore learn new words by applying grapheme-phoneme correspondences. Nevertheless, this facilitating factor is not entirely necessary, and many children can do without it. (2004: 3)

Linnea Ehri

Linnea Ehri is a professor of educational psychology in New York with a particular interest in what causes some children difficulties in becoming good readers. Her model is also developmental and consists of four stages of reading development. You will notice many similarities between Frith's model and Ehri's model.

Pre-alphabetic phase: In this stage children store in their memories connections between visual cues and words. Sometimes this is as simple as a thumbprint on the side of the page next to a word (Gough and Juel, 1991), or it may be the shapes of the letters, for example 'look', with the two eyes in the middle of the words. Many young children recognise the golden arches of McDonald's or the introduction of a favourite television show; they are not able to read the words themselves but make connections between the visual cues and the idea or meaning. They are not making connections between the letters and the sounds, hence the name 'pre-alphabetic'.

Partial alphabetic stage: In this stage children begin to make connections between letters and sounds. It is only partial however, and the most significant letters tend to be those at the beginning and end of words or letters which are meaningful to them, such as the first letter in their name. It is at this stage that children need to have some alphabetic knowledge and begin to learn correspondences between written language and sound.

Full-alphabetic stage: Now children are able to make full connections between the written letters and the sounds they represent. This means that they can decode words which are unknown. Ehri (1999) argues that at this stage reading often becomes more precise but also slows down because children are paying closer attention to accurate decoding. You may often hear children reading very slowly and deliberately word by word; Chall (1983: 10–24) describes it as being glued to the print and Stahl (1997) similarly says children are fixed on print.

Consolidated alphabetic stage: As children experience words through this focused 'sounding-out', sight words begin to accumulate in the memory and so reading speeds up and recognition of letter patterns consolidates. Children read unknown words by applying their knowledge of previously read words through the use of analogy. Meaning becomes more significant as attention to word identification diminishes. Reading also becomes faster.

Staged models of reading development are attractive to teachers of reading because they appear to define a clear linear progression and so teaching can be planned accordingly in order to facilitate this progression. Ehri (1999) has herself drawn out the implications for teachers of her staged model; these implications focus on the importance of knowledge of grapheme–phoneme relationships. Beech (2005: 56) has argued that the model is more useful as a framework which will 'bend with the winds of evidence' rather than break. In other words, Beech is arguing that Ehri's model is a useful starting point for thinking about how children learn to become readers but does not give the definitive answer. Other researchers into the development of reading have rejected a staged approach and have developed interactive models.

Adams (1990) carried out a review of the research into early reading and deduced that children build up a mental network of relations between letters through their exposure to words. Her model is better described as an interactive rather than a staged model, but there is a link to Ehri's idea of connections. Adams proposed four processors which interact which each other and so support the reader's meaning-making by giving a range of information to the reader. These processors are the *context processor*, the *meaning processor*, the *orthographic processor* and the *phono-logical processor*. Skilled fluent readers assimilate and use all this information almost automatically. Rumelhart (1985) took this a bit further by adding in a *message centre* which evaluates messages received at different levels in order to access the meaning.

Any model of reading development will struggle to provide the full picture of how all children become readers and the danger is that teachers will use a staged model as a curriculum for teaching. Kennedy et al. (2012: 82) recognise this danger and argue for a more balanced approach:

> Wide ranging attempts to synthesise the literature on early reading development have been criticised for influencing the development of instructional programmes with a heavy reliance on code-focused instruction (Teale et al., 2010). The research supports balance; balance in the elements which support early literacy development with due regard for language and vocabulary development, fluency and comprehension.

Teale et al. (2010, 2014) went on to argue that it is not enough to teach what they describe as 'constrained skills' but that they need to be contextualised within authentic reading experiences. They identify a curriculum gap in instruction in comprehension and knowledge of the content of texts. The National Curriculum (DfE, 2013a) in England states as its first overarching aim that children should 'read easily, fluently and with good understanding'. It recognises the two dimensions to reading of 'word reading' and 'comprehension' and says it is essential that pupils' competence develops in both aspects, recognising that each needs different kinds of teaching (2013a: 4). In other words, teaching children to decode is not teaching them to read.

Alexander and Fox (2004) looked at research on reading and the pedagogy of reading over the previous 50 years and, as they examined different perspectives, came to the conclusion that a much stronger idea of the complexity of reading development is needed. You might well have thought that as you have read this chapter and the first one; researchers approach the study of reading from different theoretical perspectives, and each has something to offer but also each leaves out key elements of the reading process. Alexander and Fox argued that these different approaches should be complementary and not conflicting. In addition, they argued that a model of reading development should not just focus on the early stages but should look at reading 'across the lifespan' (2004: 58). They acknowledged the changing conception of 'text' and 'reading' in the digital world and argued that our view of reading development should take that into account.

Reflective activity

Recall as much as you can of your experience of learning to read. Many of us who learned to read quite easily will have difficulty in remembering. Often we only remember the difficult times. Try and remember some key incidents of you as a child reading. What were you reading? Who were you with? Where were you?

I can recall several key incidents from my early life, although it is a long time ago now!

- My mother stuck labels on the furniture in my room – 'bed', 'wardrobe', 'chair'.
- Both of my parents read to me a lot.
- I could read when I started school and did not have to read the 'reading scheme' books.
- The teacher was reading *Heidi* to us as a class. We were allowed to bring our own copies to follow, which I did. I got frustrated however and read ahead. I became engrossed in the book and was oblivious to what was going on in the classroom. The teacher asked me a question about what she had just read; I did not hear her and then had no idea of what she was asking. I was severely told off!
- I once spent a whole day curled up on the sofa because I did not want to stop reading.

I could list many more. What do the things that you recall tell you about your development as a reader? It would be true, I would imagine, that your journey as a reader incorporates many different aspects of reading and it is not possible to identify one key focus at each stage. Becoming a reader is a holistic process and teachers of reading need to bear that in mind.

First steps

This is rather different from the models we have considered earlier. It was developed by the Education Department of Western Australia in the 1990s as a framework for teachers to look at what children actually do and plan for further development. For our purpose, we focus on the Reading Development Continuum but there is a similar framework for oral language, spelling and writing. There are six phases and for each phase there are 'indicators' or descriptors of behaviour. What is significant for me about this model is its emphasis on the context of learning. It is claimed (Education Department of Western Australia, 1997: 2) that the indicators:

reflect a developmental view of teaching and learning and are clearly related to the contexts in which development is taking place. That is, language development is not seen as a naturalistic or universal phenomena through which all children progress in the same way. Children's achievements, however, provide evidence of an overall pattern of development which accommodates a wide range of individual differences.

The underlying theoretical perspective is that learning to read is a holistic, social, active and value-laden process.

The six phases of the reading development continuum are:

1. *Role-play reading:* Young children pretend to read and tell stories for themselves. This is described as 'reading-like behaviours'. Children in this phase enjoy looking at books and texts.
2. *Experimental reading:* Young children remember stories they know well and use their memory to retell or 'read'. They know that print is constant and will talk about the books they look at.
3. *Early reading:* Now children begin to read what is actually on the page and so read more slowly, looking carefully at the details of the print. They will try and work out words they do not know.
4. *Transitional reading:* Children use a range of strategies to bring meaning to the text – letter and sound relationships, context, knowledge of what is being read and the pictures.
5. *Independent reading:* Reading is now more fluent and automatic. They will discuss what they read and sometimes even disagree with it! They will approach texts to read with purpose and intention.

In reading the brief descriptions of these phases you will see that they are much broader and do not restrict consideration to decoding skills. They include the process of meaning-making and acknowledge the relationship between the reader and the text. It may be that First Steps accommodates the views of Alexander and Fox (2004) although there is only minimal reference to multimodal texts.

Assessing Pupils' Progress: reading assessment foci

Assessing Pupils' Progress (APP) was developed from Monitoring Pupils' Progress (QCA, 2006) and published in 2008. Its main purposes are that:

> Every child knows what progress they are making, and understands what they need to do to improve and how to get there ... (and) ... Every teacher is equipped to make well-founded judgements about pupils' attainment, understands the concepts and principles of progression, and knows how to use their assessment judgements to forward plan. (DCSF, 2008: 3)

It was designed, therefore, to support the practice of assessment for learning (AfL). Strictly speaking, it is not a model of development but it does indicate a progression in reading which has been used by teachers for assessment and also for teaching, although this is not what was intended. There are seven assessment foci which specify the skills thought to be necessary for effective reading:

1. Use a range of strategies including accurate decoding, to read for meaning
2. Understand, describe, select or retrieve information, events or ideas from texts and use quotation or reference to text
3. Deduce, infer or interpret information, events or ideas from texts
4. Identify and comment on the structure and organisation of texts, including grammatical and presentational features at text level
5. Explain and comment on writers' uses of language, including grammatical and literary features at word and sentence level
6. Identify and comment on writers' purposes and viewpoints and the overall effect of the text on the reader
7. Relate texts to their social, cultural and historical contexts and literary traditions

More information about this can be found at the archived resources at http:// webarchive.nationalarchives.gov.uk/20110809101133/http://nsonline.org.uk/primary/ assessment/assessingpupilsprogressapp. We will discuss it as a resource for assessment in Chapter 10 but in this chapter I want to reflect on this as a model of progression in reading. Do these statements and foci give an authentic experience of what it means to become a better and more experienced reader? The introduction to APP describes one of its purposes to develop and refine teachers' understanding of progression.

A simple scan of the assessment foci above reveal two clear features of this description of development. First, there is an assumption that development in reading is linear, universal and easily identified. There are clear descriptive statements which purport to describe progression in reading and it is assumed that all children will progress in this way. The statements are presented in a non-problematic way, as a tick list against which each child's reading behaviours can be measured. Second, there is no mention of the impact of the text, on the reading process and of the relationship between reader and text, which will affect the understanding and creation of meaning. Neither is there any consideration given to the context and purpose of the reading behaviour. Wrigley (2010: 12) argues that, while it is to be preferred to a test, the:

> atomisation of the skills matrix is having a distracting effect on teachers' courage to plan imaginative and purposeful learning which requires the complex orchestration of skills in particular contexts. When schools are told ... – and they have been – that Jacqueline Wilson's engaging books do not exemplify sufficiently demanding language structures to raise standards, then it is time to ask the question, 'standards of what?' It appears that this may not be reading as we know it ...

Observing children as readers

The final sentence in the quote from Wrigley above emphasises the importance of being clear about what is meant when we talk about reading. In considering progression in reading it is important for teachers of reading to be careful observers of children's reading behaviours and to be able to analyse what it is that these behaviours say about children's understanding of the purposes of reading. Let us use these pictures of three-year-old Paul as an example of this.

Figure 4.1   Paul reading a map

In Figure 4.1 Paul is on a day out with his parents. He is leading the way, carefully reading the map. What does this tell us about Paul as a reader? He knows that:

- reading has a function and is useful in everyday life
- reading can give him information and help him to do things
- the marks on the page relate to the path and his surroundings
- it is his job as the reader to make the connection between those marks and the reality of where he is
- understanding what the marks mean will impact on his actions and understandings.

In Figure 4.2 is Paul, on the same holiday, looking at the writing on a monument with his dad.

Figure 4.2   Paul and his dad reading a monument

Paul is looking very carefully at the writing. He knows that the writing contains a message and he is contemplating the print to see if he can work it out. What the picture does not tell us is that his dad had asked him to identify one particular letter on this wall of print and Paul is looking carefully for that letter. His dad is waiting patiently. Paul knows that:

- print, wherever it is, contains a message
- print is there to be accessed by readers
- the details of print, for example the letters, are constant wherever they are to be found
- reading is a social activity and it helps to talk about it.

Third, we see Paul reading a book (Figure 4.3). He is in control and is holding the book correctly and is turning the pages in the conventional way. This book has been read to Paul several times and so he knows it well. This means that he is able to 'read the words'. Parents will often say to teachers that children are memorising books and not really reading them. Teachers of reading need to understand so that they can explain to parents, that reading is about understanding the message of the text. Memorising words is not the same as decoding but it is reading, as the child is understanding what the text has to offer. Paul may not yet be able to read independently,

Figure 4.3   Paul reading a book

in the sense of decoding every word, but he is well on the way and understands how readers behave and what reading has to offer.

Finally, we see Paul reading on screen (Figure 4.4). He is again recognising that there is a relationship between himself as the reader and the text on the screen. He knows that he has to respond to the instructions and is very deliberately pointing to the space on the screen. In this image Paul is surrounded by different types of texts which give him information and as a reader he has to select which will fulfil his needs and respond in order to get the information he requires. At three years old, he cannot yet do that completely independently but he is demonstrating that he understands how the texts work and the demands that are made on him as the reader.

We can see from these examples that many children come to formal reading instruction with an understanding of what print is, what it does for them and how they can use it. In playing at reading they are engaging in authentic reading experiences and so are ready to begin understanding the closer relationship between sounds and letters. Paul had already understood that reading is about getting meaning from a text and that different types of text mean different things in different contexts. He is well on the way to becoming a reader. Of course, not all children have the same experiences. Paul is fortunate that his experiences of reading closely match the experiences of reading expected in school. We have already seen that this is not the case for many children. It is the responsibility of

Figure 4.4   Paul reading a computer screen

teachers of reading to observe children's reading behaviours and then analyse their skills and understandings of reading.

Reflective activity

Take some photos of a child you know well in a variety of contexts where the child is 'reading'. Make sure you ask permission from the parent or carer. Look at these photographs carefully as we did with the photos of Paul and see what they tell you about that child's reading behaviours – their experiences with print, their understandings of the reading process and the skills already possessed. Knowing this establishes the starting point for the teaching of reading in school and teaching children to read is the topic of the next section.

Conclusion

This chapter began by considering the knowledge that children require in order to become readers. It was established that they need to know about how print works, how texts work, how language works and what the purposes of reading are. The chapter then went on to look at different models of reading development, focusing particularly on staged models. We saw how the view of reading development that was characterised by the APP grids defined progress in reading as linear, universal and non-problematic and questioned these assumptions. Finally, we looked in detail at the reading behaviours of one very young child and discussed how knowledge of this informs the teacher of reading.

The essential messages of this chapter to the teacher of reading are:

- learning to read happens long before children begin formal schooling
- children learn about reading by their encounters with print
- not every child has experiences which lead to an understanding that matches the definition of reading in school
- there are different models of reading development which assume a linear and universal progression
- progression in reading is individual, social, cultural and non-linear.

Further reading

Larson, J. and Marsh, J. (eds) (2013) *Handbook of Early Childhood Literacy*, 2nd edn. London: Sage.
This is an edited collection of papers about the development of early literacy. It takes the issues that have only been hinted at in this chapter and develops them further. It is of particular interest to those planning to work with young children but contains insights useful to all teachers of reading.

Riley, J. (1996) *The Teaching of Reading: The Development of Reading in the Early Years at School*. London: Sage.
This book combines the theory and practice aspects of reading, exploring the way in which young children develop from initial understanding of the purpose and recognition of print, through to fully developed fluent reading.

Heath, S.B. (1983) *Ways with Words: Language, Life and Work in Communities and Classrooms*. Cambridge: Cambridge University Press.
This is the account of a long-term ethnographic study of literacy in three different communities. It shows how some children have vibrant experiences of literacy but because they do not match those expected by the school they have limited success in schooled literacy. It is essential for teachers of reading to appreciate the knowledge, understanding and skills with which young children come to school.

CHAPTER 5

PROVIDING A READING ENVIRONMENT

Chapter objectives

At the end of this chapter you should:

- be aware of the importance of the reading environment
- have some strategies for talking about books with children
- know how to plan the physical environment of the classroom to support reading
- choose texts for teaching reading which engage children and build on their existing skills and understandings.

Introduction

I wonder where you go when you read. I usually read last thing at night in bed. However, the book I am reading has to be very engaging for me to be able to read more than a few pages before I fall asleep. When I have time to spare, I enjoy nothing more than curling up on the sofa with my book. I prefer silence and like to be alone. If I am reading for work then I need to be sitting at a desk or table. The nature or purpose of my reading determines the environment in which I read.

It is not only the physical environment which influences my reading. If I am reading a novel for pleasure I like somebody else to be in the room with me; this is usually my long-suffering husband who has to listen to me read out words and phrases which I particularly enjoy. If my reading is for work, I like to be alone and in silence – I am not one of those people who can work with music playing. I also have to be in the right mood or frame of mind for what I am reading and also it has to be the right time. Some books I can pick up and read just a couple of pages when I have a short moment, but with others I need to wait until there is a long period of time when I can totally immerse myself and forget my immediate surroundings.

My reading is affected by the physical, emotional and social environment.

 Reflective activity

Think back over the past few months, remembering your reading. Try and answer the following questions:

- What were you reading?
- Why were you reading it?
- Where did you read?
- How long did you read for?
- Was anybody with you when you read? If so, did you talk with them about your reading?
- What was going on in the background while you read?

As you reflect on different experiences of reading, you may well begin to identify an emerging pattern which will tell you the impact that the environment has on your reading behaviours. As a teacher of reading, how do you think the environment affects the reading behaviours of children?

The reading circle

We have already discussed in Chapter 3 the role of the enabling adult. That adult is at the centre of what Chambers (2011: 15) calls 'the reading circle'. This circle is used to describe the sequence of activities which happen when somebody reads. These activities are: selection, reading and response. These activities are circular because each influences and leads on to the other.

Your answers to the questions above will have, hopefully, been influenced by the selection of texts you made to read. As readers, we choose what we are going to read. Beginner readers need to be taught how to make that choice and to have a wide range of texts from which they can choose. This is part of the role of the teacher of reading. Later in the chapter, we will consider in more detail the impact that the selection of texts by teachers of reading has on the development of readers.

We have already considered the fact that reading is about much more than decoding and Chambers argues that we must give readers experiences of success at whatever stage they are at. There are some who use this point to argue for only allowing children to read independently texts which they can phonically decode, but Chambers points out that knowing how to handle a book, looking carefully at the illustrations while being read to and making a good choice of book are also experiences of success as a reader. Teachers of reading need to reinforce these successes and make sure there are opportunities for them to occur.

Lastly, the reading circle acknowledges that whenever we read something we have a response. I wonder what your response to reading this book has been so far. It could be one of several:

- Wow! This is amazing! Why haven't I thought of that before?
- This is interesting – I want to find out more about this.
- I wonder if Johnny has heard about this – I must tell him.
- This is all very obvious – why does someone bother to write a book about this?
- This is so boring.
- Zzzzz.

I hope that you have had some sort of response to reading this book; preferably it would have been one of the first three but even the next two would have been better than the last!

Chambers wants to help people to become 'thoughtful readers' (2011: 20). He sees reading as much more than a pastime but as a 'means of thought'. We shall return to that later, but he describes the reading in which we hope to engage children as coming out of the talk which takes place about reading. Through this:

> we break out of a limited, flat-earth view of reading, in which we only ever read the kinds of books that are familiar to us, and discover that the reading world is not flat but round, with many other interesting continents on it. Even more, that we can leave the world, which itself is small, and take off, spiralling up into a galaxy of other worlds, until eventually we can roam through the entire universe of literature, stopping wherever we want and exploring whichever strange planet takes our fancy. (2011: 21)

At the heart of all these experiences of selection, reading and response, right at the centre of the circle, is the teacher of reading. This is the person who opens those doors and shares their experiences with beginner readers.

The social environment of reading

For the purposes of this chapter we are going to consider two aspects to the social environment of reading; the first is the classroom ethos and the second the importance of talk.

 Reflective activity

Walk into the classroom in which you are working at present during a free choice time and stand in the doorway looking around. How many children are reading? Where and what are they reading? Are they reading alone or with other people? Are those other people adults or children?

Back in 1987, Frank Smith described the process of becoming a reader as 'joining the literacy club'. In doing so he was reflecting the social nature of reading and arguing that we learn by being in the company of experts, emulating them and being supported as we join in with them. Ryan and Patrick (2001) argue that it is teachers who create the social environment of the classroom by establishing the rules and boundaries, the nature of interactions and the extent to which the activities given promote collaboration. Working with adolescents, they found that the social environment plays a big role in the motivation and engagement of pupils. That must also apply to primary-aged children, and teachers of reading need to consider how they can create a classroom which inspires and motivates readers.

You are probably familiar with the work of Piaget and Vygotsky (1978), who both argue for the active role of children in the construction of knowledge. For Piaget, the key image was that of the individual child as a scientist, problem solving and making sense of the environment and experiences. For Vygotsky, however, it was the processes of socialisation and interaction which influenced development, and this sociocultural perspective places a huge emphasis on the environment in which learning takes place. What does this mean for the teacher of reading? It means that a teacher must create a classroom of opportunities for the children to behave as readers alongside more experienced readers and encourage talk and reflection on those experiences.

If this is the case, it is important to identify how it is that experienced readers behave, and Pennac (1994) identifies ten rights of readers which he claims readers accord to themselves but deny to beginner readers. These ten rights are:

1. The right not to read – there are some times when I do not feel like reading: my eyes are tired, my brain is tired or there is too much else going on. Nobody forces me to read.

2. The right to skip pages – I confess there are times when I turn over several pages because I just want to know what happens next.

3. The right not to finish a book – I used to feel guilty about this but now I know that I do not need to waste time reading something because I feel I should.

4. The right to re-read – sometimes I want to re-read a book because I love the world it portrays and want to stay in that world with those characters.

5. The right to read anything – I do not always read worthy books that could be described as 'Literature'.

6. The right to 'bovarysme' – by this Pennac means feeling. He describes it as, 'The imagination swells, the nerves vibrate, the heart gets carried away, the adrenalin pumps, identification occurs all over the place, and the brain mistakes (momentarily) the splutters of the everyday for the beacons of fiction. Such is the state we find ourselves in as readers' (1994: 165). Have you ever felt like that?

7. The right to read everywhere – curled up on the sofa, lying on my tummy on the floor, curled up in bed, sitting at a table. Where do you read?

8. The right to browse – flicking through books, picking out phrases and sentences, reading the first page and deciding if I want to go on, going straight to the last page.

9. The right to read aloud – I often read bits of books out loud to my husband, friend, colleague or whoever happens to be near – just so I can share my enjoyment. Sometimes I will read bits out loud to revel in the sound of the language and if I find something difficult to understand I will read it out loud to help me to make sense of it.

10. The right to remain silent – by this Pennac refers to the way in which for each of us reading offers an insight into life and what it means for us. That is intensely personal and sometimes cannot be expressed in words. He says, 'The few adults who have really given me something to read have always effaced themselves before the books and they've always been careful not to ask me what I understood in these books. To them, of course, I'd talk about what I read' (1994: 178).

 Reflective activity

Think back to the classroom you observed at the beginning of this section. Do you think the social environment of that classroom allowed children those rights of a reader. If not, why not? If yes, how are these rights established? How can you, as a teacher of reading, make these rights explicit to the children?

An important element of a classroom ethos which values reading and respects readers is talk. There is much evidence of the key role that talk plays in learning and I do not want to expand on that here. This next section is written with the underpinning assumption that talk is a powerful learning tool and that opportunities for talk should be an integral part of all teaching and learning. In this chapter, I want to focus on talking about books and in doing so to return to the work of Chambers.

I have recently joined a book club and am loving it. We all read the same book and then once a month we meet to discuss our perceptions of and responses to the book. Those conversations enrich my reading experience hugely; when I listen to what other people felt and said I sometimes want to go back and re-read the book. Conversations can be about our enjoyment of the book, our understanding of the book, our relationship to the plot, the setting or the characters. Every member's view is slightly different because we all come to the book with slightly different experiences and insights. To share those is part of the reading experience.

Chambers (2011) identifies what he calls three sharings and these provide a useful framework for talking about books – with adults, with children or even with yourself.

The first sharing is of enthusiasms. We often start by sharing what it is we liked best about the book:

> I liked the bit where ...
>
> It was quite scary when ...
>
> That character was so real ...
>
> I grew up in that town and I could picture where it was all happening.

Sometimes our reactions are not so positive:

> That bit in the middle was a bit too long.
>
> I don't think that character would have reacted like that.
>
> That ending was unrealistic.

As we talk about our enthusiasms, be they positive or negative, our understanding of the text begins to emerge and we construct a meaning from the shared responses.

The second sharing is of the things that puzzle us and allows readers to ask questions and seek clarification:

> I didn't understand why that happened.
>
> Can you work out why she did that?
>
> What did she mean when she said that?
>
> Why did he go there?

As these puzzles and dilemmas are talked about as a group, readers will share understandings and come to a consensus about meaning. It does not matter if everybody has a slightly different understanding because we all come to a text with different expectations, experiences and feelings.

The third sharing is that of the patterns or connections we find in the text. Chambers explains this by saying 'learning to read stories isn't only a matter of learning to recognise these verbal patterns; it is also a matter of learning to recognise the formal, narrative patterns of the story itself' (2011: 106).

Sometimes readers will make connections between what is in the book and experiences they have had in their own lives.

> I have been there.
>
> I know somebody just like that.
>
> I know just how that character is feeling – the same thing happened to me.

On other occasions readers make connections between the text they are currently reading and texts they have read before.

> That reminds me of ... in the way the author describes the setting.
>
> The narrator in this book is much more obvious than in ...
>
> This book is about ... but it deals with it completely differently.

Sometimes readers will notice language patterns for example, the repetition in *The Three Little Pigs* or the structural patterning of the text in *Titch*.

Reflective activity

Choose a children's book and read it with one or two friends. Use Chambers' three sharings as a framework for your discussions:

1. Share your enthusiasms – positive or negative.
2. Share your puzzles – the questions you have about the text.
3. Share your connections – the things that the book reminds you of.

Afterwards, reflect on how that sharing contributed to your understanding of the text.

The emotional environment of reading

Our success as readers, indeed in any form of activity, depends to a very large extent on how we feel about the activity. Is reading something which we find emotionally satisfying and rewarding or is it just a chore which has to be done? That will depend both on our relationship with the teacher and on our previous experiences of reading. Tony Martin (1989) talked to Leslie, a pupil who had failed at reading, about his experiences and his comments are salutary for every teacher of reading. Leslie remembers being given the same book to read over and over again – not because he enjoyed it but because he was not able to read all the words; he remembers having a thin reading book with lots of pictures while his peers were reading thick chapter books; he remembers being the only one in the class having to read out loud to the teacher and the feeling of embarrassment that engendered. Leslie is an example of the comment expressed by the House of Commons Select Committee (2003) in their report on the teaching of reading:

> the acquisition of reading is an extremely complex subject, which is influenced by factors outside a school's control, such as socio-economic background, neurological development, the language of instruction and the experiences and stimuli a child encounters at a very early age, as well as many others.

So much of what we have already said about learning to read will impact on how our pupils feel about reading. Those feelings come, however, not only from the experiences and relationships in the classroom but also from the home. Some parents have had very negative experiences of school themselves and as a result either do not value reading in the time and emphasis they place on it or are so keen to do nothing wrong in the eyes of the school that they do not read or talk with their children about reading. Other parents may be keen readers themselves and undermine the school 'system' by valuing other reading experiences more highly.

'Third space theory' was defined by Bhabha (1994), using the term 'third space' to identify a real or virtual space as a neutral place where differing perspectives can meet and be valued and explored. Thus, a teacher of reading can allow children to bring the knowledge and experiences of reading they have at home and relate them to the new experiences and learning they encounter at school. Moje et al. (2004) argued that when home experiences of reading are brought into school children's learning is enriched. The work of Levy (2011) demonstrates how identifying that third space can be useful for teachers of reading in recognising and valuing children's existing reading skills. Levy describes Caitlyn, who was an avid reader at home where she loved to tell the story and 'read books from her head' rather than decode each word. Even when Caitlyn had learned how to decode and also had a bank of key words which she knew on sight, she was reluctant to read the scheme books from school at home. Levy says, of Caitlyn and another pupil:

the move into Reception ... did further narrow the perception of reading ... in that they came to believe that they had to learn to decode print in their reading scheme books in order to be seen to be a reader ... this perception was met with anxiety ... the strategies that she used herself to make meaning from texts did not fit with her perceptions of a schooled discourse in reading. Subsequently, the gap between schooled reading and home reading appeared to widen. (2011: 113)

Note the anxiety Caitlyn felt, and that this was because what she could do was not recognised as being valid.

One way of incorporating the reading practices of home into the classroom is by using play to create authentic reading experiences. This means allowing children opportunities to read in the role-play area, the construction area and the small-world area among others, and creating reading that is a natural part of the context. For example, in a construction area, place instructions for building different models, information sheets about the models you can build and guidelines for putting the materials away. Ensuring classroom reading opportunities are authentic also means using a wide variety of texts in all reading situation. For example, in a shared or guided reading use a newspaper article or a web page or a text message.

Dyson (1993) describes what she calls a 'permeable curriculum' where home and school mutually support and inform each other. The aim is to build on children's successes and so make them feel good about themselves as readers, leading to more reading success. Cook (2005) describes a Year 5 visit to a local restaurant; the children noted all the reading materials and actions taking place in the restaurant, including the kitchen. Back in the classroom, they used the knowledge gained from the visit to plan a role-play centre as a restaurant. Once this was up and running, the teacher created different scenarios, for example the chef left and they needed to advertise, interview, appoint a new chef and then draw up a training manual for the appointee. As Cook (2005: 89) says:

The approach not only made meaningful use of children's out of school experience but also showed them how this experience connected to the ordinary school curriculum, especially through home-type learning strategies, such as communal recollection and representational play. It also provided for meaningful speaking and listening and problem-solving situations, which are often difficult to represent in class.

There are many opportunities within local communities – the library, places of worship, shops, doctors' surgeries or post offices to name just a few. In drawing on prior encounters and knowledge, teachers of reading can make learning to read in school a safe and recognisable experience and create a positive emotional environment. Remember that an emotional environment is one which respects those who work within it and values everybody's contribution. It also acknowledges what is important to each person, and gives everybody space to be themselves and retreat when the world gets a little too challenging.

 ## Reflective activity

Go back to the list of readers' rights identified by Pennac, earlier in the chapter. How much do you think recognising and implementing these rights would create a positive emotional environment for readers? For each point, consider a classroom practice in the teaching of reading that would exemplify the right. Share ideas with a friend. Are they all equally valid – or would you prioritise some over others?

The physical environment of reading

Many theorists have for a long time considered the importance of the physical environment and its impact on learning. A Piagetian classroom is one where children interact with the environment rather than being presented with a body of knowledge. This means that the role of the teacher is to provide these experiences and environments which allow children to discover. In the Reggio Emilia approach everything in the classroom is carefully chosen for its potential for learning. Classrooms have neutral, off-white walls, baskets for storage and wooden furniture. The colour and clutter of many primary classrooms are thought to be distracting. Natural materials are used. Collections of resources are used to stimulate children's enquiry, they are known as 'provocations', and they are displayed in a way that encourages children to explore and ask questions. Malaguzzi (1996: 40) described the classroom as the child's third teacher, saying:

> We place enormous value on the role of the environment as a motivating and animating force in creating spaces for relations, options, and emotional and cognitive situations that produce a sense of well-being and security.

Montessori (1966) believed that the classroom environment should be as close to the real world as possible in order that children have every opportunity to develop. Montessori talks about the 'prepared environment' of which the three main elements are the children, the teacher and the physical environment. Characteristics of this prepared environment must include:

- beauty, order, reality, simplicity and accessibility
- freedom to work and move around within suitable guidelines that enable them to act as part of a social group

- specifically designed materials to explore the world and develop essential cognitive skills
- mixed age groups to develop socially and intellectually at their own pace.

As Standing (1998: 267) said, 'The first aim of the prepared environment is, as far as it is possible, to render the growing child independent of the adult'.

Lipman (2010) argues that, in the twenty-first century, we can no longer consider the learner as active and the environment as passive; rather we must view both learner and environment as active. He compares the modern-day learning environment with the pedagogies of Reggio Emilia and Montessori, seeing technology as providing the modern-day tools which structure learning and guide development. He would claim that most primary classrooms are the same as they have been for hundreds of years, with an interactive whiteboard replacing a blackboard.

Consider all these arguments about the physical classroom environment in relation to the teaching of reading.

First, as Montessori used natural materials so I believe an effective teacher of reading should provide authentic reading materials for the children in the class. There should be all types of text, both printed and on screen: books, pamphlets, newspapers, magazines, comics, e-mails, letters, advertising promotions, notices, labels, etcetera.

Second, there should be the time to read all these texts and the time to browse. Browsing need not take long, a few minutes every day is enough. During browsing time, children can talk with each other and with adults about the books and share ideas, opinions and experiences.

Third, there needs to be time for children to read for themselves. This means they will read materials of their own choice, at their own speed and where they feel most comfortable. Teachers cannot be sure that children will have the opportunities for this at home and so they need to be provided at school. Some schools will have specific times in the day when everybody reads; uninterrupted sustained silent reading (USSR). Each word in that description is important and should be upheld. The time should be regarded as sacrosanct and the teacher should be reading as well rather than catching up with odd jobs. The time should be long enough for children to become immersed in what they are reading, and naturally the older the child the longer this will be and vice versa. Similarly there should be an expectation of minimum noise; again, the younger the child the less likelihood of complete silence, but there should be an atmosphere of concentration in the classroom.

It can often take as long as a term to introduce and establish a reading time in a class, but once it is part of the expected pattern of classroom life it will be a key element of your planned teaching of reading programme.

An additional facet of providing time for reading in the classroom is by becoming involved in national initiatives or devoting a block of time, for example a whole week, to book-focused activities. I want to talk about just two possibilities here.

Children's Book Week

The first full week in October every year is normally Children's Book Week and it is marketed as a celebration of reading for pleasure. It provides lots of opportunities and resources to motivate and excite children about reading and is organised by Booktrust. Some of the suggested activities on the website (www.booktrust.org.uk/programmes/primary/childrens-book-week/about-childrens-book-week/) are:

- Author and illustrator visits in schools
- Reading-themed games
- Book swaps
- Library and bookshop visits
- Writing and performing plays based on favourite stories
- Creative writing activities
- Sponsored reads
- Designing book covers
- Reading challenges such as 'try a book new to you'
- Poetry reading assemblies
- Making a film version of a favourite book.

The website includes lots of lesson plans, activities and ideas. A focused week serves to raise the profile of reading and can become a whole-community event. Other national events include World Book Day, which usually happens in March each year.

Author visits

These can be a wonderful opportunity to inspire children both to read and also to write. These can be arranged through publishers or there are agents who will arrange it for you. Contact details are available on the Booktrust website. Do not feel that you have to invite a very famous author; often local authors are willing to come into schools and children can be just as excited and impressed. When planning an author visit the first priority is to decide what the purpose of the visit is and who will be involved. Some authors will talk to the whole school, but others would prefer to run a workshop with a small group. Make sure you have prepared the children by reading the author's books before the event and putting up displays of the author's books around the school. It is often a good idea to ask a bookshop to come with lots of copies of the books which children can buy and have signed. Follow up the visit with reading, writing, drama, music or whatever the children and you feel inspired to do. It is a good idea to get the children to write thank you letters to the author.

A block of time concentrated on the promotion of reading can be a marvellous boost to the development of the reading environment of the school but it is not a substitute for a consistent ethos which values and gives time to reading. The third element in a positive reading environment is a space where books are clearly valued and displayed.

Reflective activity

Look at the reading corners in as many classrooms as possible.

- How are books displayed?
- Is it easy to see what books are there?
- Are the books displayed in a way that attracts readers?
- Is there space to read?

In my experience, book corners, if they exist at all, are dark corners of the classroom where all sorts of books are piled up and rarely are there displays introducing children to new books or making suggestions for reading. Book corners or reading areas should be areas for reading and not be taken over by other activities. They need time to be maintained; often a teaching assistant is willing to take responsibility for this. In setting up a book corner think about the way in which books are displayed to make them attractive to readers, remembering that often less is more! Use displays to focus on an author, a genre, new books, themed books, but change them frequently. Do not let displays become like wallpaper which is unnoticed.

Many schools also have school libraries, rooms which are devoted to books. It is a shame that sometimes these become rooms which are used for small group teaching or anything else rather than reading. They take a lot of maintenance and need somebody who is passionate about it. School libraries can, however, give a clear message of the importance that is given throughout the school to reading. I could write a whole chapter devoted to the use of the school library but I am not going to do so in this context. The School Library Association (www.sla.org) is worth joining as it provides lots of support and information. In 2010 there was a commission led by former Secretary of State for Education Estelle Morris to look at school libraries. The report of the commission claimed that it had 'demonstrated the powerful role a high performing school library and schools library service plays in raising pupils' literacy levels and improving their access to knowledge' (Morris, 2010: 4). The commission asked if there was any aspect of the role of a school library which could be delivered in any other way, and from their findings argued that:

> An effective school library acting as a powerhouse of learning and reading within a school is a unique resource. Our vision of a renewed school library system in the nation's schools is fundamentally about realising the potential of every child by exciting the latent reader and learner in all. (2010: 20)

The commission concluded that school libraries are often a wasted resource and do not exploit their full potential in supporting the development of readers.

Selection

At the beginning of the chapter in the discussion of the reading circle we identified selection of texts as being a key element in the teaching of reading, and it is to this that we now turn our attention. This must be clearly related to the knowledge of children's books held by the teacher of reading; this was discussed in Chapter 3 and the key points of that chapter should inform your reading of this section.

In 2006 the UKLA made a submission to the review of best practice in the teaching of reading. In that submission it was said that while phonics is necessary, educators must remember the goal of reading instruction is 'to develop effective and enthusiastic readers'. It is this goal which underpins the teaching of reading and the texts we ask children to read will affect their experiences of reading in school. Levy (2011: 82) has done some significant work in this area and she argues that 'the school context is largely responsible for shaping definitions of reading'.

Levy looked at the experiences of beginner readers in one school in depth and the relationship that developed between their understanding of reading and the books used in the classroom to support the teaching of reading. For the majority of children their success as a reader was determined by their progress through the reading scheme. In addition, the children believed that only the reading scheme books were there for the teaching of reading and other books had no part in this process. As a result, children who were still working their way through the reading scheme did not consider themselves to be readers until they had completed the scheme and became 'free' readers.

There were two implications of this self-perception. First, there was a real distinction between reading and reading in order to learn how to read. The children felt that reading meant that they had to be able to decode every word; the reading scheme books were those that they could decode and so those were the only ones they could read. Therefore, in the children's eyes, all other books were 'too difficult' and they made no attempt to read them. Second, this meant that for the children reading meant decoding; if they were not able to decode they were not able to read. Only decoding counted in relation to reading.

Improvement in reading was defined by their progress through the reading scheme, and when asked to describe what sort of reader they were children tended to answer in relation to the stage or colour of the current reading scheme book they were reading. You will remember that this happened in another school, as described in Chapter 4.

The Ofsted Report *Reading by Six* (2010) looked at the practice of 12 primary schools who were deemed successful in the teaching of reading. The report begins with a description of the teaching approach of each school; these make for interesting reading. They all use a strong phonics approach with an emphasis on decoding and only two schools made any mention of the texts that children are reading. One school said that each class listened to five 'high-quality texts' each term which means they would have experience of 15 texts during a year. The other school ensured the children were exposed to a wide range of high-quality texts. Other schools only mentioned the use of decodable texts, and in the summary, the report comments on the significance of well-structured resources. It is interesting to reflect on what message this gives to children about reading and relates to the description given by Luke et al. (2003: 249) of books being defined and used as 'pedagogical commodities'.

O'Sullivan and McGonigle (2010) argue that the use of real books which are selected and structured by their teachers is more productive in the teaching of reading than a completely free choice of books, and this is a valid point. It emphasises, however, the importance of the knowledge held by the teacher of reading about the books. It is important that the selection of books is done on the basis of the quality of the books and with the key purpose of reading for pleasure and information in mind. As Johnson and Giorgis (2003: 704) say:

> Literature is more than a resource used to teach children how to read. Literature is also one of the major reasons to become literate ... Literature is an authentic text written to tell a story, not to teach the 'short a' vowel sound.

It is also important to remember that some reading scheme books tell really good stories and can engage children in the reading process. Capper (2013) discovered that her class of seven- and eight-year-olds found the reading scheme books enjoyable and were inspired to go on to wider reading. I would argue that a key feature is the teacher of reading and their understanding of the reading process and knowledge of how books can support that process.

There is another important consideration when looking at the selection of texts in the classroom, and that is the variety of texts which are not only present but are used and valued as part of the process of learning to read. Children come to school with a wide range of reading experiences which include digital and screen media. The children in Levy's research defined reading by their experiences of reading in school, and Levy suggests some ways in which teachers can broaden definitions of reading both by the texts that they use and the way in which they talk about those texts. Her suggestions are:

- Acknowledge that reading symbols in, for example, a mathematics lesson is as much reading as is decoding letters
- Talk about reading pictures rather than 'looking at' pictures and reading print
- Encourage children to think about the reader when they are constructing texts, be those texts written, drawn or constructed as a model
- Use screen texts as reading material in shared reading, referring to hyperlinks, icons, symbols as well as 'the words'.

I am sure you have seen videos on the Internet of babies stroking the pages of books to try and change the image. This experience needs to be exploited to the full in the classroom. Burnett (2010: 16) found that 'complex interactions occur between children, technology and their wide-ranging experiences of literacy'.

Marsh (2014) looked at children's use of the virtual world *Club Penguin*, aiming to explore the literacy practices in which they engaged. She found that the purposes of literacy which were evident in the virtual world correlated highly with the purposes of literacy in the real world. Children used literacy to create and maintain social relationships and produced and read texts created by and for their peers. As a result of these findings, Marsh argues that virtual worlds could be used in the classroom in order to create opportunities for reading and writing which would motivate children.

If teachers of reading do not exploit children's existing understandings of digital media they run the risk of limiting definitions of reading and devaluing and perhaps even losing children's existing skills. As Levy says:

> for practitioners to encourage children to develop strong relationships with text, they must not only include exposure to digital technologies in the classroom, but must actively encourage children to build on the skills and strategies they develop in their homes to make sense of digital texts and use these within all aspects of their reading. (2011: 134)

This has implications for the physical environment: a classroom which incorporates digital technologies will look very different to one which has a focus on only paper-based texts. Consider the argument of Lipman (2010) discussed earlier in this chapter, and reflect on what classrooms, which are the places where reading of the twenty-first century is taught, might look like.

Conclusion

This chapter began by identifying the reading circle (Chambers, 2011) which contains all the elements of the reading process: reading, response and selection.

In considering the environment in which reading takes place we first thought about the social environment where the ethos of the class can convey important messages to children about how much reading is valued and what counts as reading. The importance of talk about books was stressed and the use of Chambers' 'three sharings' used as a framework.

Second, in consideration of the emotional environment of reading we considered how important it is to recognise the experiences, knowledge and understandings of reading that children bring to school with them and how teachers of reading need to recognise that these may not necessarily relate to 'schooled' reading. It is part of the role of the teacher of reading to validate and build on these experiences.

Third, we looked at the physical environment of reading and how the reading corner, the school library and the use of time can send messages about what is valued as reading that can either limit or extend definitions and experiences of reading.

The chapter ended with a consideration of the selection of texts and discussed the use of reading schemes and of digital media for reading.

The essential messages of this chapter to the teacher of reading are:

- Talking about books is a central and crucially important part of the teaching of reading
- The physical environment of the classroom gives messages about the value placed on reading
- It is important to give children time to browse and read
- School libraries are an important resource for the teaching of reading
- The books chosen to teach reading contribute to the children's perceptions of themselves as readers
- Children come to school with a wide range of experiences and skills in using digital media which should be built on in school
- Home reading is not necessarily the same as school reading; the teacher of reading needs to make the link.

Further reading

Chambers, A. (2011) *Tell Me: Children, Reading and Talk with The Reading Environment*. Stroud: The Thimble Press.
This is an updated and combined version of two books by Aidan Chambers. They give a clear and practical insight into how teachers can support children's encounters with books.

Levy, R. (2011) *Young Children Reading: At Home and At School*. London: Sage.
This is an account of Levy's research into the experiences of learning to read that young children encounter in school. It is powerful in accessing the voice of the child

and argues strongly that pedagogy should recognise the experiences and understandings of children.

Stone, G. (2011) *The Digital Literacy Classroom.* Herts: UKLA Minibook.
The ideas offered in this book provide a bridge between traditional literacy practice and new digital literacy pedagogy. Teachers are invited to consider the value of digital literacies while exploring practical suggestions that build on existing practice.

CHAPTER 6

TEACHING SYSTEMATIC SYNTHETIC PHONICS: SUBJECT KNOWLEDGE AND PROGRESSION

Chapter objectives

At the end of this chapter you should:

- understand why systematic synthetic phonics (SSP) is the current policy and understand the research which underpins and critiques that view
- know the terminology associated with systematic synthetic phonics
- know the grapheme–phoneme correspondences common in the English written language
- know about blending and segmenting
- be aware of the expected progression in systematic synthetic phonics and be able to relate that to children's experiences of print
- have considered elements of analytic phonics and how that relates to the teaching of reading.

Introduction

The 2014 National Curriculum identifies two aspects of reading which need to be taught: word reading and comprehension. It states that different kinds of teaching are needed for each of these and the assumption of that must be, therefore, that different kinds of knowledge are needed by the teacher of reading. This chapter focuses on the subject knowledge required by teachers in order to fulfil the requirements of that particular aspect of the National Curriculum which focuses on decoding. It begins, however, by exploring and critiquing the rationale for the emphasis on (SSP) as the first approach to reading.

The Rose review

The history of teaching reading is a long one, full of debate and argument, as researchers and practitioners look for the 'correct' way to teach reading. In Chapter 1 the many different approaches to the teaching of reading were presented and it can be seen that they often have a different understanding of what reading is and how children develop as readers.

In April 2005 a report from the all-party House of Commons Education and Skills Committee published a report called *Teaching Children to Read*. The committee had taken evidence from many proponents of synthetic phonics, such as Ruth Miskin and Rhona Johnston. Johnston and Watson (2005) based their evidence on research they had carried out in Clackmannanshire comparing synthetic and analytic phonics, which concluded that 'synthetic phonics was a more effective approach to teaching reading' (2005: 351). There has been much criticism of the methodology of this research casting doubt on its validity, but it was given strong credibility in the forthcoming review of the teaching of reading.

As a result of this Select Committee report, a review into the teaching of early reading was commissioned by the then Secretary of State for Education, Ruth Kelly. She asked Sir Jim Rose to consider what the expectations of best practice in the teaching of early reading and synthetic phonics should be; how that best practice relates to the birth to five framework and the National Literacy Framework; and how children with significant difficulties can be enabled to catch up with their peers (Kelly, 2005).

In 2006 the *Independent Review of the Teaching of Early Reading* was published. It is commonly known as The Rose Review. The review claimed that:

> Despite uncertainties seen in research findings, the practice seen by the review shows that the systematic approach, which is generally understood as 'synthetic' phonics, offers the vast majority of young children the best and most direct route to becoming skilled readers and writers. (Rose, 2006: 3)

One might feel slightly alarmed at the first six words of that sentence and within the review Rose expands on this, saying that research is often contradictory, inconclusive or too slow and therefore policy-makers must base decisions on 'replicable and sustainable best practice' (2006: 15).

There has been much criticism of the findings of the review. Richards (2006) wrote an article called 'This could be the end of teacher autonomy' summing up concerns that the review was advocating one approach to the teaching of reading for every child. Hall (2007) criticised the review because of its individualistic approach to learning, arguing that it reduces teaching to a transmission model and ignores all that we know about what children bring to the learning process. Goouch (2007) takes this argument even further; the review stresses the importance of a broad, rich language curriculum but in insisting on discrete phonic teaching assumes that children will be able to make the connections between these two types of experience themselves. She gives the example of Gabi – a child who comes into school having learned a lot about reading from her experiences at home. Goouch says:

> Let us hope that, in Gabi's early days at school, her teacher has sufficient professional freedom to take time to recognise that Gabi can write information texts, navigate the CBeebies site, find England on the map of the world, sing along with lots of songs learned from children's television, and that she has a strongly developing phonological awareness, had lots of favourite books and stories and recognizes letters in her name. The danger is that the letters in Gabi's name will not be in the initial list of sounds that her teacher is being told to teach her when she first gets to school. (2007: 56–7)

Both Hall and Goouch have hinted at the sense of compulsion that is now placed on teachers to teach phonics in one way. It is important that teachers of reading recognise that this is a political imperative and not necessarily supported by a strong research base. Back in 1993 Drummond and Styles argued that the teaching of reading was as much about politics as pedagogy, and over the years Alexander (2007) argued that educational quality is much more complex than politicians will ever admit to. In its response to the interim report of Rose the UKLA (2005: 3) gave a much more balanced view of best practice in the teaching of reading:

> Best practice in the teaching of early reading brings together two key components: the acquisition of the alphabetic principle and comprehension. These components should not be developed in isolation. Best practice integrates skills teaching with more authentic, contextually-grounded literacy activities, responding to the interests of the learner and the literacy contexts of their homes and communities.

The teaching of early reading is so important that it has a mention in the *Teachers' Standards* (DfE: 2011a) all to itself:

if teaching early reading, demonstrate a clear understanding of systematic synthetic phonics (Standard 3)

I would argue that teachers need clear understanding of much more than SSP in order to be effective teachers of reading. However, teachers of reading do need secure knowledge of the alphabetic principle, and this is the focus of the rest of this chapter.

Analytic phonics

Before looking at what is meant by 'systematic synthetic phonics', I want first to clarify what 'analytic phonics' is – the system which is thought to be less effective by government policy but in practice is implemented by many teachers of reading along with a synthetic approach and which, before the Rose Review, was the most commonly adopted approach in many classrooms.

Analytic phonics is, as its name suggests, about analysing words to identify patterns and relationships between sounds and letters. It begins with a focus on initial sounds and children would be encouraged to list words which started with the same sound – money, man, milk, mother. At first, there would be no attempt to sound out the whole word because collections of words might contain some phonically complex ones. Teachers would ask children to suggest words with the same initial sound and would write them in the list – the emphasis being on the first sound. Attention would then turn to the last sound of the word – jam, Pam, ham. Next attention would be given to the middle sound and children would focus on CVC words, that is words consisting of the pattern consonant, vowel, consonant.

The main difference between analytic and synthetic phonics lies in the size of the unit which is the main focus of learning. In synthetic phonics it is the sound or phoneme and learners put these sounds together (or synthesise them) to make words. In analytic phonics learners look at words and analyse them to identify sounds. Dombey and Moustafa (1998) describe this as part-to-whole or whole-to-part. For many young children identifying single sounds in words is challenging, and the work of Bryant (1993) argued that it is only the process of learning to read which enables children to break words up into phonemes. The syllable is seen, within analytic phonics, as the most accessible unit of sound for beginner readers; syllables can be pronounced as separate units and are the beginning of phonological awareness. You can most easily identify syllables by clapping along with spoken language and you will find that each clap will accompany a syllable. Syllables are the rhythm of language.

The work of Goswami (1986) focused attention on the idea of onset and rime. The 'rime' is the part of the syllable at the end, which includes everything from the vowel, and the 'onset' is everything which goes before the vowel. The strength of this unit of analysis is that it is easier to recognise onsets and rimes in words and that rimes are parts of words that are spelled in the same way. For example, chin, pin, spin and din share the rime '-in' but have different onsets. Star, stone, stick and stair share the onset 'st' but have different rimes. Kirtley et al. (1989) found that five-year-old children found it easier to identify the rime in words than the final consonant. The concept of onset and rime is the basis of much language play in songs, rhymes and games.

Goswami (1992) went on to argue that having identified onset and rime children use this understanding to see patterns and relationships in different words. She called this 'analogy'. If a child can recognise 'pin' and 'spin', they are likely to recognise 'chin'. The ability to look for and recognise patterns in the structure of words is helpful to a beginner reader. Dombey (1998) links this to the work of Frith which was discussed in Chapter 1; it is significant that the second phase of Frith's staged model of reading is called the 'analytic' phase.

Jolliffe and Waugh (2012) criticise analytic phonics for its lack of a systematic approach to teaching the sounds, but concede that it has a value in teaching spelling. Johnston and Watson (2007: 10) again criticise analytic phonics for its slower and less systematic approach:

> Systematic phonics is a fast-moving approach, with letter sounds being taught very rapidly, and with an early start to sounding and blending, whereas analytic phonics is typically slow-moving. It might be the case that if an analytic phonics programme was speeded up, so that letter sounds were learned equally fast, the children's reading and spelling would be as good as those taught by synthetic phonics. However, we found this was not the case.

A reflective teacher of reading needs to consider statements such as that and ask themself questions such as:

- Is speed the only criteria to judge the process of learning to read?
- Is the ability to 'sound and blend' always an indication of a good reader?

After reflecting on those two points, consider them in the light of Richmond's observation that:

> Beginner readers need the raw material on which their brains can get to work. They need to see lots of words in meaningful and interesting groups so that their powerful remembering brains can first, obviously, remember; but next, and equally important, can begin to generalise from the raw material, can apprehend patterns and similarities in words which will lead them to make hypotheses – highly intelligent guesses, which will sometimes be wrong, but are evidence of learning nonetheless – about words they've never seen before, but may have heard read to them, and very probably will already have in their stock of spoken language. (2013: 16)

However, it cannot be denied that children need to learn how to crack the code in order to become effective readers, and since the English language is based on an alphabetic system, the *Teachers' Standards* require teachers to have a clear understanding of SSP and the National Curriculum requires that 'phonics should be emphasised in the early teaching of reading' (DfE, 2013a: 4). The rest of this chapter then looks at the knowledge required by teachers of reading to fulfil this requirement.

Systematic synthetic phonics

It has already been stated that SSP is *systematic*. That means that the teaching of sound–symbol relationships is done according to a systematic plan. Children are taught sounds in a clear and predetermined order. Teachers do not pick up on an alliterative pattern that might be in a favourite book, or on the letters in a child's name for phonic teaching, but follow the order of sounds which is determined in the chosen scheme.

Second, SSP is *synthetic*. This does not mean it is artificially created like synthetic cream, but means that the emphasis is on synthesising, or putting together, smaller units or letters into larger units or words.

The alphabetic code

The teaching of phonics is based on the principle that the English language is formed by an alphabetic code. This means that letters represent the sounds of our language. There are around 44 sounds in the spoken English language, and you will quickly appreciate that there are only 26 letters of the alphabet. If there were equal numbers of each, life would be much simpler! When one letter is used to represent one sound that is called a transparent code, and this is where teaching starts. The opaque code is where there are many different ways of representing a sound.

Reflective activity

Write down as many words as you can that contain the sound /ai/ or /ie/. When you have as many as you can recall, sort them into spelling patterns. You will then begin to see evidence of the opaque alphabetic code – the same sound can be represented in many different ways.

(Continued)

(Continued)

You will have seen that I represented the sound /ie/ in two different ways. The first one uses the International Phonetic Alphabet and this can be found on page 63 of the National Curriculum for English in Key Stages 1 and 2 (DfE, 2013a). This is non-statutory and there is no need at all to learn it. You might find it easier to represent sounds in the most common spelling pattern for that sound and that is what I have done in the second way.

Phonological awareness

This refers to the ability to hear and discriminate between sounds. The teaching of phonics is all about learning how sounds are represented so it is vital that hearing and identifying sounds are well established in learners. There is no point starting systematic phonic teaching if children cannot hear and discriminate different sounds. This begins by listening to and identifying sounds in the environment. This can be done in several ways:

- A listening walk around the school or local environment, stopping at various points to listen and identify what can be heard.
- Sound lotto – children match recordings of day-to-day sounds with pictures on a card.
- Listening time – children are silent for one minute and then list all the things they hear.
- What is it? – children are blindfolded to listen to an object making a sound; they then guess what the object was from a selection on a tray.
- Making sounds – children use their voices or musical instruments to make different sounds – loud and soft, quick and slow, high and low.

You will be able to think of many more fun games and activities. The principle is that children listen to and identify sounds and develop a vocabulary for talking about those sounds.

Phase 1 of *Letters and Sounds* (DfES, 2007) is all about this element, and it describes seven aspects:

1. General sound discrimination – environmental sounds
2. General sound discrimination – instrumental sounds
3. General sound discrimination – body percussion
4. Rhythm and rhyme
5. Alliteration
6. Voice sounds
7. Oral blending and segmenting.

Teaching activities for these aspects will be discussed in more detail in the next chapter, but I hope you can begin to match the activities listed above to those aspects. What is important is that Phase 1 carries on throughout Key Stage 1 so that children's ears remain attuned to sound.

Phoneme

This is the term used for the smallest unit of sound in language. If you are a linguist you might question this and argue that a 'phone' is actually the smallest unit of sound, but for the purposes of teaching phonics it is the *phoneme*. It is important to remember that it is the sounds in a word which indicate the phonemes. It is easy to get distracted by the written form of words, but when identifying phonemes listen to the spoken word and do not look at the written word. Here are some examples:

- cat has three phonemes – /c/a/t/
- hat has three phonemes – /h/a/t
- pram has four phonemes – /p/r/a/m/
- splash has five phonemes – /s/p/l/a/sh/

If you look at the word 'splash' you will see that it has five phonemes and six letters. That is an example of the point that there are more phonemes than letters and so often phonemes are represented by different letters or combinations of letters.

When pronouncing phonemes it is very important to use pure sound; that means that when you say the sound you do not add an '-er' or '-uh' sound at the end of the letter. This is known as the *schwa* and is an unstressed vowel. It is very tempting to add that extra sound, especially with the softer phonemes, in order to make yourself heard. Resist the temptation. It makes blending impossible and can be misleading for children. The only way to make sure you are enunciating phonemes correctly is to practise; you could do this with a group of friends or you might like to lock yourself in the bathroom to practise! There are several online resources which demonstrate the correct enunciation of phonemes. Two which I like are:

www.getreadingright.co.uk/pronounce-the-phonemes/

www.mrthorne.com/44phonemes/

The second resource is one of many by a primary teacher called Mr Thorne. His website contains lots of useful resources and is worth exploring. When demonstrating how to enunciate the phonemes, he encourages viewers to watch his lips and this is a helpful point. There is a particular mouth movement associated with each phoneme; if you have trouble identifying phonemes in words a simple tip is that usually every time you move your mouth it is a new phoneme.

Reflective activity

There are two things you need to make sure you can do:

- enunciate the phonemes correctly
- identify the phonemes in words

The only way to do that is to practise so I suggest you go somewhere private and have a go!

Having practised the 44 phonemes, you might be wondering what they are and how they came about. Phonemes are either vowel phonemes or consonant phonemes. Simple vowel phonemes are:

/a/ in cat, /e/ in peg, /i/ in pig, /o/ in log and /u/ in plug

However, there are other vowel phonemes in words which are not so simple. For example, what is the vowel phoneme in fork or in car? The answers are /au/ and /ar/. You can see that it gets more complicated. This is related to the fact that some phonemes are represented in more than one way. We shall come back to this soon but firstly, need to make sure the idea of graphemes is understood.

Graphemes

The concept of a grapheme is relatively simple because a grapheme is how a phoneme is written down. A grapheme is made up of one or more letters. In the simple or transparent code there is one phoneme represented by one grapheme which consists of one letter. In the advanced or opaque code there is one phoneme represented by one grapheme which consists of two or more letters. There is always the same number of graphemes as phonemes in a word but not necessarily the same number of letters.

Consider the word 'splash' and break it down into phonemes. There are five phonemes – /s/ /p/ /l/ /a/ /sh/. This is written down with five graphemes but one of those graphemes /sh/ consists of two letters, 's' and 'h'. That is a consonant phoneme.

Consonant phonemes

There are approximately 25 consonant phonemes. It is easiest to hear them when they are said in words. You will also be able to see that phonemes can be represented in different ways. Read the following list of words aloud, being careful to enunciate pure sounds without the schwa.

Table 6.1   Consonant phonemes

Consonant phonemes	Representative words	Consonant phonemes	Representative words
/b/	ball	/s/	salt, city, science
/d/	dig	/t/	tin
/f/	fairy, photo	/v/	vote
/g/	goal	/w/	win
/h/	ham	/wh/	where
/j/	joke, giraffe	/y/	yoyo
/k/	cook, Chris	/z/	zebra, is, please
/l/	lamp	/th/	then
/m/	money, thumb	/th/	thin
/n/	nose, knife, gnat	/ch/	chop, match
/p/	pig	/sh/	shoe, chef, mission
/r/	ring, wrinkle	/zh/	measure
		/ng/	sing, pink

Source: Adapted from *Progression in Phonics* (DfES, 2001)

It is likely that as you read you became more aware of your mouth movements; if you are unsure then exaggerate these movements. This is particularly evident when you consider the difference between /th/ as in 'then' and /th/ as in 'thin'. In the former your tongue is behind your top front teeth and in the latter protrudes between the teeth. Read the words again paying particular attention to the shape of your mouth and the position of your tongue.

When looking at consonant phonemes, it is important to distinguish *blends* or *clusters*. A consonant *blend* is where consonant letters at either the end or the beginning of a word are blended or clustered together but the individual sounds can still be heard. An example is the word 'strip'. It is formed of five phonemes: /s/ /t/ /r/ /i/ /p/ which can be clearly heard as individual sounds but the first three phonemes blend together when the word is spoken. Other common blends include sp, st, sc, sn, sm, fl, br, cl, dr and gr and there are more.

Look carefully at the word 'splash'. It has five phonemes represented by five graphemes: /s/ /p/ /l/ /a/ /sh/. The first three phonemes are a blend or cluster – the individual phonemes can be heard but they blend or cluster together in the word. The /sh/ at the end of the word, however, is different. That is one phoneme represented by one grapheme which is formed of two letters. Two letters are used to represent one phoneme and this is known as a *consonant digraph*. The word 'stretch' is similar but that ends with a *consonant trigraph* – three letters which form a grapheme to represent one phoneme.

As you read you may also have questioned some of the suggested words and felt that they did not represent the phonemes as you would say them. This is because phonics is very much affected by accent. Some accents would not differentiate between /w/ in 'win' and /wh/ in 'where'. Accent, however, is particularly noticeable in the vowel phonemes, which we now consider.

Vowel phonemes

Table 6.2   Vowel phonemes

Vowel phonemes	Representative words	Vowel phonemes	Representative words
/a/	mat	/oo/	put, look, would
/e/	bed, bread	/ar/	part, bath
/i/	fig, wanted	/ur/	turn, first, term, heard, work
/o/	fog, want	/or/	born, poor
/u/	mug, glove	/au/	paw, fall, haul
/ae/	stain, play, mate, station	/er/	mother, wooden, circus
/ee/	greet, meat, thief, these	/ow/	clown, pout
/ie/	pie, fight, my, mine, find	/oi/	coin, toy
/oe/	boat, glow, drone, fold	/air/	stair, bear, hare
/ue/	blue, grew, tune, moon	/ear/	beer, near, here

Source: Adapted from *Progression in Phonics* (DfES, 2001)

I am sure that as you read through that list of words there were more occasions when you questioned the phoneme used. Do you have a bath with /ar/ or with /a/? The answer will depend on your accent. It is important to remember that phonemic awareness is not a precise science. If you are teaching in a school in which the children have different accents from yours, it is best to adapt your accent to theirs. If there are a few children with different accents from the others, do not let them think their pronunciation is wrong; children are very able to cope with difference and uncertainty.

Grapheme–phoneme correspondence

The first thing to be taught is the relationship between the phoneme (the sound) and the grapheme (the written representation of the sound). This is known as the grapheme–phoneme correspondence or GPC. In the next chapter we will explore some teaching strategies but the teaching of GPCs is something which is done quickly. There was a time when children were taught one sound a week, but in a systematic synthetic phonics approach all 44 phonemes are learned very quickly.

Blending

As GPCs are taught children also are taught how to blend phonemes together to make words. It is in blending that the true nature of synthetic phonics can be understood. Blending is for reading. Imagine you are a beginner reader and you come across the word 'sat' in a text you are reading. You will have been taught the GPCs for each of those so you will look at the graphemes and associate them with the phonemes /s/, /a/ and /t/. Your task is now to put those phonemes together to make a word. You say the phonemes in turn but stretch each one out so that it blends into the next. Try it and you will see that you are blending the phonemes together to make the word 'sat'.

Blending illustrates the importance of pure sounds and of enunciating each phoneme clearly without adding the schwa. If you sound a word out with the addition of the schwa you will get something like /suh/ /a//tuh/ and however hard you try you will never be able to make that become 'sat'.

Segmenting

Segmenting is the reverse process of blending and is for writing or spelling. If somebody says the word 'sat' to you and you need to write it down, you need to be able to hear and identify the three phonemes in the word. Once identified, you then need to know the graphemes which represent those phonemes and write them in the correct order.

There are two points arising from this process. The first is simply that letter formation is taught hand in hand with GPC so that children are writing the letters within the grapheme at the same time as recognising the sound and its grapheme. Second, children may be writing words when they have not yet learned all the alternative representations. Therefore if they spell a word in a phonically plausible way then teachers should accept it. For example, a child trying to write the word 'light' might spell it as 'lyt' because they have not yet been taught the grapheme /igh/.

Tricky words

I would not be surprised if you have been reading this chapter and thinking to yourself, 'But there are lots and lots of words which do not fit into this'. This is correct and these words tend to be called 'tricky words'. Unfortunately, many of these words are some of the most common words in usage in English. Some of these words are decodable but not at the early stages of a phonic programme, and some are not decodable at all. Examples of some of these words are: he, she, go, said, because, the. There are many more; they are the words which form the glue in language and it is difficult to write meaningfully without them. There is nothing else to do but to teach these holistically: there are various strategies which can be adopted to teach them and they will be discussed in the next chapter. Fortunately, because most of these words belong to the set of most common words they are words which children will tend to know and encounter in their reading.

Decodable texts

There is an argument strongly expressed that children in the early stages of reading should be given books to read which they are able to decode independently. The justification for this is said to be that children will experience success and so pleasure in reading and will also have practice in decoding skills.

The immediate problem is that at the early stages children's knowledge of GPCs will be very limited and several 'tricky words' will need to be introduced as well.

Reflective activity

The first phonemes children learn are /s/ /a/ /t/ /p/ /i/ and /n/. Try and create a decodable text using words only made from those phonemes and a few tricky words. You will be able to create quite a few short simple sentences and maybe even put them together to form a story. Reflect on that story in the light of what you have already discovered about the reader's role in interacting and making meaning from the text. I would hazard a guess that the text you have written is not the most engaging book to read!

Wyse and Goswami (2008) argue that the teaching of reading is all about teaching children how to make meaning from and understand texts. Dombey (2010) states that as teachers of reading our central concern must be meaning so that children 'develop a habit of mind that expects the words they decode to make sense' (2010: 4). However, Jolliffe and Waugh (2012) claim that decodable texts should only be a small part of children's reading experience. They quote the National Reading Panel (2000) which states that children must understand the purpose of learning letter-sounds and can apply their skills in daily reading activities. Teachers of reading need to ask themselves if these decodable texts do help children understand the purpose of reading.

Non-words

Many schools have now begun teaching children how to read what are described as 'non-words' or 'pseudo' words. This came about since the introduction of the phonic screening check for all Year 1 children in June 2012. More will be said about this in Chapter 11, but practising reading non-words with children seems to me to be a bizarre thing to do. This practice has been justified as providing a focus on decoding skills so that children are not distracted by anything like meaning. UKLA undertook a review of Year 1 teachers in July 2012, a month after the first screening check, asking if new issues were identified that were previously unknown to teachers and if the check gave a valid reflection of children's abilities as readers. Responses overwhelmingly indicated that schools felt the phonics screening check was 'costly, time-consuming and not necessary'. Teachers felt that it impeded fluent readers and often undermined their confidence as readers; these able readers were beyond the level of decoding required by the test and were held back by having to comply with the requirements of the test. The non-words were confusing for children who knew that reading was supposed to make sense and so tried really hard to create meaning from the nonsense words.

The clear message for teachers of reading is that the purpose of reading is for pleasure or information, and knowing and experiencing that is a central part of the process of learning to read. Learning to decode is vital but only within the context of the whole reading process.

Progression in phonics

Letters and Sounds (DES, 2007) identifies six phases in phonic teaching and learning and in each phase the content of what is to be taught and the length of time it is supposed to take is specified. It is so designed that children complete all six phases by the end of Key Stage 1. The phases and what they contain are as follows:

1. Phase One starts in Reception and continues throughout Key Stage 1. As already indicated, its focus is on listening, remembering and manipulating sounds. During this phase you may well find that the games and activities are spread thoughout the day and do not form part of a discrete lesson. However, some schools do teach this phase in discrete lessons. Remember that the focus is on listening to sounds. Blending and segmenting are taught orally.

2. In Phase Two children are introduced to letters and GPC. The phase lasts for six weeks and 19 letters and their simple graphemes are taught at a rate of approximately four a week. Children are also taught how to blend and segment with letters and to use these skills in the context of letters. As *Letters and Sounds* says, 'It must always be remembered that phonics is the step up to word recognition. Automatic reading of words – decodable and tricky – is the ultimate goal' (2007: 48).

3. Phase Three lasts for 12 weeks and 25 graphemes are taught, representing about 42 phonemes. Most of these graphemes have two letters.

4. Phase Four lasts for four weeks and is a consolidation phase. Children are taught how to read and spell words containing adjacent consonants and polysyllabic words.

5. In Phase Five children learn alternative spelling for phonemes and also look at alternative pronunciations of graphemes. This phase lasts 30 weeks and takes most of Year 1.

6. Finally, Phase Six emphasises fluency and accuracy in reading and spelling while looking at more complex spelling. This goes through Year 2.

You can see that the pace is rapid. Many children do not manage to keep up this pace of acquiring phonic knowledge and some schools teach phonics in mixed age ability groups. We shall consider that in the next chapter. The progression in phonics is very similar in most schemes with only very slight variations.

Letter names

It has been shown that letters are the tools of both reading and writing. Phonics is about learning the phonemes and the graphemes which represent those phonemes. Children should not be taught that the letter 'a' is called /a/ because it will soon become apparent that that particular letter is a part of several other graphemes and does not always represent the phoneme /a/. It is important, therefore, that children are taught letter names alongside the phonemes and graphemes.

Knowing the alphabet is an important part of becoming a reader because the alphabet is the tool of both reading and writing. There are lots of fun ways to incorporate the alphabet into classroom life:

- sing the alphabet song in spare moments
- arrange things in alphabetical order and talk about how this is done with the children
- use alphabet books for reading aloud and shared and guided reading

UNIVERSITY OF WINCHESTER
LIBRARY

- make alphabet books related to whatever topic you are studying at the time
- make collections of words starting with each letter
- make illuminated letters
- use alliteration whenever possible.

Conclusion

It is fitting to close a chapter on the subject knowledge required to teach SSP with a section on the alphabet. It is because English is an alphabetic system that phonics is a central part of the process of learning to read. It is a complex code, however, and so it is important that teachers of reading are secure in their own subject knowledge and their own phonemic awareness.

This chapter began by putting the emphasis on systematic synthetic phonics into a historical and political context and has compared that approach to analytic phonics. The chapter then described and explained the essential elements of systematic synthetic phonics: phonemes, graphemes, GPCs, blending and segmenting. It concluded by considering the importance of teaching the alphabet.

The essential messages of this chapter to the teacher of reading are:

- pedagogy is often determined politically
- teaching phonics is about teaching children how to decode and is far from being all there is to teaching children to read
- teaching phonics is about learning the relationships between the sounds of spoken language and the symbols of written language
- teachers of reading need to be secure in their own phonemic awareness
- learning about the alphabet should be fun and integrated into other aspects of learning and teaching.

This chapter began by showing how the teaching of reading has become a big political issue in England at the start of the twenty-first century. It seems appropriate to close this chapter by quoting the first recommendation from the All Party Parliamentary Group (2011: 4) in their report, *Overcoming the Barriers to Literacy*. It says:

> Literacy is an essential life skill which begins when pupils start reading for pleasure. The Department for Education needs to acknowledge that literacy is more than a mechanical skill. Literacy is the key skill enabling active participation in all areas of life. Schools need to develop a culture of reading. It should be acknowledged that there is no one way to teach reading and so a single focus on systematic synthetic phonics is a false one. The phonics test at age six is likely to de-motivate children rather than ensure that they become eager and fluent readers.

Further reading

Dombey, H. and Moustafa, M. (1998) *Whole to Part Phonics: How Children Learn to Read and Spell*. London: Centre for Language in Primary Education.
This puts the teaching of phonics into a broad context, drawing on research and showing how it relates to classroom practice.

Jolliffe, W. and Waugh, D. (2012) *Teaching Systematic Synthetic Phonics in the Primary School*. London: Learning Matters.
This is a very useful book which sets out all you need to know about SSP and how to teach it. It acknowledges other perspectives but is firmly in the camp of supporting government policy.

Richmond, J. (2013) *Teaching Reading: How To*. Leicester: UKLA.
The blurb on the back of this short book says that 'it challenges recent UK governments' preoccupation with synthetic phonics as the only method which teachers should employ in order to teach children to read'.

CHAPTER 7

TEACHING DECODING: THE PEDAGOGY OF PHONICS

Chapter objectives

At the end of this chapter you should:

- know the typical structure of a daily discrete phonics lesson
- have some teaching strategies for teaching GPCs, blending and segmenting
- know the criteria for selecting resources for teaching phonics
- be able to track children's phonic knowledge, ensuring progression.

Introduction

In this chapter strategies for teaching synthetic phonics are explored. The expectation is that there will be a daily discrete phonics lesson. It is important to be clear about how this works. First, the lesson is short, lasting no more than 10 to 15 minutes.

It is only a part of the reading lessons that children will be having and should not dominate children's experiences of reading in school. Second, it should be discrete; that means it is focused and clear and during that lesson teachers of reading do not allow themselves to be distracted by other things. Last, the lesson should be fast-paced, interactive and use multisensory resources; in other words the lesson should be fun, engaging and relevant to all teaching styles. This chapter explores how these phonic lessons can be planned in order to meet these criteria.

The chapter then goes on to look at how teachers can track children's phonic knowledge both formatively during lessons and summatively at the end of the phase. The Year 1 phonic screening check is revisited and discussed as a means of monitoring decoding skills. Finally, the chapter looks at how to choose an effective phonic scheme and explains the government criteria for choosing resources to teach phonics.

Teaching about sounds and letters in the early years

It is clearly established in the research literature that children's knowledge of letter names when they start schools is one of the best predictors of their ability as readers at the end of their first year at school (Bond and Dykstra, 1967), and the research also argues that knowing letter names helps in learning letter sounds. Work by Treiman et al. (1998) found that children learned the sounds associated with the letters whose names they already knew much more quickly.

Stuart (2006) discussed the question of when children should start to receive formal phonic teaching and how quickly they will transfer their knowledge of grapheme–phoneme correspondences to their reading. She looked at one group of five-year-old children who were given phonic teaching on blending, segmentation and GPCs using the *Jolly Phonics* scheme and another group who were taught using 'big books' looking at sound–symbol relationships. She found that more of the *Jolly Phonics* group were able to relate phonemes to graphemes and vice versa. From this, Stuart concludes that five-year-old children were able to be taught about letter sounds and GPCs in a systematic and structured way. One might want to argue, however, that knowing that one group had learned what they were taught does not necessarily imply that they were ready to be taught it.

Phase One of *Letters and Sounds* (DES, 2007) falls mainly within the Foundation Stage and should be embedded within a rich curriculum of language and texts. Much of the teaching and learning will take place with informal activities within a play-based curriculum, and others will be teacher-initiated activities which are available during free choice. Some of these activities were listed in the previous chapter.

The Tickell review of the Early Years Foundation Stage (DfE, 2011b) emphasises the importance of embedding learning potential in opportunities which are genuine and supported by a real awareness of the intended outcomes and of the way in which children learn best. The review states that 'playing and exploring, active learning, and creating and thinking critically, are highlighted in the EYFS as three characteristics of effective teaching and learning' (2011b: 27), and this applies equally to teaching and learning about letters and sounds. What does this look like in practice?

One of the most important characteristics of teaching and learning with all ages, but particularly with young children, is that talk and conversations between practitioners, teachers and children are the key to learning about the alphabetic code of the English language. In Chapter 5 the importance of an environment for reading was discussed, but however good an environment is, it loses some impact if there is no talk about it or within it. Adults should be talking about the books on display, reading signs, notices and captions and drawing children's attention to the letters. As adults write in front of the children they will talk about the print and articulate how they know which letter to put. For example, 'I am going to write "apples" on our shopping list. Can anybody hear the first sound in apple? … So, I write the sound /a/ with a letter "a"'.

Displays of print around the room and an alphabet chart, alphabet books, letter cards, magnetic letters and letters made out of soft material, sandpaper, salt dough, card, plastic and any other material can be available for free play resources. Sometimes letters can be hidden in the sand or water tray, and sometimes different examples of the same letter can be hidden around the room or outside for the children to find and sort into a collection of a particular letter. Children can use computers to explore the shape of letters using different fonts and can draw or paint letters – small letters in paper or whiteboards and huge letters on wallpaper or in water on the playground. Alongside all these activities there will be adults talking to the children about the letters:

> Look! All the letter 'g's have a long curly tail.
>
> Do you notice how tall and straight the letter 'l' is.

We have already mentioned in the previous chapter how children are fascinated by their names. I once watched a little girl who spent about 20 minutes looking at her name on her name card and comparing it to her friends. She counted the letters, found letters which were the same and traced over the letters with her finger. Names are highly significant to young children and to them their name is a signifier of their identity within the classroom. They will frequently call the first letter of their name 'my letter' and that will be the first letter they attempt to write. Early years' teachers need to exploit this interest. Do not worry if the first letter is not one of the letters stipulated within the order of teaching in your phonic scheme; exploit the children's interests and talk about the shape of the letter, look for it in other places and words and relate the shape of the letter to the sound. However, if the child's name is written in the opaque code, for example 'Geraldine', I would not put too much emphasis on that. I wonder if I am the only teacher who when friends name their new babies think how easy or not it will be for the child to learn how to read and spell their name!

Using books can help focus on rhyme, rhythm and alliteration. Alliteration is when all the words of a phrase start with the same sound. Great fun can be had thinking of alliterative words to describe characters in books or children in the class. Remember we are talking about sound and so the activity should be an oral one. Some books provide a powerful starting point for this activity, for example *Some Smug Slug* (Edwards, 1996) contains lots of wonderful words starting with /s/ – slimy, succulent and suspense, and they are used to describe several 's' animals. Note that some of these words might be thought quite difficult for young children, but their meaning is clear within the context of the story and they are wonderful to say out loud, revelling in the sound.

Other books are brilliant for encouraging rhyme and rhythm and one of the best I know for this is *Tanka Tanka Skunk* (Webb, 2004). This is a book which is impossible not to read out loud and impossible to read while keeping still! It has a strong rhythm and is superb for learning about syllables and the beat, pulse and rhythm of language. On one page the words are:

Cat-er-pill-ar, Big Gorilla, Yakety, Yakety, Yak

The words are accompanied by bold animals dancing across the page. Read those words aloud and bang on the table, clap your hands, stamp your feet, shake a musical instrument, stomp around the room or do anything which helps you to feel the rhythm of language. Young children cannot help but join in and in so doing are learning about the sounds of language – an early phonics lesson!

Another important element of early years phonic teaching is the use of rhymes, poems and songs. These can be fitted into short periods of time and used to draw attention to the sounds of language. Traditional nursery rhymes can draw children's attention to rhyme using the illustrations and prior knowledge to predict the words and then focus on the rhyming pattern.

Hickery dickery dock,
The mouse ran up the ?

There are many collections of rhymes and songs for young children which will help them to hear and talk about sound patterns in language. Look on the Booktrust website (www.booktrust.org.uk/books/children/poetry/) and you will find lists of poetry books for different ages and some examples of interactive books and games with an emphasis on rhyme.

Reflective activity

List as many traditional nursery rhymes as you can remember and make sure you can sing/say them. Look up in a nursery rhyme book to discover some new ones and also to find some traditional rhymes from other stories. Practise these so that you can use them easily and fluently in a classroom.

The structure of a lesson

There is a clearly established pattern for discrete phonics lessons which is useful to follow as it ensures that each required element is covered and the balance of time on each is appropriate. As with any structure, it should not be adhered to too rigidly but used as a framework to be adapted in order to suit the purpose of each lesson. There are six parts to the lesson, but as the whole lesson should only last for about 15 minutes you will see that each part does not last long.

First, as with any lesson the learning objectives and success criteria are established. This is important so that both the teacher and the pupils know what the purpose of the lesson is and how they can tell whether or not the lesson has been successful. It is important that these are expressed in child-friendly language so that they are easily understood by the children.

An example might be:

> In this lesson we are going to make sure you remember the letter 'm' we learned yesterday and we are going to learn the new letter 'd'. By the end of the lesson you should be able to say the letter and the sound, find the letter in words and read and spell some words which have that letter in them.

This could be displayed on a whiteboard and read to the children. It can then be referred to again at the end of the lesson so that the children can make an assessment of their own learning.

Second, the previous days' learning is quickly revisited. Often this is done by showing letter cards quickly and asking the children to say the phoneme written on them. Alternatively, children could be asked to orally blend words in order to read them.

Third, the new letter is taught; the letter shape is displayed and the letter name and the phoneme are introduced. Children look for examples of the letter in words and practise sounding out simple words containing the letter. Next, children practise their new skills by writing words containing the new letter and reading different words.

Last, children apply their new skills by writing a dictated text or reading a short text out loud. At the end of the lesson the success criteria are revisited and children can reflect on their own learning in relation to the objectives of the lesson.

To recap, the common structure of a discrete phonics lesson is:

1. Specify learning objectives and success criteria
2. Review previously learned phonemes and graphemes
3. Teach the new GPC or tricky words
4. Practise those letters in context
5. Apply them by reading or writing a short text
6. Assess learning against the success criteria.

We shall now consider different teaching strategies for the different elements that need to be taught.

Teaching GPCs

When teaching the relationship between phonemes and graphemes it is extremely important to be clear because there is great potential for confusion, as I am sure you have already realised. As has already been made clear, lessons should be short, focused and multisensory. The next section of this chapter looks at how different letter sounds from different phases can be taught. We begin with Phase Two. The first letters to be taught in the first week are 's', 'a', 't' and 'p'. In *Letters and Sounds* (2007: 51) a very clear outline of a lesson to teach the letter 's' is given. We are going to see if that pattern will work for teaching the letter 'a'.

First, let us be clear what we want the children to be able to do at the end of the lesson. We want them to be able to:

- Say the letter name 'a'
- Say the /a/ sound
- Identify which letter represents the /a/ sound
- Say the sound when shown the letter
- Find the letter when hearing the sound
- Form the letter 'a' according to the description given by the teacher.

What do we need to teach this letter? We need:

- An apple and/or a picture of an apple
- A card showing the plain letter on one side and on the other an apple superimposed on the letter shape
- Whiteboards with pens and wipes
- Phonic fans.

Many resources for teaching this can be downloaded for free from the *Letters and Sounds* website (www.letters-and-sounds.com/) and there are many other websites with lots of ideas. Be selective and choose carefully.

Letters and Sounds identifies three stages in learning a letter sound.

1. Hear it and say it. Show the children the apple and open your mouth wide making a repeated /a/ sound as you pretend to bite it. Ask the children to pretend to hold an apple in their hands and say /a/ as they pretend to bite it. Identify any children whose name begins with /a/ and say their names, emphasising the initial sound. Have pictures or objects which also begin with /a/ and as you hold them up ask the children to tell you what they are (ant, axe). Say some words which have /a/ in the middle and ask the children to say the sound with you when they hear it.
2. See it and say it. Show the card with the picture of the snake and the apple. Move your finger round the apple saying /a/ and then saying 'apple' when you have finished. Write the letter 'a' on the white board and say /a/. Encourage the children to say /a/ when you write the letter.
3. Say it and write it. Move your finger around the apple describing the shape as you write it. If you are unsure of how to form the letter ask for the school's handwriting policy and copy that style. If you are not yet in a school the site www.doorwayonline.org.uk/letterformation.html gives some useful animations on how to form letters and numbers. Ruth Miskin (1999) suggests you use the words 'round the apple and down the leaf'.

Once the children have been introduced to the phoneme and its grapheme there is a rapid fire practice in identifying the sounds when the letters are shown. As /a/ is the second sound learned there will only be two to identify, but by the end of the first week children should have learned four sounds and the number to be revised will rapidly increase.

Children then have to identify the grapheme when they hear the phoneme. For this they can use phonic fans or cards and hold up the correct letter when the teacher says the sound.

That is the basis for teaching grapheme–phoneme correspondence. It can be used for any GPC but of course there are lots of variations and teachers of reading should be careful not to repeat ideas too often so that they become stale.

Most schemes associate an object with a phoneme as a way of helping children to remember the sound. It is certainly better to put an abstract concept such as 'phoneme' in the context of a real object to which young children can relate. Not all schemes use the same object however! While most associate the phoneme /a/ with an apple, *Jolly Phonics* uses 'ant' as its way of remembering and associates the sound with tickling movements up the arm to represent the movement of ants.

There are lots of games which help children to recognise phonemes and their appropriate graphemes. Here are ideas for just some of them. A lot more can be found in *Progression in Phonics* (DfES, 2001).

- Tray game: each child has an object and they sit in a circle with a tray in the middle. The teacher holds up a card on which is written a grapheme. If the object starts with that sound the child puts it on the tray.
- Swap shop: children in a circle each holding up an object. When the teacher says 'Swap shop!' the children swap objects with somebody who has an object starting with the same phoneme.
- Jump in the hoop: two large hoops are placed on the floor with either a grapheme card or an object in each one. The teacher holds up an object and the children have to jump in the hoop which starts with the same phoneme.

Whatever activity or game is done, teachers need to remember that the object is the matching of the sound with the letter (the phoneme with the grapheme) and so it is essential that the phoneme is spoken by both teacher and children in order to reinforce the sound.

The principles for teaching GPCs remain the same at whatever phase you are working, but it becomes slightly more complex when teaching alternative spellings or split digraphs, as in Phase Five. At whatever level you are teaching though it should be interactive and multisensory.

To teach the split digraph it is best to show the children visually how it works. *Letter and Sounds* (2007: 135) is very clear about how to do this. Start by counting the phonemes in the word 'tie'. Use phoneme buttons, a phoneme chart or fingers to show how many there are. Write the word on the whiteboard or put grapheme cards on the floor – /t/ /ie/. Ask the children what phoneme needs to be added to make the word 'time'; they are likely to say /m/ and put it at the end of the word – /t/ /ie/ /m/. Tell the children that it is not spelled like that but we need to cut or split the grapheme /ie/ and put the /m/ in the middle. Cut the grapheme card in half and physically place the /m/ card in the middle. When this is done join the /i/ and the /e/ with string or an arrow to show they are still one grapheme. It can be effective to get children to hold the grapheme cards and the ones holding /i/ and /e/ hold hands behind the child holding the /m/ card.

By Phase Five teaching begins of alternative spellings. *Letters and Sounds* (2007: 136) suggests having a list of words containing the same grapheme but with different phonemes – milk, find, wild, skin, lift, child. The children sound out the words and guess which is the correct pronunciation for a real word. This is a useful strategy and one that has worked well for many years. However, since the introduction of the Year 1 phonic screening test some schools are teaching children to read non-sense words, so this strategy might not be so helpful!

Reflective activity

Look at different phonic schemes and practise the mnemonics used to teach the phonemes and the graphemes which represent them. These might be actions, pictures, characters or rhymes. Reflect on which suits your learning style best and consider how you might use it with children.

Teaching blending

Very soon after the teaching of only a few GPCs children are taught how to blend phonemes and read words. Blending is an important process to enable children to decode independently. In Phase One children will have been blending orally so will have articulated the phonemes in turn and then put them together to make a word, for example /c/ /a/ /t/ cat. Doing this emphasises the importance of pure enunciation without adding the schwa.

Blending needs to be demonstrated both orally and physically. Orally, it is important to draw out each phoneme – stretching it so that it runs into the next one. This means that one sound is produced which is the word. This takes practice so that you are actually blending phonemes and not just inserting a schwa in between! Liberman and Liberman (1990) describe this process as 'co-articulation'.

The process of blending also needs to be modelled physically, and magnetic letters or grapheme cards are useful for this. Put the appropriate magnetic letters on the board with quite a large space between them. Take the first letter and ask the children to say the phoneme, stretching it out while you are holding it. As they do so slide the letter towards the next letter and when they are close move your hand to the second letter and slide both letters to the third letter. The theory is that the three phonemes will blend together smoothly to make the word! As I have already said, however, it may take a bit of practice. If it is challenging, start with two phoneme words (at) before moving on to CVC words.

Alternatively, or in addition, ask children to stand at the front holding grapheme cards and to move together as the phonemes are sounded.

There are two important points to remember about this process. First, the phonemes are stretched and not repeated. Children are not saying /s/ /s/ /s/ /a/ /a/ /a/ /t/ /t/ /t/; that will never blend to make the word 'sat' but are stretching out each phoneme in turn until it runs into the next one. Second, when children are moving magnetic letters or grapheme cards all movement should be from left to right. There is a tendency to move letters to meet in the middle and this is not how it works – remember reading in English always goes from left to right.

Teaching segmenting

Segmenting is the reverse process of blending and is used for spelling when writing. In order to segment children need to be able to hear a whole word and break it down into its constituent phonemes. They have to remember the order of the phonemes, remember the grapheme which represents each phoneme and then blend the phonemes together to check that the written word is the same as the spoken word.

Again, magnetic letters or grapheme cards are the most useful for this. Children need to have whiteboards with some magnetic letters on the top. The teacher says, 'We are going to write the word "sat". Say the word with me. Now say the first sound in the word. Find the letter which represents that sound and put it on the board'. This process is repeated for the second and third letters. When all three letters are on the board, ask the children to blend the sounds and read the word to make sure the written word is the same as the original spoken word.

Phoneme frames can be useful for teaching segmentation. These are just frames drawn on a whiteboard so that children can write or place magnetic letters in the box. For example see Figure 7.1:

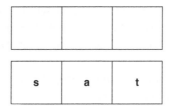

Figure 7.1   A phoneme frame

More simply, children can put the graphemes on their fingers – writing or sticking stickers – to show how many phonemes are in a word.

Children need lots of practice in segmenting as some can find it quite difficult. One fun game is called 'Full circle'. Each pair of children has a whiteboard and a chosen selection of magnetic letters. The children are given the first word and they make it with their magnetic letters. They then have to change one letter to make another word. They keep going, changing one letter at a time until they come back to the word 'sat' when they shout out 'full circle!' One example of a group of letters is 's, a, t, p, i,' from which the children can make sat, sit, sip, tip, tap, sap, sat. Other examples are on page 63 of *Letters and Sounds*.

Reflective activity

Choose one game to teach blending and another to teach segmenting. Practise these – see if you can persuade a group of friends to play them with you! Make sure you can identify where blending and/or segmenting is a part of the game. As a teacher of reading you need to be able to identify these two skills and to carry them out.

Teaching tricky words

There are many words with spellings that do not conform to expectations, and often these words are high frequency and encountered regularly by children in books. How are these to be taught? They cannot be read by blending as they are not phonically reliable. Often, they can be deduced from the context or children can use their knowledge of how language works; this has been described as 'semantic' (meaning) or 'syntactic' (grammar) knowledge. Some teachers will teach these words using flash cards – rectangles of card with the words written on. These require children to memorise the words focusing on the physical shape of them. Johnston and Watson (2007: 36) do not like this approach: 'Any teaching using flash cards, where the children are expected to read words visually, seriously undermines the synthetic phonics method'.

I do not think any method of teaching reading requires such unquestioning devotion and fidelity. All children are different and will learn in different ways. If one way works with a child when no other way does, then use that method. What really matters is that children understand what reading is all about and are motivated and enthusiastic to read.

Jolliffe and Waugh (2012) are not quite so rigid, but they too do not recommend learning whole words at the early stage, arguing that it relies too much on visual memory and the number of these words means that too much demand will be placed on the memory. Johnston and Watson (2007) suggest looking for the 'pronounceable bits' of tricky words and drawing children's attention to those parts of the word they will be able to decode. They give the example of the word 'yacht', saying that children will be able to identify the first and last phoneme of the word. Johnston and Watson do not suggest what happens then, as knowing /y/ and /t/ will not help you to read the word 'yacht'; dare I suggest that most children would use the context of either the story or the illustration and test their hypothesis by looking at the first and last sounds. Jolliffe and Waugh (2012) suggest that two or three words are taught each week and a display of them is kept in the classroom and continually referred to.

It is true that many of these tricky words are high frequency, so if children are read to lots and talk about books and the language in them they will soon come to recognise and know these words. Good teachers of reading will take every opportunity to point them out to children and talk about how they are spelled.

Choosing a phonics scheme

There are many different published commercial schemes for teaching SSP. As a trainee or beginner teacher of reading you will have very little say over the scheme chosen by your school and will have to comply with it. Some schemes offer the whole package and claim to be all you need for literacy teaching, including the training to use it. I would advise caution over using those; often because schools invest a lot in these schemes they are committed to them and so lose the flexibility and adaptability that characterise good teaching. Sometimes best practice means a teacher will choose resources and methods to suit individual needs at particular times. Other schemes are more flexible and can be used on a pick and mix basis.

Letters and Sounds (2007) was a government publication sent free of charge to all schools. It is a very good resource giving a systematic sequence of teaching phonics and a structured programme of teaching strategies, games and activities. It is no longer recognised as a government publication as there has been a change of government and policy since its publication. You might find a copy in school – my experience is that a lot of schools still use it as their basic resource for teaching phonics. If you cannot find it, at the time of writing, it is available online at https://www.gov.uk/government/uploads/system/uploads/attachment_data/file/190599/Letters_and_Sounds_-_DFES-00281-2007.pdf.

In 2010 the government outlined what are described as 'core criteria' by which effective synthetic phonics programmes can be judged. In the introduction to these criteria it says that:

> Phonic work is best understood as a body of knowledge and skills about how the alphabet works, rather than one of a range of optional 'methods' or 'strategies' for teaching children how to read. For example, phonic programmes should not encourage children to guess words from non-phonic clues such as pictures before applying phonic knowledge and skills. (DfE, 2010: 2)

I hope you appreciate from reading this book this far that phonic work is not the exclusive way of teaching children how to read. It teaches children how to decode and that is only part of learning how to read. It is an important part and teachers of reading need knowledge of how the alphabet works in order to teach it effectively. 'Non-phonic clues' are a useful resource for readers and in many texts are an essential element of the text; children need to be taught how to read pictures as well as how to read the print. In the next chapter, we will discuss how understanding texts often involves more than reading only what is on the page or screen.

The criteria for effective phonic programmes are not surprising. These programmes should:

- Present high-quality SSP work as the prime approach to decoding print, i.e. a phonics 'first and fast' approach.
- Enable children to start learning phonic knowledge and skills using a systematic, synthetic programme by the age of five, with the expectation that they will be fluent readers having secured word recognition skills by the end of Key Stage 1.
- Be designed for the teaching of discrete, daily sessions progressing from simple to more complex phonic knowledge and skills and covering the major GPCs.
- Enable children's progress to be assessed.
- Use a multisensory approach so that children learn variously from simultaneous visual, auditory and kinaesthetic activities which are designed to secure essential phonic knowledge and skills.
- Demonstrate that phonemes should be blended, in order, from left to right, 'all through the word' for reading.
- Demonstrate how words can be segmented into their constituent phonemes for spelling and that this is the reverse of blending phonemes to read words.
- Ensure that children apply phonic knowledge and skills as their first approach to reading and spelling, even if a word is not completely phonically regular.
- Ensure that children are taught high-frequency words that do not conform completely to GPC rules.
- Provide fidelity to the teaching framework for the duration of the programme, to ensure that these irregular words are fully learnt.
- Ensure that as pupils move through the early stages of acquiring phonics, they are invited to practise by reading texts which are entirely decodable for them, so that they experience success and learn to rely on phonemic strategies.

The criteria certainly require fidelity by teachers to the 'framework', which means that the stated progression is used systematically and rigorously. This allows for children's progress through the framework to be monitored and tracked.

 Reflective activity

Choose one phonic scheme used in a school you know and evaluate it against the government criteria.

If possible, ask teachers why they chose the scheme and compare their answers with the criteria.

Several commercial schemes have completed a self-assessment against these criteria and these are published on the Department for Education (DfE) website. The government has reviewed all these forms to make sure the programmes and products meet their criteria but are emphatic that they do not endorse any particular programme.

You will have noticed that there is a strong emphasis on the notion of 'systematic'. In its review, *Reading by Six,* Ofsted says, 'the diligent, concentrated and systematic teaching of phonics is central to the success of all the schools that achieve high reading standards in Key Stage One' (2010: 4).

A critically reflective reading of that statement might want to ask what is deemed to constitute 'success' and what determines 'high reading standards'? These questions are important ones for teachers of reading who aim to create readers rather than just children who can decode.

Tracking phonic knowledge

It is evident that teachers of reading need to know how effective their teaching has been and how much impact it has had on children's learning. In the context of a tightly structured systematic teaching programme teachers need to assess what children know so that teaching can be accelerated or decelerated to address children's needs. With such specific teaching it is difficult to work in mixed ability groups and some schools group children according to their phonic phases across age groups. This means that a whole school will teach phonics at the same time and that teaching assistants also take responsibility for a group. Children are assessed at the end of a specific period of time and the groups adjusted.

There are some advantages to this method of organisation. First, it means that teaching can be very focused and directed at individual children. It means that the adult responsible for each group knows the children's phonic knowledge and ability well and can adapt teaching strategies accordingly. Second, it means that phonic teaching is consistent across the whole school. It ensures that the discrete phonic lessons *are* discrete and there is no danger of them becoming longer than they should. It also means that class teachers can draw on a wide range of phonic knowledge within their other lessons. Third, it means that children's learning is continually reviewed and so the risk of children not being stretched or falling behind is minimised. It does have the disadvantage of the effect on the self-esteem of an older child of being in a group with younger children and this needs to be carefully and sensitively monitored. It also means that senior teachers need to ensure that the quality of teaching is of a high standard in every group and sometimes teaching assistants will need additional training to augment their personal subject knowledge.

Many schemes build in assessment activities to their teaching programme and provide pro formas for tracking pupils' phonic knowledge and skills. It is important to remember that phonic tracking is a record of children's knowledge of GPCs and their ability to blend and segment. It is not a record of their skill as readers. That will be monitored and recorded in other ways, and we will return to that in Chapter 10. Phonic knowledge is basically hierarchical and cumulative. Some children will be secure in a phonic phase and others will be working within that phase. Security means that they consistently know the phonemes associated with that phase, and can blend and segment the GPCs taught before and during that phase.

Much of the evidence of children's phonic knowledge can be gained through observation, but sometimes teachers will work with individual children, asking them to find the grapheme for a given phoneme, say the phoneme for a given grapheme, read a given word by blending and write a given word by segmenting. Most teachers will keep detailed records specifying what GPCs are known securely by each child and how successful the children are in blending and segmenting.

It was in this context that the Year 1 phonic screening check was introduced in 2012. It consists of 40 words in two equal sections. Each section contains some real words and some pseudo or non-words. Next to each pseudo word is a picture of an imaginary creature. This is explained as a way of contextualising the experience for the children – they are naming an imaginary creature and not trying to match the non-word to a real word. The test is progressive, that is the words in the second section are phonically more complex than those in the first. Words in the check include those such as tord, thazz, blan, steck, bild, quemp, shin, gang, week, chill and grit in Section 1 and blurst, bron, stroft, day, slide and newt in Section 2.

The test is to be administered on a one-to-one basis by a qualified teacher over a period of a stated week in June. The pass mark was 32 and headteachers are required to inform parents of the mark their child achieved and if they passed or failed the test. If a child fails the test at the end of Year 1 they are required to take it again at the end of Year 2.

The DfE website describes the phonic screening check:

> The phonics screening check is a short, simple assessment to make sure that all pupils have learned phonic decoding to an appropriate standard by the age of 6. All year 1 pupils in maintained schools, academies and free schools must complete the check.

> The phonics check will help teachers identify the children who need extra help so they can receive the support they need to improve their reading skills. These children will then be able to retake the check in year 2. (DfE, 2013c)

In the years since the check has been introduced many schools have started teaching children how to read non-words and several popular parenting websites give guidelines to parents on how to prepare your child for the check. Some of these parenting websites also offer support to anxious parents who wrote in because their children did not do well in the check. One mother said that she was going to write the words on card, laminate them and stick them up all over the house so her child could practise through the summer holidays. I wonder how you, as a professional teacher of reading, would respond to that parent?

The government commissioned a review of the check and this was carried out by the National Foundation for Educational Research (NFER). The latest report of the review was published in May 2014. The purpose of the review was twofold; first to look at the confidence of teachers and how schools prepared for the check, and second on the impact of the check on the teaching of phonics and also on the broader teaching of literacy. The review came up with some significant findings:

> One of the key messages to emerge from the evaluation so far is that many schools believe that a phonics approach to teaching reading should be used alongside other methods. Responses from teachers in both the survey and case-study schools revealed that almost all schools are committed to teaching phonics to some degree, and that, within literacy teaching, considerable emphasis is placed on phonics as a method of teaching children to learn to decode. However, the findings indicate that most teachers do not see a commitment to systematic synthetic phonics as incompatible with the teaching of other decoding strategies. (Walker et al., 2014: 11)

Most teachers felt that the check told them nothing new about the children's ability as readers. The only significant impact the check had on phonics teaching was that schools taught children to read non-words, but in most cases, they did this in a rather cynical way. As one Year 1 teacher told the researchers:

> It [the check] hasn't really impacted on the teaching of phonics. It's just led to more work on the teaching of nonsense words, but I am not sure this will help with their reading and writing skills. (Walker et al., 2014: 27)

The review also revealed that most teachers and literacy co-ordinators relied more on teachers' ongoing assessment of children's phonic knowledge and skills to make judgements about individual children's needs for additional support.

On 20 June 2014 an open letter was sent to the then Secretary of State for Education, Michael Gove, from the chairs of nine professional teachers' associations plus academics in the field of literacy education. The letter concluded:

> Thus the phonics check is methodologically flawed, undermines confidence of children, particularly some of the more able, is negatively impacting on how reading is taught and is an inefficient, and expensive and time consuming, way of assessing an aspect of children's reading ability. It is time to abolish it. (UKLA, 2014)

On 15 July 2014 Michael Gove was removed from office. At the time of writing, nothing is known about the direction that his successor intends to take.

Conclusion

The story of the phonic screening check is another reminder of the political nature of the teaching of reading. The start of the twenty-first century has seen a widening of the gap between politicians who make policy, and teachers and researchers who understand how children learn to become readers and what best helps them to do so. The teacher of reading not only needs secure subject knowledge and sound pedagogy but also a confidence in their own skill. That confidence should give them the courage to affirm their professional understanding and so be able to speak out loudly their informed views on the teaching of reading.

The key messages of this chapter are:

- learning about letters and sounds in the early years should take place within the context of play
- phonic lessons should be short, discrete, multisensory and structured
- children need to be taught GPCs and the skills of blending and segmenting
- teachers should ensure that their phonic teaching is systematic and fast
- teachers need to continually monitor and keep track of individual children's phonic knowledge
- government policy is not always in line with professional knowledge.

Further reading

Jolliffe, W. and Waugh, D. (2012) *Teaching Systematic Synthetic Phonics in the Primary School*. London: Learning Matters
This is a very useful support for the teaching of SSP. It presents SSP teaching as unproblematic but gives some helpful ideas for teaching and support for subject knowledge.

Dombey, H., Moustafa, M., Barrs, M., Bromley, H., Ellis, S. and Kelly, C. (1998) *Whole to Part Phonics: How Children Learn to Read and Spell*. London: Centre for Language in Primary Education.
This was published quite a while ago but puts the teaching of phonics into a broader theoretical context, contrasting analytical and synthetic phonics.

Richmond, J. (2013) *Teaching Reading: How To*. Leicester: UKLA.
A small book which looks at the current policy on the teaching of reading in relation to what research tells us.

CHAPTER 8

TEACHING COMPREHENSION

Chapter objectives

At the end of this chapter you should:

- have considered the relationship between response and comprehension
- understand the different ways of comprehending a text
- be able to reflect on your own comprehension skills as a reader
- know some strategies for teaching children to comprehend
- know the place of comprehension in the National Curriculum.

Introduction

So far, this account of the journey towards becoming a teacher of reading has looked at the knowledge and the skills needed for effective teaching. In looking at the skills, the focus has been on teaching decoding as that is the strong policy of the current government. Teachers of reading are required to teach pupils to use phonics as their first strategy when reading a text. Assessments of six-year-olds focus purely on their ability to decode words, even to the extent of using non-words. However, when the reading process was discussed in the first chapter the importance of understanding was stressed; it is possible to decode a text without understanding and that cannot be described as reading. Comprehension, therefore, is at the heart of what it means to become a reader, and this chapter looks at how the teacher of reading can help children to access and create meaning when they read. This might be the only chapter in the book entitled 'Teaching Comprehension', but I hope you realise by now that the whole perspective of the reading process which underpins this book means that understanding is key to effective reading.

What is comprehension?

When I was at school, comprehension was a regularly timetabled lesson and it involved a lot of writing. We were given a passage to read and then had to answer questions about the passage – always answering in a complete sentence of course. I am sure that some of you can remember doing that as well.

Reflective activity

Read this passage carefully and then answer the questions below.

> The blonke was maily, like all the others. Unlike the other blonkes, however, it had spiss crinet completely covering its fairney cloots and concealing, just below one of them, a small wam. This particular blonke was quite drumly – lennow, in fact, and almost samded. When yerden, it did not quetch like the other blonkes, or even blore. The others blored very readily. It was probably his bellytimber that had made the one blonke so drumly. The bellytimber was quite kexy, had a strong shawk, and was apparently venenated. There was only one thing to do with the venenated bellytimber: givel it in the flosh. This would be much better than to sparple it in the wong, since the blonkes that were not drumly could icchen in the wong, but not in the flosh.

1. When does the blonke not quetch like the others?
2. According to the passage, what has made the blonke drumly?
3. What should the blonke do about his problem?

I would imagine that you did not find the questions too difficult to answer, although probably finding the answer became slightly harder with each one. However, I expect that you still are not completely sure what the passage is about. You read the passage; you answered comprehension questions about it; you did not really understand it. How did that happen? Probably, you used your knowledge of how language works grammatically in order to match the wording of the question with the grammatical structure of the relevant section of the passage. To answer the first question, a reader would look for the word 'quetch' in the passage because this is clearly the key word of the question. The fact that the first word of the sentence containing the word 'quetch' starts with 'when', the question word, indicates that this is the answer to the question. Knowledge of how the English language works helped you to answer the question even though you did not really know what it was talking about!

So, answering so-called 'comprehension questions' does not demonstrate under-standing; so what are teachers of reading looking for when they want to know if children have understood what they have read? Washtell (2008) says:

> comprehension is a multilayered and multifaceted business: it is about the relationship between the writer, the text and the reader. It is highly interactive and reciprocal in nature. The writer is working hard to influence the way we read, so that we get the intended meaning of the text whilst we are bringing our own experiences and prior knowledge to the task in order to interpret the text. (2008: 63)

There are several key words to pick up on in that quotation. First, comprehension is about a '*relationship*' – a reader cannot fully understand a text unless they are fully engaged with it. Second, comprehension is '*interactive and reciprocal*' – a reader has an important role in the sense-making process; it is not just about working out what the writer intended but also involves bringing what the reader already knows and has experienced to the text. These points are developed further in the chapter.

Pardo defined comprehension as 'a cognitive process in which readers construct meaning by interacting with the text through a combination of prior knowledge and previous experience, information in the text, and the stance the reader takes in relationship to the text' (2004: 272).

Again, comprehension is defined as an active process where the reader plays as much a part as the text and the writer and where a certain amount of cognitive activity is involved. Comprehension is what the reader *does*, not something that just happens or is gained. This implies that readers need certain knowledge, skills and experiences in order to comprehend. They need to have had a range of dif-ferent experiences in life, a knowledge of how texts work and a knowledge of how language works, in its simplest and most complex forms. As has already been indicated, they also need to be engaged with the text – reading it intentionally for pleasure or for a specific purpose. These needs will be returned to when teaching strategies are considered.

In 2006 the Primary National Strategy published a paper on *Developing Reading Comprehension* (2006a) which was designed to provide a theoretical underpinning for the more practical booklets published in 2005 (DfES, 2005a, 2005b, 2005c). This paper relates teaching comprehension very closely, as one might expect, to the simple view of reading, arguing that reading comprehension is the product of word recognition and listening recognition skills. It claims in the very first paragraph that readers cannot achieve the 'ultimate goal' of comprehension unless they can recognise the words on the page. I am not sure how that would apply to somebody reading *Tuesday* by David Wiesner (1999) – a book with no words but a tremendously magical, exciting and humorous story. A reader will certainly make meaning from that text after engaging in powerful cognitive activity but is unlikely to have recognised many words.

Kirby and Savage (2008) ask if the simple view of reading can account adequately for the complexities of language, whereas two years earlier in 2006, Nation and Angell argued that the 'searchlights model' (and its cue systems of context, grammar, phonics and meaning) could not accommodate the complexities of the comprehension process! Stuart et al., (2008), in justifying what they describe as the 'reconstruction' of the searchlights model, argued that the model does not account for the hierarchical development of reading, 'because word reading is a prerequisite for text comprehension' (2008: 60).

Let us return briefly to the relationship claimed between reading and listening comprehension in the DfES *Primary National Strategy* (2006a) paper. Listening comprehension is related to the linguistic skills of vocabulary knowledge, grammatical skills and pragmatic abilities. The latter refers to pragmatics, which is the communication system of language. It is argued that listening comprehension (that is understanding what you hear) is a strong predictor of individual differences in reading comprehension. That concerns me, as personally I have great difficulty in understanding complex texts when I just listen; I need to see the written form of the text or write it down as I listen. My husband, however, is the exact opposite; he prefers to listen as he finds it easier to understand even complex texts that way. That is just simple anecdotal evidence of the complexity of the process and the difficulty of claiming that any perspective is universal and will apply to all readers.

Teaching comprehension

In 2000 the National Reading Panel examined 230 research studies about teaching comprehension and from these drew out three main elements which they deemed to have high significance when teaching comprehension. These were:

- increasing vocabulary and learning about words
- adults who were modelling and teaching comprehension strategies
- children actively engaging with texts.

There are several research studies which have looked at the different elements in the comprehension process (Pressley, 2000; Pardo, 2004; Lewis and Tregenza, 2007) and Warner (2013: 56) has synthesised what she sees as the most essential. These are:

- activating prior knowledge
- prediction
- questioning and clarifying
- visualisation and imagination
- summarising
- drawing inferences
- monitoring understanding.

We will explore each of these in turn and relate them to classroom pedagogy. In order to do this I am going to use a classic text called *The Velveteen Rabbit* by Margery Williams. It was published in 1922 and has been described as one of the first modern picture books. It is available as an e-book on www.gutenberg.org/files/11757/11757-h/11757-h.htm. This is a good example of a text which can be

The cover of the first edition

The first illustration in the book

Figure 8.1   Images from the first edition of The Velveteen Rabbit (illustrated by William Nicholson, 1922)

read at several levels and as we explore part of the text I hope you will begin to see that comprehension is multifaceted and multidimensional.

Activating prior knowledge

As you look at the cover of the book what do you think the book is about? What sort of book do you think it is? Does it remind you of anything? It is clearly an old picture – the design is simple and only a few colours are used. There is a clear framing around the edge of the picture – why did the publishers decide to do that? For me, it gives the impression that this book is contained – it is a story unrelated to anything else.

When I look at this cover the image of the Rabbit dominates. He is standing tall and proud and looks as though he is saying, 'Here I am. Who are you?'. Looking closely at his face, however, the initial confident appearance weakens; his face looks a bit more uncertain and this gives the Rabbit more of an air of approachability.

The first illustration inside the book confirms my second impression. Again there are not many colours but the dominant ones are red and gold – indicating that it is Christmas. The picture is shaded and rather vague – unlike the simplicity of the Rabbit's picture on the cover, this image is more confused and busy. The background is striped – is that wallpaper? It looks a little like bars – is the Rabbit in prison? Certainly, I can only see the Rabbit's head; the rest of his body appears to be tightly bound within a sock. He is a present for somebody; that tells me he is an object who has no choice over what happens to him. The edges of the image are blurred and objects within it are not clearly defined; for me that emphasises the unreality of that which is portrayed. There is holly sticking out of the sock along with the Rabbit's head. Holly is prickly and can hurt; the Rabbit must be very uncomfortable in the sock if he is able to feel things at all. His face suggests that he does feel something because he looks rather worried and uncertain. He looked like that on the cover though so maybe that is how he was made and he is not real at all. There are strong shadows in the picture and they make me feel that something a bit scary is going to happen; it is strange because Christmas is usually a happy time but this picture does not feel happy to me.

Were your reactions like mine or different? I drew on my knowledge of the conventions of using colour to convey emotions, of celebrating Christmas and of books I have previously read. What prior knowledge did you draw on? Asking children to do the same exercise reveals the knowledge they have as they come to read the text. That knowledge is the filter through which their comprehension of the text will grow. Teachers of reading will ask children to justify their ideas and say where they come from, and then use that to illustrate how understanding a book is as much about creating meaning themselves as trying to guess what an author intended. With younger children the same effect can be gained by asking them to say as many words as they can which come into their mind when they see the cover and hear the title. Older children can look at the different covers of different versions and create a cumulative understanding of what the book is about, considering why different editors chose different covers.

In the activity above, children are drawing on their prior knowledge to make sense of the text and so understanding a little more of what is involved in comprehension. It is partly formed by prior knowledge and experiences, and children need to learn that they already know much of what will help their understanding. That prior knowledge may not be just factual information but also affective experiences which relate to the emotion of the text.

The book begins by describing how the Boy took the Rabbit out of the stocking and that for a while the Rabbit was his favourite toy. Then other presents arrived and the Rabbit was discarded and eventually taken up to the nursery where there were lots of other toys:

> For a long time he lived in the toy cupboard or on the nursery floor, and no one thought very much about him. He was naturally shy, and being only made of velveteen, some of the more expensive toys quite snubbed him. The mechanical toys were very superior, and looked down upon every one else; they were full of modern ideas, and pretended they were real. The model boat, who had lived through two seasons and lost most of his paint, caught the tone from them and never missed an opportunity of referring to his rigging in technical terms. The Rabbit could not claim to be a model of anything, for he didn't know that real rabbits existed; he thought they were all stuffed with sawdust like himself, and he understood that sawdust was quite out-of-date and should never be mentioned in modern circles. Even Timothy, the jointed wooden lion, who was made by the disabled soldiers, and should have had broader views, put on airs and pretended he was connected with Government. Between them all the poor little Rabbit was made to feel himself very insignificant and commonplace, and the only person who was kind to him at all was the Skin Horse. (Williams, 1922)

There are lots of words in this extract which children may not understand, but comprehension of the whole text is about more than knowing definitions of individual words. When I read this part of the text it brings back feelings I have had when I have been the new person in a situation and felt like an outsider. I am sure you too will remember times when everybody else seemed to know what was happening, what to do and what things meant and you felt alone and vulnerable. This is what it was like for the Rabbit and children can share those feelings with him, and so learn to empathise. Talking with children about those feelings can be a powerful activity and needs to be handled sensitively by a teacher; in discussing the feelings of the Rabbit children are able to explore their own feelings in a less threatening way, and this is an illustration of the power of fiction to develop understanding and empathy.

Discussion might begin with a very open question such as, 'How do you think the Rabbit was feeling?' leading on to, 'Have you ever felt like that?'. Older children can be encouraged to identify words and phrases in the text which give them clues, for example 'snubbed', 'insignificant' and 'superior'.

Predicting

As most readers read they are consciously or subconsciously making predictions about what is happening and what will happen next. Teachers of reading will help them to do this more effectively by showing them how to draw on clues from the text. Children can look at the other toys, maybe find illustrations of similar toys, and consider which the Boy would enjoy playing with and why. Which do they think was the favourite toy? Why do they think this was? How was the Skin Horse different from the other toys? What do you think he looked like? Maybe children could be encouraged to draw him or search for pictures of a toy horse from the time? What clues do we get about his appearance from his name? Why do you think he was kind to the Rabbit?

It is important that all suggestions are accepted as valid; children are creating hypotheses and problem solving, not trying to guess what was in the author's mind.

The text continues:

The Skin Horse had lived longer in the nursery than any of the others. He was so old that his brown coat was bald in patches and showed the seams underneath, and most of the hairs in his tail had been pulled out to string bead necklaces. He was wise, for he had seen a long succession of mechanical toys arrive to boast and swagger, and by-and-by break their mainsprings and pass away, and he knew that they were only toys, and would never turn into anything else. For nursery magic is very strange and wonderful, and only those playthings that are old and wise and experienced like the Skin Horse understand all about it.

'What is REAL?' asked the Rabbit one day, when they were lying side by side near the nursery fender, before Nana came to tidy the room. 'Does it mean having things that buzz inside you and a stick-out handle?'

'Real isn't how you are made,' said the Skin Horse. 'It's a thing that happens to you. When a child loves you for a long, long time, not just to play with, but REALLY loves you, then you become Real.'

'Does it hurt?' asked the Rabbit.

'Sometimes,' said the Skin Horse, for he was always truthful. 'When you are Real you don't mind being hurt.'

'Does it happen all at once, like being wound up,' he asked, 'or bit by bit?'

'It doesn't happen all at once,' said the Skin Horse. 'You become. It takes a long time. That's why it doesn't happen often to people who break easily, or have sharp edges, or who have to be carefully kept. Generally, by the time you are Real, most of your hair has been loved off, and your eyes drop out and you get loose in the joints and very shabby. But these things don't matter at all, because once you are Real you can't be ugly, except to people who don't understand.'

'I suppose you are real?' said the Rabbit. And then he wished he had not said it, for he thought the Skin Horse might be sensitive. But the Skin Horse only smiled. (Williams, 1922)

Questioning

Both the activities above have involved questions and this is an important element to be developed further. Questions that the teacher asks are very important, and those which only require the repetition of information retrieved from the book should be used as a starting point to help orientate the children into the text. For example, 'What did Rabbit ask the Skin Horse?'. Further consideration will be given to teachers' questioning later in the chapter.

For now, I want to focus on the questions the children as readers ask about the text, and we have already suggested what some of those questions may be above. Teachers need to model this process of constant questioning to them so they are aware of what happens as readers read. As I read the above text I have questions of it: What is nursery magic? What has happened to Skin Horse that makes Rabbit think he understands? Why does Rabbit want to know what Real is? Is Skin Horse Real? Children can be encouraged to generate their own questions and this can be done in several ways:

- Hot seating. The teacher takes on the role of a character from the text, for example, Skin Horse. The children think of questions they want to ask the character who responds in role; children can be encouraged to ask follow-up questions which probe more deeply.
- Ask the author. Children list questions they would like to ask the author about the book and maybe send an e-mail or write a letter to the author with their questions.
- Children think of questions about each section of the text and then try and find at least two possible different answers to each question.
- Annotate the text. Children engage in a conversation with the text, underlining, highlighting and commenting on particular sentences, words or phrases.

In creating and asking questions the aim is to encourage children to immerse themselves in the text and begin to see beyond what is actually written to make sense of the whole text.

There are different levels of understanding. The literal is about recalling and knowing just what is directly stated in the text. For example, Skin Horse and Rabbit were different kinds of toys from the mechanical toys, the Boy plays with different toys at different times, Nana tidied up the toys. Deductive or inferential understanding requires readers to look beyond what the text actually said and to 'read between or beyond the lines'. For example, there is something different about Skin Horse, the Boy's life is very different from our lives, something is going to happen to Rabbit. Evaluative understanding requires readers to make a response to the text and to establish connections between the text and other texts read or the text and experiences the readers has had.

Interrogating the text is almost like encouraging the reader to look at it sideways and think of alternative explanations. The teacher might read a sentence to the class: 'Between them all the poor little Rabbit was made to feel himself very insignificant and commonplace, and the only person who was kind to him at all was the Skin Horse'. Children then give different perspectives on why Rabbit felt like that: he had no machinery inside him, he did not know about real rabbits, he was made out of old-fashioned materials. All are feasible and readers do not know if any are true.

Visualisation

The extract is a very visual piece of writing and there are lots of images and ideas which can be conveyed in other ways:

- Draw the scene inside the nursery, making sure that all the details given in the description are included.
- Draw the scene on Christmas day when presents were being opened. What other presents do you think Boy received that made him forget about Rabbit?
- Find and cut out pictures of the other toys.
- Create a story board of the events that led up to this moment.
- Make a freeze frame of Rabbit sitting alone and others looking at him. Photograph it and add captions and speech or thought bubbles.
- Write the scene in the nursery as a playscript. Older children might like to consider the set they would create for this if it were a play. There is a useful resource pack by the Unicorn Theatre available on www.unicorntheatre.com/files/1-Unicorn%20Theatre%20The%20Velveteen%20Rabbit%20Resource%20Pack.pdf.
- Imagine this was a film: compose or choose the sound track for this opening scene.

These are just some strategies for helping children's comprehension of a text. Most of them are taken from a series of three booklets published in 2005 by the DfES on what they describe as 'reading comprehension'. It is helpful, at this point, to explore the concept of inference a little further. It has been mentioned throughout this chapter as an important element of comprehension but needs to be defined and explained and related to pedagogy.

Inference

To make an inference means that a reader uses two or more pieces of information from a text to gain a third piece of information which is implicit within the text. It can be very simple, such as looking at the pronoun 'she' and inferring that it refers to a female character. It can be much more complex such as identifying values or subtle messages which are not explicitly stated. The ability to infer understanding is an important element of comprehension. Kispal (2008) found that poor inferencing skills cause poor comprehension and not vice versa, so they are an important element of the teaching of reading.

Kispal (2008) carried out a detailed review of the research relating to inference and found that readers who are good at making inferences:

- are active readers engaged with the text
- monitor their comprehension of a text as they read and correct misunderstandings
- have an extensive vocabulary
- have a good working memory
- possess a wide background knowledge
- share the same cultural background as the writer of the text.

The review found that there was limited research evidence of the best teaching strategies to improve inference skills, but did identify some strategies which help. Most of these have already been discussed in this chapter but it is worth repeating them in order to stress their effectiveness. They are:

- teacher modelling – thinking aloud, asking themselves questions, making explicit the thinking process
- reinforcing strong decoding skills and extending vocabulary
- making explicit the structure of a story, emphasising the possibility of multiple interpretations
- questioning by the teacher, justifying answers, not interrupting during reading
- questioning by pupils
- activation of prior knowledge
- prediction and contextualisation
- aural work – listening to stories
- choosing the right texts – not too easy or too explicit
- cross-curricular work.

All of these are strategies which the review found supported the emergence of inference, but there was no evidence to suggest which was the most effective. Neither was there any evidence to suggest a progression in learning to infer when reading texts. However, it was found that children who are unable to decode can infer from picture books and talk is a valuable way of developing inference skills orally.

Reflective activity

Look again at the passage from *The Velveteen Rabbit* and list everything that you know about the scenario portrayed in that scene. Think about the setting, the characters and the events. How many of those did you know directly from the text and how much did you infer? What knowledge did you draw on to make your inferences?

Comprehension or response?

The *Primary National Strategy* (DfES, 2005a) defined comprehension as making meaning from texts which incorporates understanding the text, engaging with the text, critically evaluating the text, making connections with existing knowledge, reflecting upon responses and monitoring own understanding, making decisions about which strategies will help clarify understanding. This is the only mention, in definitions of comprehension looked at so far, of the response of the reader to a text, and it is important therefore to further consider the relationship between response and comprehension.

Rosenblatt argues that:

> The reader can begin to achieve a sound approach to literature only when he reflects upon his response to it, when he attempts to understand what in the work and in himself produced that reaction, and when he thoughtfully goes on to modify, reject or accept it. (1978: 76)

Meehan (1998) relates her own experiences as a beginner reader to Rosenblatt's definition. She recalls having to answer lots of questions, just like the ones about the blonke passage at the start of the chapter, but being given no opportunity to be 'interactive, inquiring or introspective' about what she read (1998: 314).

Nicholson (2004) describes some work done with a Year 6 class looking at *Bridge to Terabithia* by Katherine Paterson, which won the 1977 Newbery Medal, and in this unit of work it could certainly be argued that the children were interactive, inquiring and introspective. To begin, the children were given the cover and asked to note what the title was and what they felt about the book from those two things. Ideas were shared and the children were beginning to draw on their creative and interpretive skills.

Note how this is different from the activity I suggested with *The Velveteen Rabbit*. Nicholson was asking for the children's response, which was completely undirected. The focus was on what they thought and felt. Martin (2011) develops this idea even further and argues that, as Rosenblatt said above, it is a reader's response to a text which matters and that response is about reflection. Readers understand by thinking about what they have read. As Martin says:

> Reader response is about reflection – thinking about what has been read. However, its starting point is not just the text ... but also the way in which the reader responded to it and found it exciting, sad, funny or frightening. The interesting question then is 'Why did the text provoke the particular response? (2011: 88)

Responding to a text is a powerful tool for young readers who are developing understanding of what reading can offer them. They will see that different responses are not a problem but are welcomed as giving deeper insights into a text. Response invites tentativeness because it knows there is no right or wrong answer. As readers share responses and talk about and discuss how they feel, so they mutually support each other and create a shared understanding of a text. This is exactly what happens in my book club when we discuss a book. I will read it and share my own responses but as I listen to those of other people, I will frequently modify my response to take into account the different viewpoints. Far from feeling that my understanding is wrong and discarding it, I will modify my thinking in the light of the responses of other readers.

Many years ago, Harding (1977: 391) said 'response is a word that should remind the teacher that the experience of art is a thing of our making, an activity in which we are our own interpretive artist'. Responding to a text is active and creative and yet is also in one way entirely personal and in another entirely social.

Let us look at how one six-year-old child responded to his favourite book. Neil is a great fan of the *How to Train your Dragon* series of books by Cressida Cowell and eagerly devours anything to do with them, including the film. Such is Neil's engagement with the book that he regularly writes letters to the hero, Hiccup, who occasionally writes back, helped by Neil's parents. Here is one letter written by Neil:

With corrected spellings, it reads:

> To Hiccup. I am sorry that we have not sent you a letter for a long time. Speaking of feelings, we like Toothless bringing our letters. I do not go to dragon school. Unfortunately I do not live in a world of your fire breathing friends. Love Neil.

What does this tell us about Neil as a reader and his understanding of the books he is reading at home with his parents? As a reader Neil has a relationship with Hiccup which for him is very real. He writes to him and in his letters he responds to events in the book. His responses are both interactive and creative. However, while fully engaged with the book, Neil is also able to distance himself and recognise that he does not fully share in Hiccup's world. As a relatively inexperienced

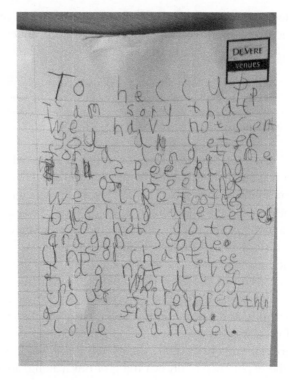

Figure 8.2   Letter to Hiccup

reader, Neil knows a lot about the book and understands the relationships between the characters in the books. He uses this understanding to write his letters. Neil's writing is an illustration of the relationship between comprehension and response. How can teachers of reading exploit this relationship in order to extend and challenge children's comprehension of texts?

Martin (2011) argues that teachers should allow for response before they 'rush' into a consideration of the print. A first reading of a text must be followed by response and engagement. The implication of this is that children's reading is mediated by an adult or a more experienced reader and belies the view that comprehension comes after decoding. This happens when we, as adults, read and there is no reason why it should not happen for children as well. Lesser (2014) describes the process in this way:

> There will always be a gap of some kind. It may be located in places as small as the sentence, or even the individual word; it may govern entire relationships – among characters, between characters and author, between author and reader. It may be a purely metaphorical absence, or it may involve an actual cut or deletion. But it is always there. (2014: 41)

Lesser is arguing that the role of the reader is to fill in the gap in whichever way makes most sense for them. There are echoes here of Iser's 'implied reader'. In Chapter 3 we discussed how Iser saw it as the reader's responsibility to build bridges to create meaning and believed that each reader might well create a different meaning. How can this happen at a collaborative level within a classroom? The extent to which children are supported in creative meaning-making depends on the skills of the teacher of reading in asking questions and engaging in dialogue.

Teachers asking questions

Martin (2011) aligns himself with the importance of the reader in creating meaning when he encourages teachers of reading to ask children 'reader questions'; that is, questions which focus on the reader. The question which asks 'What do you want to happen next?' is a 'reader question' as opposed to 'What do you think will happen next?' which is a 'text question'. The former requires the reader to share an emotional and personal response rather than searching for the answer in the text. In his letter, Neil is responding to the text at an emotional and personal level.

When planning a conversation with an individual pupil, a small group or the whole class about a text which has been read, it is important first to establish the purpose of the conversation and ensure that all questions work towards that purpose. Bloom's (1993) taxonomy is a useful tool for ensuring that the questions asked are at the right level. The taxonomy looks at the three different domains within which learning takes place; these are the cognitive, the affective and the psychomotor. In simple terms, these can be described as the head, the heart and the hand. In reality, teachers tend to focus only on the cognitive domain, although for readers all three domains are important. However, in relation to teachers' questions, the cognitive domain is considered.

The taxonomy starts with the simplest or the lowest order of thinking and moves on to the more complex or the higher order thinking.

1. Knowledge. Questions start with Who? What? Where? When? How? and are about remembering and recalling facts. This relates to the literal level of comprehension we discussed earlier in the chapter. There is nothing essentially wrong with this sort of questioning, but teachers need to recognise that this is a starting point for future learning and should not be the only type of questions asked.
2. Comprehension. These questions look for the understanding of facts and ideas by organising, comparing, translating, interpreting, giving descriptions and stating the main ideas. They start with words like, 'What do we mean by ...?' 'Explain ...'.
3. Application. This requires readers to apply what they know to new situations and to problem solve using their knowledge. 'What other examples are there of this?'

4. Analysis. Here we begin to look at inferential comprehension as readers are asked to make inferences and to find evidence to support generalisations. 'What is the evidence for ...?'
5. Synthesis. This requires readers to create a new pattern or an alternative solution or proposal. What if the other toys were friendly to Rabbit?
6. Evaluation. Readers are asked to make judgements about what they have read. 'What do you think about ...?' 'On what basis do you think that?'

Kagan (2005) disputes the hierarchical nature of Bloom's taxonomy, arguing that all thinking can be simple or complex at whatever level it occurs. He prefers to think of three types of thinking: understanding information, transforming information and generating information. Within each type of thinking Kagan identifies five different thinking skills:

- Understanding information: recalling, summarising, symbolising, categorising and shifting perspective.
- Transforming information: analysing, applying, inducing, deducting, calculating.
- Generating information: brainstorming, synthesising, predicting, evaluating, questioning.

What is key is that these are not hierarchical, and that teachers need to use all of these thinking skills at different times and in varied contexts to ensure that they are challenging the thinking of their pupils.

 Reflective activity

Choose one of your favourite children's books and plan a conversation you might have with a group of children about that book to develop the children's literal, inferential and deductive comprehension. Use either Bloom's taxonomy or Kagan's thinking skills to help you to identify questions. Afterwards, reflect on what was the most useful tool for you.

Dialogic teaching

However carefully thought-out teachers' questions are, there is always the danger that the conversation becomes one-sided and that pupils respond in ways which they think will please the teacher. They may no longer be trying to guess the meaning from the text, but they might well be trying to guess the meaning that the teacher holds. Rosenblatt (1978) believes that it is in the first encounter a reader has with a text that expectations are created and that these can lead to frustration or fulfilment. It is in dialogue with a more experienced reader about the language, subject, ideas and themes of a text that fulfilment is more likely to be achieved.

Dialogic teaching (Alexander, 2004) recognises talk as the bedrock of thinking and learning in children's development. The justification of this is well-established in the research literature and this is not the place to expound on it. It is enough to say that Sinclair and Coulthard (1992) found that most exchanges in classrooms were the basic 'initiation-response-feedback' (IRF) exchange. That means that the teacher initiated through a question, a pupil responded and the teacher followed up, with brief praise, repetition of what the pupils said or exhortation. The result of this is that most of the talk in classrooms is done by teachers and most of the talk done by pupils is very limited and constrained.

Reflective activity

When observing in a classroom, look out for examples of the IRF exchange. Look also for examples of longer exchanges between pupils and teachers. Reflect on what you observe and consider how it impacts on pupils' learning and achievement.

Alexander asked the question, 'How can the power of talk to promote and enhance children's learning be strengthened?', and answered it by affirming the power of dialogue to challenge learners. He quoted Bahktin (1981: 168) who said that 'if an answer does not give rise to a new question from itself, it falls out of the dialogue'. The essence of dialogue is that it is a two-way conversation and for Alexander, the key element for teachers is that they respond to children's answers and comments through clarification, summary and prediction. Teachers' responses comment on the children's answers and justify their comments. Five key characteristics of dialogic teaching have been identified (Alexander, 2004: 28):

- Collective – teachers and children are addressing learning tasks together
- Reciprocal – teachers and children listen, share ideas and consider alternative viewpoints
- Supportive – no worry about 'wrong' answers and mutual support to find understanding
- Cumulative – build on ideas from each other to create coherent thinking
- Purposeful – planned with particular goals in mind.

We shall return to this in the discussion on guided reading in the next chapter, but let us now consider these characteristics in relation to comprehension.

If I am looking at a text with a group of children, my aim, as a teacher, would be to allow each child to express their own response and propose an understanding of the text, supporting them to do this. In addition, a teacher might want to identify a mutual understanding of that text from the whole group. In order to do that, every member of the group, including the teacher, needs to listen to what that text means to all the other members of the group. In so doing, different viewpoints will be respected and valued and the prior experiences and knowledge that led to those understandings will be shared. As the discussion develops, understandings will be modified and challenged until eventually a consensus is agreed. This is not a quick process; it needs time for everybody to feel at ease and confident to share, and it needs a teacher who will support, encourage and value all contributions, seeing their own as one among equals.

Warner (2013) identifies some strategies to facilitate effective talk about books:

- Ground rules. We must not assume that young children know how to take part in a fruitful group discussion and there needs to be explicit teaching on how to do this.
- Model thinking aloud and proposing tentative ideas.
- Give children the vocabulary for reasoning and problem solving, for example 'I like that idea because ...' 'I'm not sure about that because ...'
- Express misunderstandings – model uncertainty, checking understanding and problem-solving.
- Demonstrate that reading invites multiple interpretation.
- Model how to respond to each other's ideas.
- Discuss alternatives and develop strategies to reach consensus.

You will see that most of these strategies are designed to teach children how to discuss and listen so that listening comprehension is enhanced because ideas are shared, justified and explained.

As children read books, talk about their personal responses to them, listen to the responses of others and come to an agreed understanding of the text, they will be expressing opinions about that text, considering its language, structure, authenticity and other aspects. In other words, they will be acting as critics. Chambers (2011) is adamant that children can be critics and quotes many examples of children talking about books to prove his point. He cautions against using books as starting points for talk about all sorts of topics and ideas that might have been stimulated by the book but in reality had nothing to do with the text itself:

> Surely it is this passionate adventure with language we want for our children before all else. We therefore help them explore literature as its own story, and the story of literature is discovered in the story of our own and others' reading of it ... our reading is a construct of the language we use in telling ourselves about it. (Chambers, 2011: 129)

Conclusion

The National Curriculum (DfE, 2013a) places comprehension at the core of the English curriculum, alongside word reading. The introduction to the programmes of study states that:

> Good comprehension draws from linguistic knowledge ... and on knowledge of the world. Comprehension skills develop through pupils' experience of high-quality discussion with the teacher, as well as from reading and discussing a range of stories, poems and non-fiction. (2013a: 4)

In this chapter we have explored different elements of comprehension and seen that it is more complex than some might believe. The essence of understanding a text is bringing prior knowledge and experience to the text and through talk, with oneself or others, coming to a meaning which could be very personal.

The key messages of this chapter are:

- comprehension is a complex process
- comprehension takes place at different levels: literal, inferential and deductive
- reader response is at the heart of comprehension
- teachers can support comprehension through providing response opportunities and dialogue
- talk is vital in understanding texts
- readers draw prior knowledge and experiences to inform their meaning making of texts.

Further reading

Warner, C. (2013) *Talk for Reading*. Leicester: UKLA.
This is a little book which not only justifies talk as an integral part of the reading process but also gives some good ideas and strategies for teachers to support the use of talk.

Goodwin, P. (2004) *Literacy Through Creativity*. London: David Fulton.
This collection of chapters on ways of teaching literacy creatively gives lots of examples and ideas of how creativity leads to understanding.

Chambers, A. (1985) *Booktalk: Occasional Writing on Children and Literature*. London: Bodley Head.
This is a book full of ideas and thinking about talking about books with children. If you were ever in any doubt that talk is an important element of reading, read this book!

CHAPTER 9

TEACHING STRATEGIES FOR READING LESSONS

Chapter objectives

At the end of this chapter you should:

- be reminded of theories about how children learn
- be able to justify reading aloud to children of all ages
- know how to plan whole-class and small group reading lessons
- understand how to create opportunities for independent reading
- have strategies for giving children individual reading practice.

Introduction

This chapter aims to address the question which most readers will have been asking, 'How do I actually teach reading?'. Previous chapters have looked at what we are teaching when we teach reading by hoping to provide some insight into the reading process; others have explored what teachers of reading need to know and understand in order to become effective teachers. We have looked in some detail at the teaching of decoding but stressed continually that while this is a really important part of reading, it is not the whole story. Lastly we thought about what we mean when we talk about comprehension and how teachers of reading can help children to go beyond a surface understanding of texts.

Reading is something which is an integral part of life in a modern society, and it is even more central within a primary classroom. Children who struggle with reading will struggle with most elements of the curriculum, and it is the role of the teacher of reading to support them and minimise that struggle. Children learn to read all the time; when they share a book with a more experienced reader, when they find where the breakfast cereals are in the supermarket, when they read the road signs and know which direction to take and when they play that game on their tablet. Life, for many but not all children, is full of implicit reading lessons. In school, those reading lessons need to be explicit and the skills and strategies of fluent reading need to be modelled, demonstrated and taught to children, and then their attempts at reading need to be scaffolded and supported until they are fully independent.

This chapter considers some ways in which teachers of reading can do just that. Five key ways of explicit reading lessons are explored: reading aloud to children, shared reading, guided reading, independent reading and practising reading.

Before we go into detail however, it is helpful to remind ourselves of what we know about how children learn so we can ensure that our reading lessons are as strategic and intentional as possible.

Children learning

The main learning theorists who have impacted on primary education are Piaget, Vygotsky and Bruner. Piaget's work tells us that children are problem solvers. They are engaged in a continuous process of making sense of the world and of accommodating new knowledge to what is already known. Vtgotsky reminds us that this sense-making process is both social and cultural. The cultural aspect means that children bring to the learning situation the language and behaviour from their own culture. We have already seen how this applies in the learning of reading, from different book-handling skills to understanding of the nature and purpose of reading. Teachers need to incorporate these cultural understandings and behaviours into their teaching.

Second, learning is seen as a social process and the role of the other person who is more knowledgeable and/or more experienced is crucial. Vygotsky's concept of the *zone of proximal development* (ZPD) is crucial here. The zone identifies the learner's ability to make sense and identifies the appropriate next steps in learning in relation to existing knowledge. There is no point trying to teach something that is already known but there is also little point in trying to teach something that is way above the learner's current understanding. The notion of 'potentiality' is central to this concept. Vygotsky argued that children can achieve much more highly from working in collaboration than they can do alone.

Bruner took this intervention from the teacher within the ZPD further and looked at what best supported the children. He used the concept of 'scaffolding' to describe how children are supported in their learning. Consider how scaffolding is used in the construction of a building. In the early stages the scaffolding is in place first and forms the shape of the required building. Construction takes place within the support of the scaffolding; as the building becomes more secure so the scaffolding is removed until eventually the building is able to stand alone. The process is the same with young learners and it is the intervention, talk or questioning which provides the scaffolding.

It is these key ideas in relation to children's learning development which underpin the explicit teaching of reading set out in this chapter. As you read about each strategy, relate it back to what you know about children's learning:

- it is active and about problem-solving and making sense
- it is social and a more experienced learner will provide support within the ZPD
- scaffolding will enable the learner to achieve at a higher level and as it is gradually removed the learner becomes more independent.

Reading aloud

Tucked away at the back of the *Primary Framework for Literacy and Mathematics* (DES, 2006) were overviews of learning for each year group in the primary school. The literacy section of these overviews for each year group mentions the existence of a 'planned read-aloud' programme. In Foundation Stage and Key Stage 1 it is described as 'one key to the development of early readers' (2006: 107 and 112) and in Key Stage 2 it is said to 'continue to support independent reading' (2006: 122 and 132). In the current National Curriculum (DfE, 2013a) the programme of study for reading comprehension in Year 1 includes the statement that pupils should be taught to 'develop pleasure in reading, motivation to read, vocabulary and understanding by listening to and discussing a wide range of poems, stories and non-fiction at a level beyond which they can read independently' (2013a: 11).

In Year 2 the curriculum includes books 'that they listen to' (2013a: 18) in relation to understanding and in Key Stage 2 mention of children being read to is restricted to the non-statutory guidance. It is a shame that the idea of a 'planned read-aloud' programme has gone because this, as we shall see, is an important part of teaching children to read.

It is part of the 'folk tradition' of primary English teaching that reading aloud to children is a worthwhile activity in which to engage. However, it is often perceived as something to be done at the end of the school day and its benefits are often articulated in terms of its calming influence rather than as a strategy for teaching reading. Anecdotal evidence from trainee teachers and teachers on Postgraduate Professional Development (PPD) suggests that it is more common with younger children and rarely occurs in the final two years of Key Stage 2. This is supported by UKLA research (Cremin et al., 2008b) on teachers as readers which identified that 70 per cent of the respondents reported having read a book aloud during the previous month or reported that they were currently reading a book aloud to the class. Nine per cent had last read aloud over six months ago or never; 45 per cent of Key Stage 2 teachers had either only read a complete book to their class within the past three or six months or had never done so; reading aloud diminishes considerably in older classes. Results also demonstrated that teachers in their early years of teaching read aloud most frequently and teachers with longer experience less frequently. No explanation is given for this finding.

The Ofsted report entitled *Reading for Purpose and Pleasure* found that few schools were 'successfully engaging the interest of those who, though competent readers, did not read for pleasure' (2004: 4). Following on from this, there have been government initiatives to remedy the situation, including the National Year of Reading (2007–2008), Reading Champions and Reading Connects. These reports all emphasise the importance of providing the appropriate texts and of providing role models of readers. None of them mentions reading aloud to children.

Chambers (1991) referred to the work of Vygotsky and Bruner to argue for the value of reading aloud in helping children to become readers. Meek (1988) raised the profile of literature in the classroom by highlighting what it is that texts themselves teach children about the reading process, and this was echoed by Flynn and Stainthorp (2006) when they emphasised the importance of reading aloud to children for not only being an enjoyable experience but also teaching children about the nature of print. Perera (1987), from a linguist's perspective, argued that being read to is an important stimulus for children's language development.

Other research (Raikes et al., 2006) has shown how maternal book reading has a positive effect on children's vocabulary development. There have been other small-scale research projects which have looked at the contribution that reading aloud makes to children's literacy development (Lane and Wright, 2007; Ranker, 2007; Auerbach, 2006; Lesesne, 2006; Yopp and Yopp, 2006), but none of these look at current pedagogy in England.

Think back to Vygotsky's sociocultural perspective on literacy learning discussed above, in which the social, cultural and historical context defines the perspective of what reading is (Barton and Hamilton, 2000). Literacy learning is therefore a social activity; the knowledge acquired by learners will be based on a shared view of what the world is like. As Hall states, 'Learning to read is concerned with how reading is done' (2003: 137). In reading aloud to children, it is thought that a teacher is sharing views both of what it means to be a reader and of what reading does for the reader.

Wenger's notion of 'communities of practice' (1998) is central here because it puts the emphasis, in Vygotskian terms, on the interactions between the reader, the listener and the text, but also in Bruner's terms between the individual and the culture of the listening/reading community. In reading aloud the teacher is both sharing and communicating meaning and meaning-making processes. The text that is chosen to be read and the way in which the teacher reads will indicate the parameters of that community of culture. Bruner said 'Pedagogy is never innocent. It is a medium that creates its own message' (1996: 63). The teacher's own interpretation of the text producing a 'subjectivity' of understanding will lead to the creation of an 'intersubjectivity' – a meaning created within the context of the reading aloud by the listeners, the reader and the text. Thus a discourse (Gee, 1999) is created whereby the children are apprenticed into the practices of a literate community.

However, the nature of being read to allows listeners to make their own personal response, drawing on their own 'cultural capital' (Bourdieu, 1993) to create understandings. It could be argued that the dominant discourse within the reading aloud experience belongs to the teacher, who may have chosen the text and interprets and mediates it through the reading. However, each listener will have their own personal emotional response and it is the emotions which are the powerful key to learning. Gerrig (1998: 2), in a book on the psychology of experiencing narrative, uses the metaphor of 'being transported' to another time and place. The images of displacement, movement and journeying are powerful metaphors for the learning process – a process which must involve change in all aspects of the being – cognitive, social, emotional and physical. Illeris (2007) states that for too long learning has been seen as the concern of psychology but that it must now be considered within a broad range of disciplines and influences. Oatley, in a paper arguing for the inclusion of fiction in psychological study, echoes this viewpoint: 'Emotions are at the center of literature because they signal situations that are personally important but that might be either inchoate or just beyond the edge of easy understanding' (1999: 112).

Research on the brain within the discipline of neuroscience has confirmed that listening to stories increases brain activity because of the way in which listeners create pictures in their imagination as they listen, thus making and strengthening neural connections in the brain (Sigman, 2005).

Booth says, 'We know that things happen to people when they hear stories' (2006: 67). He goes on to list the emotional intensity of the shared experience, the stimulation to personal and collective memory, the awareness of the anatomy of story, the hearing, understanding and learning words, understanding the role of tolerance, understanding and empathy. He concludes by saying, 'We become human through our stories' (2006: 67), echoing Hardy's famous description of narrative as a 'primary act of mind' (1997: 13).

And so we come full circle back to the view of reading as a sociocultural process where knowledge is social and is learned within a 'community of practice'. Teachers of reading need to see reading aloud to children as a powerful learning experience rather than just a pleasant social time. They need to give time to reading aloud and to choose carefully what they read.

It is clear that there is strong theoretical justification for reading out loud to children, but there are some very practical reasons in relation to the pedagogy of teaching reading as well. Let us consider those now.

First, reading aloud to children models to them what fluent phrased reading is like. That means that teachers of reading need to be expert readers aloud. Reading aloud is not as easy as you might imagine; if somebody were to ask you to read a page from this book out loud right now I can guarantee that most people would make several errors. Therefore, reading aloud is something that should be planned and prepared. Practise reading to your friends and family or read to yourself in the bathroom. A planned read-aloud programme is necessary so that teachers of reading can practise to ensure their reading is of the highest possible standard.

Second, reading aloud to children allows them to experience texts which they are unable to read independently and so inspires and motivates them to develop their reading skills. This can be particularly useful when non-fiction texts are read because children are introduced to sources of information and the language of different types of information books; reading loud can model the use of index and contents pages and the use of subheadings and captions.

Third, reading aloud to children introduces children to a broader repertoire of authors and genres of books. If the majority of children are already reading a particular series of books, there is no point in reading them one of those during the read-aloud reading lesson. The purpose of reading aloud is to introduce them to other authors or genres which they may not know. This implies that teachers of reading have an extensive knowledge of children's books to draw on.

Lastly, reading aloud allows children to hear the patterns and rhythms of written English. Written English is not spoken English written down but is very different in its sound and use of language.

Hearing written language spoken out loud will help children in their own independent reading and also in their writing.

In Key Stage 2 many teachers will select a class novel which they read to the class over a period of time. This is good practice as it teaches the children sustained concentration and listening and is a useful way of developing reading stamina.

It also allows older children to experience hearing whole texts, as in shared and guided reading there can be a tendency to use extracts from texts. When reading a class novel it is important to plan carefully so that the stopping points are thought through and prepared. Stopping at the right place can maintain attention and allow children to focus on the structure of story and how authors maintain momentum.

Traditionally, reading aloud to children takes place at the end of the school day. This can be appropriate and is a good opportunity to draw the class together for a calm focused time before everybody goes home. However, it does not always have to be at this time and it is good to vary the times. Younger children often come and sit on the carpet for the read aloud time while older children will stay sitting at their tables. You might consider allowing children to doodle on paper while listening as this can help to maintain concentration. They might be encouraged to mind map what they are hearing, or relate it to the introduction the teacher might have given before reading. Identifying something to look out for is a way of maintaining concentration.

While reading aloud by an adult is the best, do not forget that audio books can be a useful substitute. You can use commercial ones or you can ask friends and relatives to read books for you; this can enable you to have books read in a variety of voices and accents.

I hope the importance of regular reading aloud to children has been clearly established. Teachers should have a planned read-aloud programme, serving the purposes outlined above. Clay (1991) talked about the power of reading aloud to children:

> When a story is read ... the shape of the story is created, the characters emerge, and the style of discourse and the literary turn of phrase are heard ... new language forms are introduced to the ear...and meanings can be negotiated in discussion before, during and after the story reading. (1991: 171)

Reflective activity

Make a recording of yourself reading aloud from a book suitable for older children. Consider where the natural breaks might be. Listen to yourself reading and identify ways of improving.

Shared reading

Reading aloud to children is a reading lesson where the prime responsibility and action lies with the teacher. The teacher is demonstrating to the children the reading process and what it can offer. Shared reading is the next move towards independent reading as teacher and pupils share in the process of making sense of a text.

Shared reading as a teaching strategy was first devised by Holdaway in 1979. It is a reading lesson which is carried out with the whole class; it is led by the teacher but is collaborative and interactive. Burkins and Croft (2010: 14) say, 'Direct instruction finds a logical home in shared reading, offering us opportunities to teach toward understanding the reading process'.

Shared reading is where aspects of the reading process are made explicit and effective strategies for reading are modelled. Holdaway saw shared reading as a way of replicating with a whole class the experiences that many children have with a shared bedtime story. It provides children with a demonstration of the reading process and gives instruction which is firmly contextualised. Justice and Pence (2005) argue that in shared reading the teacher is very intentional in their encouragement and support of the pupils' engagement with the text.

As shared reading is a reading lesson, it will be planned with clear and focused learning intentions decided by the teacher. These could relate to either the decoding or the comprehension aspect of reading; it might be thought that the former is more frequently to be found when working with younger children. Once the learning intentions are decided the choice of text is important. The text needs to contain clear examples of the elements being taught. The text might be in the form of an enlarged text or 'big book', in which case a stand or easel is required. Alternatively a smaller text might be used with a visualiser or an e-book on the interactive whiteboard; sometimes the children might be given copies of extracts from the text. It is often the case that the same text is used several times, maybe each day over the period of a week, and so the text chosen must be of sufficient quality to withstand such prolonged and in-depth analysis.

On the first reading the teacher will read the whole text to the children focusing on the whole story. While reading however, the teacher will be pointing to the print and allowing a finger or pointer to move smoothly underneath the print from left to right. This serves several purposes – it shows the children which bit of the text is being read, it demonstrates the direction of reading and the smoothness of the movement emphasises phrased fluent reading as opposed to stilted word-by-word reading. After the reading children should be given the opportunity to make a personal response to the text, talking about it as discussed in the previous chapter.

On the second and subsequent readings children are taught reading strategies, that is what a reader needs to do in order to read the text independently. For younger children the focus might be on using phonic skills to blend for reading. The teacher can cover words and gradually reveal them grapheme by grapheme as they are blended. The teacher might teach other strategies to adopt when finding a word you do not know: missing the word out and reading on to the end of the sentence, re-reading the sentence, or looking at the illustrations for support. It is the current government policy that phonics should be taught as the first strategy but there are many occasions when this does not work and children need to know other strategies.

Sometimes, the focus could be comprehension. The teacher might explore character or setting, identifying words and phrases used by the author to describe these; they might focus on a particular aspect of punctuation, for example question marks, remembering that punctuation is there to show the reader how the text is to be read; the focus might be story structure, looking at the text to identify different elements of the story and perhaps recording this on a story map. If the text is non-fiction the focus might be skimming and scanning to find the required piece of information or on using the contents or index to find information.

It is important to remember, however, that not all of these elements will be covered at once in one lesson! Each lesson will have a clear learning intention and the focus of the shared reading will address that learning intention. It may well be that the same text is used over a period of a week and that a different learning intention is used each day, but this need not necessarily be the case.

Teachers of reading need to continually bear in mind that the purpose of shared reading is to show children what readers do, in other words to make explicit the reading process. Shared reading is a clear example of working within Vygotsky's ZPD. The text chosen will be one that the pupils could not read independently but the teacher is supporting them in reading it together.

Reflective activity

Choose a non-fiction text and plan a shared reading lesson which teaches children how to use the contents and index. Reflect on the type of text which is best suited for this and the sort of questions from the teacher that would best focus children's learning.

Guided reading

Guided reading represents a further step towards independent reading in strategies for teaching children how to become readers. It was first introduced to most primary teachers in England by the *National Literacy Strategy* (DfEE, 1998) although it had been practised in New Zealand since the 1980s. The NLS imposed a rigid 'literacy hour' in which every minute was accounted for and the emphasis was on pace of teaching in order to meet precisely defined objectives. Guided reading was part of this strategy; teachers were required to devote 20 minutes each day to working with one small group on guided reading while the other children were engaged in independent activities. Many teachers found it challenging to meet the requirement that the majority of the class were working completely independently so that the teacher could focus on the guided reading.

Teachers were told that guided reading was supposed to replace the traditional approach of hearing every child read every day from their 'reading books'. There was strong evidence to suggest that this practice was not an effective strategy for teaching reading (Southgate et al., 1981; Bennett et al., 1984; Francis, 1987), but it was deeply embedded in the culture of primary schools and many teachers found it difficult to let go. In her observations of primary teachers during the first two years of the National Literacy Strategy, Fisher (2002) saw that teachers found guided reading difficult to manage; many teachers removed it from the literacy hour to elsewhere in the day and increased the number of extra adults in the class to read with children individually.

In 2003 the Primary National Strategy, *Excellence and Enjoyment,* was introduced and with it more flexibility in pedagogy (DfES, 2003). In contrast to the strong directives from the NLS, teachers were now advised to look for teaching strategies which exhibited 'fitness for purpose'. Much greater variety was seen in the practice of guided reading from then on and this variety is still evident in schools today.

It is helpful, however, to return to the key principles of guided reading and to explore what is the theoretical foundation of this approach. Hobsbaum et al. say:

> In guided reading, children read the text themselves while the teacher acts as the expert who guides them through the text, by providing signposts to the most important and most helpful features of the textual landscape. It follows from this that teachers must know the landscape well. Teachers must know not only the text but also the processes of learning they have the responsibility to develop. (2006: 3)

Guided reading is a challenging teaching approach and it is not surprising that some teachers find it confusing. It requires a high level of knowledge and expertise on behalf of teachers.

As with shared reading, the theoretical basis for guided reading is Vygotskian. In a guided reading session the more experienced reader is guiding the less experienced reader and providing scaffolding to support their learning. Guided reading is about helping children to become independent readers who can decode, understand and respond to texts on their own. Groups for guided reading are ability-based because the teaching needs to be closely aligned to the learners' needs.

In spite of the good and useful new flexibility, it is still helpful to look at the basic structure of a guided reading session, but always remember that it needs to be adapted according to the objectives of the lesson and the needs of the individual children within the group.

First, the teacher introduces the text to the children. In doing so, it is not read to them but 'talked through', giving the children the framework of the story structure and introducing any new words which might prove challenging. Second, the teacher reminds the children of what they do if they encounter a word they do not know. Generally, teachers will cover all strategies but might focus on one in slightly more depth. The children will then read the text to themselves. Younger children will read aloud and the teacher will 'zone in' to each one in turn, but older children will read silently. The group will then discuss the book together – both their response to it as readers and articulating the strategies they used to understand the text – whether decoding or comprehension.

With older Key Stage 2 children guided reading often follows a different format. The children will have been asked to read a chapter or two of the book before the session, and during the session responses are shared and discussion held concerning a particular element of the text, for example character development.

In order to make guided reading more manageable, publishers have responded by producing sets of levelled books. In classrooms you will see boxes of books, usually colour coded according to the level they are at and stored in sets of six. Teachers then have to just pick up the next set of books to use with the group. Life is made even easier for teachers by publishers giving suggested lists of activities or questions to use in the back of the books. Other teachers use the Assessing Pupils' Progress (APP) grids to plan guided reading. These grids will be discussed further in the next chapter, but it is to be remembered that they are an assessment tool and not a planning tool. The danger of using pre-prepared questions and activities is that the person who wrote them does not know the children in the group. To be truly effective guided reading needs to be precisely focused to the needs of the children and the skill of the teacher of reading used to adapt and change plans according to the children's responses. Fountas and Pinnell (2012), in commenting on these developments, say:

> The deep change we strive for begins with the why and not the how, so our practices can grow from a coherent theory ... to change our practices in an enduring way, we need to change our understandings. If we bring our old thinking to a new practice, the rationales may not fit. (2012: 271)

What does good practice in guided reading look like?

1. The first crucial element is the selection of texts. The selection is made by the teacher and books are chosen according to the reading strategy that the teacher wants to teach, the difficulty of the text and the general interests of the group. Children should be able to read the text with minimal support from the teacher.
2. Setting targets for guided reading groups is key to assuring progression. Targets will allow the teacher to plan questions carefully and then they need

to be flexible. Good questions could lead anywhere and exciting things might happen. This is where the power of guided reading lies, in its ability to allow for the development of 'interthinking' – creating ideas and patterns of thought together (Mercer, 2000).

3. Guided reading groups should be formed according to current attainment and identified next steps. Groups should not be too large or too small, but the similarity of ability is more important than always having six children in a group.
4. Following the basic structure of the session as outlined above but being flexible enough to adapt according to the needs of pupils.

Reedy (2011) argues that talk is the key factor in a successful guided reading session. He discusses the teacher's role, which is dialogic and not a didactic transmission model of teaching.

> The teacher's contribution frames the discourse and gets it going. However, she takes a much more facilitative role here. The questions and contributions she makes are there to nudge the discussion forward and to position herself as part of the group. The questions she asks are genuine; she doesn't know the answer to a question that asks for a personal response ... Thus, discussion during a reading session is a powerful opportunity to model and develop response as well as understandings that go beyond the literal. (Reedy, 2011: 64)

Reedy recognises that this is a challenge for teachers and offers some advice for practice:

- Wait to give pupils opportunity to share their ideas first
- Encourage pupils to ask their own questions
- Use paired talk
- Encourage pupils to reply to each other rather than always going through the teacher
- Facilitate and summarise, asking pupils if they agree (2011: 65).

Burkins and Croft (2010) give an example of how a teacher of younger children supports the children in their move towards independence in reading. During shared reading sessions the teacher had taught the children to predict the word by looking at the first letter, and then the illustration and then to blend all the way through the word to check their prediction. In guided reading she continually reminded them of this teaching, 'You know how to figure that out; I have seen you do it in shared reading'. During a guided reading session the teacher observed a child use the strategy she had been teaching. She asked him to explain how he worked out that part of the story. She reinforced what she taught, praising the child and saying to the group:

When he got stuck on a word today, Jo did exactly what we practised in shared reading. I watched him look at the letters and search the picture and come up with a word. And then, and this was really something, he went back to the letters and looked at the whole word. I didn't even remind him to check. After that, he remembered to reread the whole sentence again and think about the story. He remembered from shared reading. (Burkins and Croft, 2010: 20–1)

This is an example of how in the teaching of reading teachers are enabling children to become independent readers and providing them with the support they need to do that. Iaquinta (2006) also stresses the importance of the role of the teacher; she says that skilful teachers use their knowledge of development in reading and the reading process in relation to their knowledge of the children's skills and understandings, to decide where to go next and how to model and explain strategies. She argues that this must always be independent of commercially produced materials. Villaume and Brabham (2001) use the analogy of learning to drive for the process of learning to be a reader, and sees guided reading as the time when the learner is put in the driving seat.

Reflective activity

Choose a book which you think you might use in a guided reading session. Go through the book, annotating it with all the possibilities for talk and teaching which are in the book. Remember you would not use all these possibilities in one session but as a teacher of reading, you need to be aware of the potential within books for teaching.

Independent reading

Children need opportunities to read independently without being guided by a teacher or adult. In Chapter 5 we talked about creating environments which are sympathetic to reading and allowing time and space for personal reading. In this section of this chapter we are going to consider literature circles, the use of other adults to read with children and home–school links.

Literature circles

These are established in schools in the USA and are becoming more common in English primary schools. The name 'literature circle' was first used by Harste et al. (1984) and it refers to a group of children who all read the same book and talk about it. It is very similar to the book groups that many adults attend. The underlying view of literature circles is that reading is a social activity, but alongside that they allow children to behave as independent readers. Strong proponents of literature circles are King and Briggs (2005), who argue that circles provide children with the opportunity to try new texts and authors and to share their enthusiasms with others. They also develop reading stamina because children have to have read in order to take part in the discussion and encourage children to persevere with texts they might not enjoy at first. The discussion introduces them to different responses and ideas and may well challenge their own thinking.

Hobsbaum et al. (2006) identify some key characteristics of literature circles which distinguishes them from guided reading groups. In literature circles:

- children are required to be critical readers and co-construct new understandings of texts
- children choose the text they read
- readers with similar interest but not necessarily of similar skills talk together
- texts which challenge children in many ways are read
- texts are read to children or they can read them independently
- the teacher participates as an equal reader member
- texts can be thought about through discourse, art, music, drama or in any other way.

Allan et al. (2005) looked at the experience of four primary schools in Scotland who were using literature circles. They found that the children gained autonomy as readers and also became more enthusiastic. They were talking about the books at home and wanting to set up more groups. There was also an increase in their receptive vocabulary, particularly that of the boys.

The teachers in the project, however, identified some management problems to do with running literature circles but also found ways to overcome these issues. The groups worked best when the teachers had prepared the children for them, when the children chose the books themselves and when the groups had a regular meeting time which was known by everybody and stuck to.

Literature circles are certainly a good way of generating enthusiasm for reading and are relatively easy to implement in a class. Why not ask a teaching assistant to run a literature circle while the teacher takes a guided reading group?

Reading to another adult or more experienced reader

In the section on guided reading we saw that research has shown that hearing children read is not the most effective strategy for teaching reading. This is certainly true, but that does not mean that children do not need opportunities to practise reading. We have seen that in shared and guided reading children are taught how to read – they are taught the strategies they need in order to both decode and comprehend a text. In shared reading children are taught as members of the whole class group and in guided reading they are taught and given the opportunity to practise with scaffolding from an informed adult. They also need to have opportunity to practise these skills on their own.

This is for practise and is not a teaching session as such. Therefore, they do not need to read to somebody with the professional expertise of a teacher, but they do need to read to somebody who is a more expert reader than they are. The person hearing children read does need some training, however; they need to know how to encourage a child when s/he comes to a word s/he does not know and what strategies the child might be encouraged to use. It is the responsibility of the teacher of reading to do this and to make sure the book from which the child is reading can be read independently.

If the children reading are very young or inexperienced they may not have the skills to read independently at all but they can still benefit from time spent sharing a book with an adult. Often young children will enjoy listening to a story being read; if the adult pauses at the end of a sentence the child will often 'read' the last word or sometimes the child will echo-read – articulating the words about ten seconds after the reading adult. Other children will want to read the book themselves and will do so, engaging in reading-like behaviours. They may tell the story from memory or by looking at the pictures. This is still a valuable part of learning how to be a reader.

Sometimes younger children read to older children and in some schools this is a whole-school policy where Key Stage 2 classes pair up with Key Stage 1 classes. This is not only useful practise for younger children but can also be helpful for older children who struggle with reading, giving them an authentic purpose for reading. This can require quite a lot of organisation, but it is worth doing because it is another way of making a school into a true reading environment.

The teacher of reading has an active part to play in these sessions. They need to be constantly observing, prompting, intervening and supporting where necessary. They may remind everybody of strategies to adopt when encountering an unknown word, reinforcing the idea of using phonics as the first tactic. They can also draw everybody together at the end and give people yet another opportunity to talk about books and their reading.

Reflective activity

Imagine that as a teacher, you are training a new teaching assistant to read on a one-to-one basis with children in your class. Plan what you would say to them and what the key principles are.

Parental involvement

If you go past any primary school at the end of a school day, you will see the children coming out of school clutching their 'book bag'. In this will be their current 'reading book' and a home–school liaison book. There will be a strong expectation that children will read some of their reading book at home with their parents or carers, who will then write an appropriate comment in the liaison book. This practice has been going on for years in English primary school. My children are grown up but I can still remember the importance of hearing them read; it did not matter how much they read from books at home or how much they talked about books, it is those few pages from the school reading book that really count. I also have to confess that there were times when life got busy that I would be driving my children to school with them beside me reading from their school reading book!

For parents this can be a challenging expectation – they may lead busy lives and want to spend precious time with their children doing other things; they may struggle with reading themselves; they may not speak or be literate in English; they may be working; they may have no idea of what is expected and get angry with their child when they think the child is not reading as well as expected; they may think the book the child is reading is too easy or too hard or the child has been reading it for too long; they may worry that their child seems on a lower-level book than her/his older sister or her/his friend's child; they may have no idea what to do when the child struggles with the reading or does not want to read. With all these potentials for difficulties, one wonders why schools bother to send reading books home.

We have already seen how for some children their experiences of reading at home are very different from the expectations and experiences of reading at school. It can only be a good thing to bridge that gap, but this requires great sensitivity on the part of the teacher of reading. The work of Heath (1983), Minns (1990) and Gregory (1996) are just some examples of research which demonstrates how home reading practices can differ enormously. There are very few homes where there are few examples of reading behaviour. The teacher of reading needs to find out what reading traditions are in the home. Many schools do home visits before children start school and this is a useful way to find out something about children's prior experiences.

The home–school liaison diaries can make for interesting reading and analysis. How (unpublished research) has looked at examples of these from several different schools. She found that in most of them the voice of the child was silent; the most dominant voices were the parents (usually but not exclusively the mother) and the teacher. The general tone of the diaries was congratulatory, with lots of examples of generic praise. What is significant is that a large majority of the comments are related to the school 'reading books', and so there is very little indication of the sort of reading experiences children have outside school.

Many schools hold parent evenings to inform parents about the reading policy of the school. The difficulty with meetings such as these is that it is usually the same parents who always come and they are the ones who are very involved with the school anyway.

How can schools try and inform and involve parents more in the reading development of their children? Here are just a few ideas:

- Ask parents to comment on home reading in the liaison diary.
- Hold parent information evenings in a local pub or coffee shop; for many parents the school building has negative connotations.
- Hold parent book clubs where parents can come and talk about reading – it might be about reading at their own level or it might be looking at children's books.
- Put colour-coded bookmarks into the books that the children take home – yellow means 'Please read this to me'; purple means 'I will have a go but please tell me the word if I get stuck'; green means 'I can read this by myself'.
- Do not expect children to read to their parents every day but have other reading-focused home learning activities – take a page of newspaper and see how many letter 'p's you can find in one minute, asking somebody to time you; tell somebody at home all about your favourite book and ask them about theirs; on your way home find three notices and read them; when you watch your favourite television programme put the subtitles on and read them. There are many more things you can ask children to do at home which involve reading and take the pressure off the steady progression through the reading scheme.

Conclusion

Reading is not a natural activity and it needs to be taught. There are some children who will learn to read relatively easily and for them it almost seems a natural process. There are others for whom it is more of a struggle, and they need a lot of explicit teaching and many opportunities to practise. The aim of teaching children to read is that they become independent readers; that means that they can access texts and understand and respond to them by themselves. In this chapter we have considered different strategies for teaching reading and seen how they each provide more or less scaffolding as is deemed appropriate for the needs of the learner.

The key messages of this chapter are:

- reading aloud is a vital ingredient in teaching children to read and should be a regular feature in the timetable.
- shared reading is the opportunity to teach reading strategies explicitly in the context of a text.

- guided reading allows children to practise reading strategies, knowing they are supported by scaffolding provided by a knowledgeable teacher
- talk is an essential part of learning to read
- children need lots of opportunities to practise reading independently
- most parents need support and guidance about how to best help their child become a reader.

Further reading

Graham, J. and Kelly, A. (2008) *Reading Under Control: Teaching Reading in the Primary School*, 3rd edn. London: Routledge.
This is an edited collection of chapters about different facets of teaching reading. The first chapter gives a particularly interesting historical overview of the teaching of reading.

Goodwin, P. (2011) *The Literate Classroom*, 3rd edn. London: David Fulton.
Another edited collection of chapters about the teaching of reading and writing which give some interesting insights into the relationship between the two.

Hobsbaum, A., Gamble, N. and Reedy, D. (2006) *Guided Reading: A Handbook for Teaching Guided Reading at Key Stage 2*, 2nd edn. London: Institute of Education.
Do not be put off by the title – it contains lots of useful information for Key Stage 1 teachers as well.

CHAPTER 10

KNOWING AND RECORDING CHILDREN'S DEVELOPMENT AS READERS

#VILLAINS

Chapter objectives

At the end of this chapter you should:

- know what is happening currently with respect to assessment and be able to contextualise it within the recent past
- be familiar with the level descriptors for reading
- understand how children progress as readers and the factors that influence progression
- have some strategies for finding out about children's achievements as readers
- know the difference between formative and summative assessment
- have begun to contemplate life without levels.

Introduction

I thought long and hard about the title of this chapter, and originally was going to include words such as 'assessment' and 'tracking' and 'monitoring'. All these things are addressed in the chapter, but I wanted to convey what is really important to teachers of reading. This goes back to things we have already discussed – the subject knowledge held by teachers of reading about the reading process and the journey that children make as they become readers. Teachers of reading need to know about the children in their class; they need to know where they are and where they need to get to. You could compare a teacher to a satnav. The curriculum and external requirements show where the end of the journey is; the teacher knows what the starting point is and has to work out the most efficient and effective route. There are times when the journey does not go according to plan and the teacher has to re-evaluate and adjust the route. Not all children travel on the motorway and go by the fastest route; some take many diversions and are held up by road works, but the job of the teacher is to ensure that they get to the required destination. This chapter looks at how teachers know where children are, what happens to them en route and how the best route is decided.

The chapter begins by looking at the current situation regarding assessment and the measurement of progress. At the time of writing, there is much debate as to what schools will do and so much of what this part of the chapter says is speculative. The chapter does however look at how teachers can know what children are like as readers and how this can inform future planning and teaching.

The current state of play

It was in 1988 that England first had a National Curriculum and the associated regime of assessment. This was initially complex with ten level descriptions under attainment targets; there was one attainment target for reading. The DES said 'We shall use the word level to define one of a sequence of points on a scale to be used in describing the progress of attainment' (DES, 1988: 32).

The introduction of levels established a clear relationship between the curriculum and assessment, and as a consequence the use of criterion-referenced assessment of pupil performance became the norm. This means that pupils were assessed against stages of progression as defined by the curriculum.

The system was revised and in 1995 there were eight levels, each with their own level descriptor. Level 2 became the expected standard of achievement at the end of

Key Stage 1 and level 4 at the end of Key Stage 2. Since then, level-based assessment has been embedded in current practice and teachers talk with confidence about the level at which children are operating. Level descriptors are used for both formative assessment (day-to-day informal monitoring of learning) and summative assessment (end of Key Stage formal testing). It is assumed among teachers, parents and others that the use of levels gives a shared understanding of achievement.

However, the research literature does not see levels as so unproblematic. NFER (2007) questioned the judgements that were being made and there were debates about the feasibility of reliable and consistent judgements that a child was working at a particular level (William, 2003; Newton, 2003, 2009). Stobart (2009) questioned the equivalency of, for example, a level 3 at the end of Key Stage 1 and a level 3 at the end of Key Stage 2. In recent times levels have been subdivided to, for example, 2a, 2b and 2c, and there has been an expectation that pupils would make two levels of progress over a key stage which is described in terms of six sub-levels. This finer division was generally profession-led.

In 2013 the DfE decided to abandon levels:

> We believe this system is complicated and difficult to understand, especially for parents. It also encourages teachers to focus on a pupils' current level, rather than consider more broadly what the pupil can actually do (DfE, 2013b: 2).

The government is proposing a return to norm-referenced assessment in relation to the summative assessment at the end of each key stage. This means that the proportion of pupils achieving the same grade in an assessment remains constant from year to year and it is therefore possible to tell how an individual pupil is performing in relation to all the other pupils who have been assessed. The government proposes ranking by decile (a decile would be a group consisting of 10 per cent of the national cohort); each pupil would be placed within a decile. It will be interesting if this system actually does make it easier for parents to understand. Another feature of the removal of levels is that the relationship between the reporting of achievement and what has been taught is weakened. In the National Curriculum there is no mapping of pupil progress towards the end points; the route of the journey is not defined.

This decision has caused concern among teachers and schools despite the fact that teachers and schools now have more freedom to devise their own way of accounting for progress. Brill and Twist (2013) argue that schools have been given an opportunity to develop their approaches to formative assessment and to take greater control of the shape and structure of assessment. There is evidence that this can have a positive impact on pupil achievement (Ofsted, 2011b; Loughland and Kilpatrick, 2013). However, Brill and Twist propose that in order for this to happen, there needs to be a strong shared understanding both of assessment and of progress. This would entail both a lot of work and a lot of professional development for schools, and anecdotal evidence at present suggests that many schools are going to continue using levels.

The National Association of Headteachers (NAHT) commissioned a review on assessment (2014) in response to the changes in policy. The Commission echoes the views of Brill and Twist (2013) that there needs to be a closer link between curriculum, assessment and pedagogy. The Commission also warned against the government's too strong reliance on external end of key stage tests. It argued that this led to a distortion of the curriculum and, because of the accountability through Ofsted and performance management, too much temptation to 'teach to the test'. In its response to the consultation on assessment procedures the UKLA (2013) also argued this point; the National Curriculum views learning as based on discrete knowledge, if assessment looks only at knowledge transfer there will be a lack of emphasis on engaged learning. Judgements of children will be made on the basis of retained knowledge rather than strengths in learning.

It is within this context that this chapter attempts to consider the assessment of reading. It is a time of uncertainty and nobody can know how schools will react or if there will be a national system. However, we can look at progression in becoming a reader and how teachers can find out about children as readers, and that is what the rest of the chapter addresses.

 ## Reflective activity

Ask a teacher about the pupils in their class. Ask them to tell you how they are doing as readers and what sort of readers they are. Listen carefully to the words that are used. Does the teacher talk in relation to levels? What other criteria do they use for this assessment? Ask them how they know about their children as readers. What sources of information do they use?

Progress in reading

In Chapter 4 of this book we discussed in some detail the development of reading and the stages that children go through. I do not intend to repeat any of that here, I want to focus in on descriptions of progress which particularly support teachers of reading as they look to evaluate achievement.

First, let us revisit the knowledge, skills and understandings which very young children have as they come to understand what reading is and what it can do for them. Holdaway (1979) first used the phrase 'reading-like behaviours' to describe the play activities that young children engage in when they pretend to be readers. Children not only do that in relation to books and the printed word but, as Millard (2006: 234) says, they experience many 'globalised, multimodal literacy encounters in the home'. Kelly (2004) described the behaviours of a four-year-old boy who was demonstrating computer games to his grandmother. She describes how he 'makes predictions, hypothesises and interprets different symbolic systems, while engaging in reading both visual images and print' (2004: 71).

Kelly suggests that these experiences with his grandmother on a games console are similar to the bedtime book sharing experiences described by Holdaway many years ago.

Vygotsky (1978) argued that children learn about symbolic representation first through play when they turn a stick into a sword, and then when they learn how abstract symbols represent words and ideas. It is only when children have fully assimilated that concept of symbolic representation and know and understand the nature and purpose of reading that they truly begin the journey towards becoming a reader.

DEPENDENCE

Beginner reader 1	Does not have enough successful strategies for tackling print independently. Relies on having another person read the text aloud. May still be unaware that text carries meaning.
Non-fluent reader 2	Tackling known and predictable texts with growing confidence but still needing support with new and unfamiliar ones. Growing ability to predict meanings and developing strategies to check predictions against other cues such as the illustrations and the print itself.
Moderately fluent reader 3	Well-launched on reading but still needing to return to a familiar range of texts. At the same time beginning to explore new kinds of texts independently. Beginning to read silently.
Fluent reader 4	A capable reader who now approaches familiar texts with confidence but still needs support with unfamiliar materials. Beginning to draw inferences from books and stories read independently. Chooses to read silently.
Exceptionally fluent reader 5	An avid and independent reader, who is making choices from a wide range of material. Able to appreciate nuances and subtleties in text.

INDEPENDENCE

Figure 10.1 Becoming a reader: reading scale 1

Source: CLPE (1988)

The Primary Language Record (CLPE, 1988) is an old but unequalled system of monitoring and recording children's reading development. The record contains two reading scales, used to evaluate children's achievements as readers. The first scale is about the level of independence in reading and is shown in Figure 10.1.

You can see from the descriptors on this scale that 'dependence' is not measured just by the ability to decode. The beginner reader is completely dependent on a more experienced reader to access a text. Look at the descriptors and you will see that the underpinning model of reading for this is one which recognises all sources of information to support the sense-making process; it does not see decoding as something separate from comprehension – the two are inextricably linked.

Another interesting feature is that this scale is advised to be used with six- to eight-year-old children. In 2014 a six-year-old child is expected to be able to sound out words independently and this is tested by the phonic screening check. It would be interesting to compare the reading dependence of a six-year-old in 2014 who has passed the screening check against the CLPE scale. An essential difference, however, between the screening check and the CLPE reading scale is that the former is based on testing and the latter on observations. Observations give evidence of learning and identify what it is that children can do in an authentic context.

Afflerbach (2005) outlined some principles about assessing reading which should inform our thinking:

> First, reading assessment is a useful tool in the service of improving the teaching and learning of reading. Assessments allow us to understand the strengths and needs of each of our students so we may teach them well. Second, all reading assessment must be clearly and carefully tied to an informed understanding of what reading 'is.' We are fortunate to have a rich knowledge base that describes the nature of reading and its development (Clay, 1979; Heath, 1983; Snow, 2002). From this research we are able to construct an understanding of reading that should guide our efforts to design and use reading assessment effectively. Third, reading assessment must reflect our most current knowledge in the science of assessment. The historical progress in our understanding of reading is paralleled by enhanced understanding about how to develop and use effective assessments (2005: 152).

Note that what we assess when we assess reading is crucial, and this is the problem when it comes to measuring or describing reading in these times of great accountability. The CLPE reading scale describes reading behaviours and yields rich observational data. The screening check gives a number of correctly decoded words and it is easy to assume that a child who decodes 30 words correctly is a better reader than one who only decodes 25 correctly. Teachers of reading have to ask themselves what knowledge from assessment will help them to teach and support further development. If a child fails to decode enough words then teachers need to teach more and give them more practice in decoding words until at the next check a higher score is achieved. Does that mean the child is a better reader?

INEXPERIENCED

Inexperienced reader 1	Experience as a reader has been limited. Generally chooses to read very easy and familiar texts where illustrations play an important part. Has difficulty with any unfamiliar material and yet may be able to read own dictated texts confidently. Needs a great deal of support with the reading demands of the classroom. Over-dependent on one strategy when reading aloud; often reads word by word. Rarely chooses to read for pleasure.
Less experienced reader 2	Developing fluency as a reader and reading certain kinds of material with confidence. Usually chooses short books with simple narrative shapes and with illustrations and may read these silently; often re-reads favourite books. Reading for pleasure often includes comics and magazines. Needs help with the reading demands of the classroom and especially with using reference and information books.
Moderately experienced reader 3	A confident reader who feels at home with books. Generally reads silently and is developing stamina as a reader. Is able to read for longer periods and cope with more demanding texts, including children's novels. Willing to reflect on reading and often uses reading in own learning. Selects books independently and can use information books and materials for straightforward reference purposes, but still needs help with unfamiliar material, particularly non-narrative prose.
Experienced reader 4	A self-motivated, confident and experienced reader who may be pursuing particular interests through reading. Capable of tackling some demanding texts and can cope well with the reading of the curriculum. Reads thoughtfully and appreciates shades of meaning. Capable of locating and drawing on a variety of sources in order to research a topic independently.
Exceptionally experienced reader 5	An enthusiastic and reflective reader who has strong established tastes in fiction and/or non-fiction. Enjoys pursuing own reading interests independently. Can handle a wide range and variety of texts, including some adult material. Recognises that different kinds of text require different styles of reading. Able to evaluate evidence drawn from a variety of information sources. Is developing critical awareness as a reader.

EXPERIENCED

Figure 10.2   Experience as a reader across the curriculum: reading scale 2

Source: CLPE (1988)

For teachers, as Afflerbach says, assessment should be a tool which supports teaching and learning. Achievement is often a product of experience and the CLPE Reading Scale 2 (Figure 10.2) looks at the progression from experienced to inexperienced.

This is an important consideration for teachers of reading; it is too easy to label a child as 'low ability' when actually they may not have had the relevant experiences. The scale not only looks at ability to read but also at attitudes to reading and behaviour as readers. Again, close observation of the descriptor for an inexperienced reader shows how the understanding of the reading process influences the assessment tool. An inexperienced reader is said to be 'over-dependent on one strategy when reading aloud, often reads word by word'. It may well be that a child who has been taught to always use phonics as the first strategy will remain inexperienced according to these terms.

One crucial element is the text. I may behave as an experienced reader when reading some texts but as a very inexperienced reader when reading others. Teachers of reading need to be aware of the context in which judgements are being made and the impact that will have on the level of achievement. The knowledge necessary to make an assessment against the CLPE reading scale can only come from continual focused observations of reading behaviours, and later in the chapter we will explore some strategies for doing this. We now turn to another scale of reading development; one which is more recent and commonly used in schools – the APP grids for reading.

Assessing pupil progress

The APP grids can be found online at http://webarchive.nationalarchives.gov. uk/20110809101133/nsonline.org.uk/node/20683.

They were developed from a QCA project in 2006 and were published in 2008. They were developed to support Assessment for Learning (AfL). AfL is about formative assessment and is 'the process of seeking and interpreting evidence for use by learners and their teachers to decide where the learners are in their learning, where they need to go and how best to get there' (Black, Harrison, Marshall and William, 2002: 2).

There are ten key principles of AfL:

- AfL is part of effective planning for teaching and learning
- focuses on how children learn
- is central to classroom practice
- is a key professional skill for teachers
- is sensitive and constructive
- fosters motivation
- promotes understanding of goals and criteria

UNIVERSITY OF WINCHESTER
LIBRARY

Reading assessment guidelines: levels 1 and 2

Pupil name _____   Class/Group _____   Date _____

	AF1 – use a range of strategies, including accurate decoding of text, to read for meaning	AF2 – understand, describe, select or retrieve information, events or ideas from texts and use quotation and reference to text	AF3 – deduce, infer or interpret information, events or ideas from texts	AF4 – identify and comment on the structure and organisation of texts, including grammatical and presentational features at text level	AF5 – explain and comment on writers' use of language, including grammatical and literary features at word and sentence level	AF6 – identify and comment on writers' purposes and viewpoints, and the overall effect of the text on the reader	AF7 – relate texts to their social, cultural and historical traditions
Level 2	In some reading: ■ range of key words read on sight ■ unfamiliar words decoded using appropriate strategies, *e.g. blending sounds* ■ some fluency and expression, *e.g. taking account of punctuation, speech marks*	In some reading: ■ some specific, straightforward information recalled, *e.g. names of characters, main ingredients* ■ generally clear idea of where to look for information, *e.g. about characters, topics*	In some reading: ■ simple, plausible inference about events and information, using evidence from text, *e.g. how a character is feeling, what makes a plant grow* ■ comments based on textual cues, sometimes misunderstood	In some reading: ■ some awareness of use of features of organisation, *e.g. beginning and ending of story, types of punctuation*	In some reading: ■ some effective language choices noted, *e.g. "slimy" is a good word there* ■ some familiar patterns of language identified, *e.g. once upon a time; first, next, last*	In some reading: ■ some awareness that writers have viewpoints and purposes, *e.g. 'it tells you how to do something', 'she thinks it's not fair'* ■ simple statements about likes and dislikes in reading, sometimes with reasons	In some reading: ■ general features of a few text types identified, *e.g. information books, stories, print media* ■ some awareness that books are set in different times and places
Level 1	In some reading, usually with support: ■ some high frequency and familiar words read fluently and automatically ■ decode familiar and some unfamiliar words using blending as the prime approach ■ some awareness of punctuation marks, *e.g. pausing at full stops*	In some reading, usually with support: ■ some simple points from familiar texts recalled ■ some pages/sections of interest located, *e.g. favourite characters/events /information/pictures*	In some reading, usually with support: ■ reasonable inference at a basic level, *e.g. identifying who is speaking in a story* ■ comments/questions about meaning of parts of text, *e.g. details of illustrations diagrams, changes in font style*	In some reading, usually with support: ■ some awareness of meaning of simple text features, *e.g. font style, labels, titles*	In some reading, usually with support: ■ comments on obvious features of language, *e.g. rhymes and refrains, significant words and phrases*	In some reading, usually with support: ■ some simple comments about preferences, mostly linked to own experience	In some reading, usually with support: ■ a few basic features of well-known story and information texts distinguished, *e.g. what typically happens to good and bad characters, differences between type of text in which photos or drawings used*
BLIE							

Overall assessment (tick one box only)   Low 1 ☐   Secure 1 ☐   High 1 ☐   Low 2 ☐   Secure 2 ☐   High 2 ☐

Figure 10.3   APP reading assessment guidelines: levels 1 and 2

- helps learners know how to improve
- develops the capacity for self-improvement
- recognises all educational achievement.

This is not the place to go into detail about AfL, but looking at the work of Shirley Clarke (2008) will help you to find out more.

APP was first piloted for English but is now used in all the core subjects. The grids are devised according to the levels of the previous National Curriculum and are detailed in Figure 10.3. The first thing to notice is that they are much more detailed and specific than the CLPE scale. Reading is broken down into seven assessment foci:

- use a range of strategies, including accurate decoding of text, to read for meaning
- understand, describe, select or retrieve information, events or ideas from texts and use quotation and reference to text
- deduce, infer or interpret information, events or ideas from texts
- identify and comment on the structure and organisation of texts, including grammatical and presentational features at text level
- explain and comment on writers' use of language, including grammatical and literary features at word and sentence level
- identify and comment on writers' purposes and viewpoints, and the overall effect of the text on the reader
- relate texts to their social, cultural and historical traditions.

Teachers have to consider evidence from ordinary classroom activity which demonstrates what children can understand and do. Guidelines aim to help teachers assess this evidence in relation to National Curriculum levels. In May 2010 an article appeared in the *Times Educational Supplement* claiming that although at first glance it seems straightforward, 'behind the title lays a raft of confusing guidelines that demand ever more paperwork from overstretched staff' (Barker, 2010). Other people argued that APP does not improve learning or achievement but simply indicates gaps which teachers then fill in. This emphasises the tension in the relationship between assessment and the curriculum.

Let's follow just one assessment focus through from level 1 to level 5. We will look at AF3: deduce, infer or interpret information events or ideas from texts. According to the APP grid, progression in AF3 looks like Table 10.1.

The first thing to notice is that there is progression in the frequency and consistency with which these behaviours occur, from 'in some reading with support' to 'across a range of reading'. One presumes that by reading in this context it means 'texts', but this is not clear. It is also important to realise that the nature of the text will determine the inferences and deductions that can be made. Are these inferences to be made from the printed word only or from the whole text, including

Table 10.1   Assessment Focus 3: Levels 1–5

Level 1	In some reading, usually with support:
	• reasonable inference at a basic level, e.g. identifying who is speaking in a story • comments/questions about meaning of parts of text, e.g. details of illustrations, diagrams, changes in font style
Level 2	In some reading:
	• simple, plausible inference about events and information, using evidence from text, e.g. how a character is feeling, what makes a plant grow • comments based on textual cues, sometimes misunderstood
Level 3	In most reading:
	• straightforward inference based on a single point of reference in the text, e.g. 'he was upset because it says "he was crying"' • responses to text show meaning established at a literal level, e.g. '"walking good" means "walking carefully"' or based on personal speculation, e.g. a response based on what they personally would be feeling rather than feelings of character in the text
Level 4	Across a range of reading:
	• comments make inferences based on evidence from different points in the text, e.g. interpreting a character's motive from their actions at different points • inferences often correct, but comments are not always rooted securely in the text or repeat narrative or content
Level 5	Across a range of reading:
	• comments develop explanation of inferred meanings drawing on evidence across the text, e.g. 'you know her dad was lying because earlier she saw him take the letter' • comments make inferences and deductions based on textual evidence, e.g. in drawing conclusions about a character's feelings on the basis of their speech and actions

the illustrations? This places big demands on the subject knowledge of teachers of reading about the texts that are used. The differences between levels are not always obviously apparent and I find it difficult to work out a significant difference between level 4 and level 5.

APP is now firmly established in the practice of primary schools and is frequently used as a tool for planning, particularly for guided reading. The statements above are often turned into what are known as 'I can' statements, which are designed to make the criteria explicit to children and to enable them to see what they need to do in order to progress. Here are the 'I can' statements for AF3 as produced by one local authority (Lancashire Primary Strategy, 2006):

Table 10.2   'I can' statements for AF3: Levels 1c–5a

Level 1c	I can guess what is going to happen in a story that has repeated patterns.
Level 1b	I can guess what might be happening in my books with help from my teacher. I can guess what might happen to the characters in my books.
Level 1a	I can say what I think about a character in a story. I can say who is bad and who is good. I can say what I think about the events in a story.

(Continued)

(Continued)

Level 2c	I can guess what might happen in a story by what has already happened.
	I can compare settings and events to my own experience.
	I can compare stories and say why they are similar and different.
Level 2b	I can find clues in a text to help me explain the meaning.
	I can say what I think, and find parts of the text to say why I think it.
	I can talk about what characters might be thinking or feeling using clues in the text.
Level 2a	I can talk about the theme of a story.
	I can discuss the reasons for events in a story.
	I can understand how certain words and phrases make texts funny, spooky or create moods.
Level 3c	I can explore the themes and ideas in texts and find references to support my views.
	I can make sensible predictions based on knowledge of the text.
	I can discuss the actions of the main characters and justify my views by referring to the text.
	I can summarise the main points from a text.
Level 3b	I can identify the language the writer has used to create moods and build up tension.
	I can guess why events and actions have happened using evidence from the text.
	I can guess what will happen because of what I already know about the text.
Level 3a	I can tell the difference between fact and opinion.
	I can read between the lines using clues in the text.
	I can use the way in which the author uses dialogue, action and description to help me understand.
	I can judge why the characters act in the way they do.
Level 4c	I can understand why characters feel and act the way they do.
	I can read between the lines using evidence from the text and my experience of the wider world.
	I can use clues from the way characters speak and act to help me understand.
	I can use the author's descriptions to help me understand.
Level 4b	I can identify points of view whether they are hinted at, or stated clearly.
	I can discuss messages, moods, feelings and attitudes by reading between the lines and using deduction.
	I can identify the key points in a text at my level.
Level 4a	I can explain and comment upon hinted or clearly stated points of view.
	I can describe, using examples from the text, how the author has chosen vocabulary to create various effects.
Level 5c	I can compare and contrast points of view which are hinted at with those that are openly stated.
	I can analyse how an author has created messages, moods, feelings and attitudes.
Level 5b	I can identify the techniques the author has used to create moods, feelings, messages and attitudes.
Level 5a	I can identify and evaluate the techniques an author has used to create moods, feelings, messages and attitudes.

The first thing you will have noticed is that the levels have been broken down into sub-levels which presumably is to make the stages of progress even more finely defined. 'I can' statements are designed to be used as targets and given to children at the start of a lesson so that they know exactly what is to be achieved in that lesson. Consider the difference this makes to assessment of children as readers. The teacher plans what is to be learned, the lesson is tightly focused on one aim, the children know what they are expected to learn and at the end of the lesson both children and teacher decide to what extent it has been achieved. Contrast that with the much broader statements in the CLPE reading scales and evidence that is based on observation of children as readers in a variety of contexts and with a variety of texts over time. The point needs to be made again that when assessing reading, teachers need to be sure what it is they are assessing and how that helps them build a picture of children as readers.

 Reflective activity

Choose one or all of these books:

The Conquerors by David McKee

Not Now Bernard by David McKee

Three Cheers for Inventors by Marcia Williams

Come Away from the Water Shirley by John Burningham

Open Very Carefully by Nick Bromley

Read the book through several times to yourself. Reflect on your response to it – did you like it? What were the best/worst bits? What questions did the book raise in your mind? What patterns could you see?

Now self-assess yourself against the 'I can' statements above. What level reader are you? Why is that (not) a fair assessment of you as a reader? What would help you become a better reader?

It is important that any assessment of children's achievements is both valid and reliable. A valid assessment means that it measures what it is supposed to measure. We have already mentioned how challenging this can be when assessing reading, but it can be helped by collecting a range of evidences for each statement. A reliable assessment means that the same decisions or conclusions are reached over time with a group of similar pupils. Benchmarking against the judgments of other teachers is one way of achieving this, and teachers hold moderation meetings where they meet and discuss children's achievements together to ensure that everybody is working from the same understanding. On the website for APP there are case studies of children working within the same level and this is another way of ensuring consistency. Attending a moderation meeting is a good way to become familiar with the criteria for assessment.

We now turn to some strategies which will help teachers find out more about the children in their class and their reading.

Miscue analysis

Goodman (1969) was the first to develop the idea of miscue analysis as a way of knowing how children tackle texts and what their needs for further development are. A miscue is when a child says something when reading aloud that is unexpected and does not match with the written text. Looking at what the child actually says helps the teacher to know how the child is attempting to make sense of the text. The term 'miscue' comes from the 'cues' which Goodman believed readers use. These cues are:

- the graphophonic system – the relationship between letters and sounds
- the semantic system – the meaning of the whole text
- the syntactic system – the way in which language fits together
- the contextual system – the illustrations, the layout, the type of text and the familiarity with the content of the text.

When carrying out a miscue analysis the teacher listens very carefully to what the child actually says and decides what sort of miscue it was. Goodman (1969: 123) described miscues as a 'window on the reading process'. In order to carry out a miscue a child needs to be able to read fairly fluently but maybe is having some difficulties about which the teacher is concerned. The chosen text needs to be something which the child can read fairly independently but is slightly more challenging than the book they are currently reading. It needs to be a book which is unknown to the child. The text on which the miscue analysis is done needs to be approximately 300 words long and the teacher needs a copy of the text on which they can record what the child says.

The child is told that the teacher is going to be listening very carefully to his reading; if he finds a word he does not know he must try his very best to work it out himself because the teacher is not going to help him. The teacher reads the first paragraph and then the child takes over. The teacher listens and records the miscues. Possible miscues include:

- Substitution. This is where the child reads something which is not written. The teacher writes what is said over the word.
- Omission. A word is left out completely. The teacher circles what is left out, even if it is only part of a word.
- Insertion. The child puts in an extra word which is not written in the text. The word is written above the text.
- Reversal. Words are read in the wrong order. This is indicated by arrows.

- Self-correction. The child reads an incorrect word and then self-corrects. Write the incorrect word above and then put 'SC' by the side.
- Repetition. The child repeats a word; this is shown by a double underlining.
- Pause. If the child pauses for a long time in between words, double parallel lines are written between them.
- Sounding out. If a child attempts to sound out a word but does not succeed in blending to the whole world, record above the word the graphemes that are sounded.

After the reading the teacher discusses the book with the child in much the same way as any other book talk session. This enables the teacher to assess the child's understanding of the text as a whole and their personal response to it.

The teacher can later look at the recording of what the child read and analyse it. The key question is whether what the child read made sense. If the meaning of the text remains clear then the child is probably reading with understanding. They might have missed out a word and read to the end of the sentence, re-read the sentence, paused to look at the illustration or self-corrected. If, however, the child's reading did not make sense then the teacher will look at the miscues to find what they were actually doing. For example, the child may not self-correct even though it is obvious that the word read does not make sense; the child may read a word which is phonically or visually very similar to the written word but does not makes sense (house for horse) or the child may read word by word and ignore punctuation.

The pattern of miscues made will give the teacher a clear indication of whether the child is reading for meaning or not. This will indicate what teaching is needed to address this. For example if a child is not reading for meaning the teacher might continually remind them to check for meaning; give them cloze procedure exercises (texts with some words missing which the child has to fill in); continue to read to them a lot so that s/he experiences meaningful texts and make sure they are reading books which interest them. Miscue analysis can also indicate what area of phonics a child needs further work on.

Running record

Running record was devised by Marie Clay (1985). It is very similar to miscue analysis which is described above, but is best for younger children who are just beginning to read on their own. The text chosen should be one known to the child but not known so well that they can read it without looking! The child reads aloud to the teacher who records what is said. Every word recorded correctly is recorded with a stroke /. A 'T' indicates that the teacher told the child the word. A substitution is recorded above the written word and a circle shows when a word is left out. If a child self-corrects the letters 'SC' are written next to the original miscue.

When analysing the errors Clay (1985) suggests teachers ask themselves, 'Why did he do that?'. Looking carefully at every miscue enables teachers to see if the child pays more attention to visual cues than to meaning, reads for meaning but pays little attention to the detail of the printed word or ignores meaning.

Reading conference

Every now and then it is helpful for teachers of reading to spend some time in conversation with individual children about their reading. This can tell you a lot about the child's attitude to reading and his/her perception of him/herself as a reader. You can find out about what they read at home and you may get some surprises. I once talked to a seven-year-old boy whose teacher was concerned about his reading in school. He was very unenthusiastic about his reading and frequently did not read when he took his book home. It turned out that this child was in fact a very enthusiastic reader; he was a sports fan and every evening read avidly the sports pages of his dad's newspaper. He knew everything about what was going on in most sports but was not interested in what happened to Biff, Chip and Kipper. The teacher would not have known that if the reading conference had not taken place.

Reading logs

It is helpful for children to keep a record of what they have read; if this consists of all reading then it informs the teacher again of their outside school interests. It is not a good idea to ask children to write a review of every book they read; if I had to do that I would very soon start reading less. It is good though just to record the title and author and give it some sort of rating – graded 1–5, red, orange or green, smiling or frowning face or any other symbol which appeals. This can be done online – a computer can be kept open in the book corner and children can log on and record their opinions. As the teacher monitors this, they can then recommend books. This works best with older children, but younger children can cope with a simplified version. Each book might have a card in it and children write their names and put a symbol indicating their response.

Observation

Observation is a much under-valued assessment tool outside the early years, which is a shame as it can yield a lot of information about children as readers. It is useful for a teacher of reading to sit near the book corner and just observe what happens. A teaching assistant could also be carefully briefed and asked to do this. Teachers can see who goes in there and for how long they stay; what books they read and whether they flick through a lot or concentrate on one. Do they talk to others about their reading or are they quiet on their own? How often do they visit the reading area?

Reading tests

There are some commercially produced reading tests which are thought by some to give more valid and reliable assessments. Those who like them claim that they are more reliable. Most reading tests do not look at reading holistically but tend to assess just one small part of it – phonics, word reading, sentence reading, cloze procedure.

A test which is commonly used in schools is the *Neale Analysis of Reading Ability*. This claims to measure accuracy (decoding), comprehension and rate of reading in children between the ages of 6 to 12. It also gives an indication of a pupil's interest in reading. However, Spooner et al. (2004) claimed that accuracy and comprehension cannot be assessed separately as Neale claims. They found that performance in the comprehension aspect of the test was mediated by the decoding element. The *Neale Analysis of Reading Ability* is a reading and comprehension test. The children read short stories and are asked questions about each story. If they make 16 or more errors when reading one of the stories the test is stopped. For every mistake they make when reading they lose a mark which in turn reduces their raw score. The child's raw scores are converted to give a reading age and a comprehension age. These ages can then be compared with the child's actual age: if there are significant differences it could indicate (not definitely show) some difficulty with reading and/ or comprehension.

Lots of schools still use the '*Salford*' test, which is a set of sentences of increasing complexity that the child reads. The child is stopped after 'x' number of mistakes and the teacher calculates the score which turns into a reading age. It doesn't include any measure of reading comprehension skills.

It is important to remember that standardised reading tests only look at one aspect of the reading process and much more contextualised information is required if a teacher of reading is to make an informed assessment. If using a reading test, teachers need to examine it carefully: look at the date of publication, the underpinning view of reading and what the test claims to assess. If you work in a strongly multicultural context look carefully for any cultural bias in the test. Finally, consider what the test will tell you and ask if that will help you become a more effective teacher of reading.

Many standardised reading tests use the term 'reading age', as mentioned above. These are very unreliable ways of describing children as readers and mean nothing to teachers of reading to inform pedagogy. The danger is that if a six-year-old child has a reading age of nine, parents will get very excited thinking their child is highly intelligent and operating in school like a nine-year-old. This, of course, is not the case. Fortunately, reading ages are slightly less prevalent since the introduction of levels. It is interesting though that numbers are liked as an assessment outcome as it is felt they give a stronger indication of achievement.

End of Key Stage summative assessments

In early 2011 the government asked for a review of the end of Key Stage assessments as they currently stand. The Bew Report was published in June 2011 and indicated that teachers and headteachers were keen that the summative assessment should take the form of moderated teacher assessment. The commission considered this very carefully but concluded that:

> We feel that a system entirely based on teacher summative assessment would not be sufficiently reliable for the purpose of providing school accountability data. While we believe ongoing and high quality assessment is crucial to ensuring pupils make good progress, we do not believe that schools should be held accountable through a system wholly based on moderated teacher assessment (Bew, 2011: 53).

It is interesting that the link between school accountability and pupil achievement is determining the nature of the assessments. There is more mention of the impact on the school than on the journey of the individual child towards becoming a reader. However, this changes later in the report when it says:

> We also suggest that the current assessment foci in reading could be reconsidered – they currently encourage schools to concentrate teaching on interpreting texts and understanding authorial intent. We feel that there is a possibility that this may lead to unhelpful test preparation. We feel there is a risk that being forced to over-interpret texts may take pupils away from reading for pleasure and could potentially restrict their love of reading. Pupils at Key Stage 2 should concentrate on reading fluently and regularly; and we believe it is essential that they enjoy their reading and read widely and often with texts becoming increasingly challenging (Bew, 2011: 59).

This is a positive and encouraging comment and it will be interesting to see how it works out in practice with the new assessments.

In their guidance to test developers for the 2016 assessments the government (Standards and Testing Agency, 2014a and b) declares the stated purpose of these assessments to 'ascertain what children have achieved in relation to the attainment targets outlined in the National Curriculum for reading'. They also say that these tests will:

- hold schools accountable for the attainment and progress made by their children
- inform parents and secondary schools about the performance of individual children

- enable benchmarking between schools, as well as monitor performance locally and nationally.

Teachers in Key Stage 1 will mark the test internally. The test will consist of two elements – one booklet containing a text with questions interspersed throughout, and one booklet containing a text with another booklet containing the questions. The latter is deemed to be more challenging and teachers will decide when to withdraw a child from the test. The Key Stage 2 reading test will last for an hour and will consist of a reading booklet with an associated answer booklet. The content of both tests is drawn directly from the programmes of study.

Working without levels

Anecdotal evidence at the time of writing indicates that most schools will continue to label their children according to the level descriptors. Teachers are now confident in this system and feel it is understood by all stakeholders. There are some notable exceptions to this, however, and one is Wroxham Primary School in Hertfordshire. The underlying aim of the school is to 'create conditions in which children could surprise their teachers and themselves, inviting the development of richer and more complex ways of thinking and talking about learning than the reductive language and concepts of ability and levels' (Swann et al., 2012: 24).

The school does not label or group children and involves them closely in their own assessment. It is hoped that more schools will be bold enough to focus on the learning potential of each child rather than another method of stratification to replace levels. Swann et al. describe how Wroxham School talks a lot about the capacity of children to learn within any given situation and of how teachers and the school experience help pupils to 'become more powerful, enthusiastic learners' (2012: 122).

Another innovative and exciting school is The Wyche School in Worcestershire. The headteacher, Geoff Rutherford, talks about the dilemma of the requirement to continually raise standards: 'the school believes there is a lot more to raising standards than simply seeing scores rise in two subjects, based on a test that barely lasts an hour taken by one cohort of children in a week in May' (Rutherford, 2012: 44).

It is important that teachers of reading bear that in mind. Enabling children to become readers is more than teaching them how to read; it is about creating those conditions which allow children to discover for themselves what reading can offer.

At the time of writing we do not know what will happen when there is no longer the requirement to assess children according to levels. One can only hope that schools will take the opportunity to rethink what progress in reading really looks like.

Conclusion

Ability as a reader depends so much on what you are reading, when you are reading and why you are reading – that is difficult to measure through one fixed summative assessment. Assessment should inform teaching and learning; not in the sense of 'teaching to the test', which has been the result of the phonic screening test, but in the sense of knowing what is needed for readers in the twenty-first century.

The key messages of this chapter are:

- when assessing reading be very clear about what is being assessed
- performance as a reader is dependent on the text being read and the context in which it is being read
- assessment of reading needs to be holistic
- progress in reading does not happen in a smooth upward trajectory.

Further reading

Clarke, S. (2008) *Active Learning through Formative Assessment*. London: Hodder Education.
This is not a book about reading but about AfL. It provides some good ideas and strategies which can be transferred to the teaching of reading.

Swann, M., Peacock, A., Hart, S. and Drummond, M.J. (2012) *Creating Learning without Limits*. Maidenhead: Open University Press.
This is not about reading either but is an inspiring read that will make you rethink your views about teaching and learning.

CLPE (1988) *The Primary Language Record: Handbook for Teachers*. London: CLPE.
Although this was written over 25 years ago, there is still much that we can learn from it. It reminds us that parents and children should be involved in assessment and that good assessment is contextualised, holistic and takes place over time.

CHAPTER 11
SUPPORTING INDIVIDUALS

Chapter objectives

At the end of this chapter you should:

- be aware of the responsibilities of teachers towards children with special educational needs
- be able to provide for precocious readers within your class
- have some strategies for encouraging reluctant readers
- know the needs of children for whom English is an additional language and be able to support them
- know the support available for children with dyslexia
- be familiar with some intervention strategies to support struggling readers.

Introduction

The National Curriculum (DfE, 2014) states:

> A wide range of pupils have special educational needs; many of them also have disabilities. Lessons should be planned to ensure that there are no barriers to every pupil achieving. In many cases, such planning will mean that these pupils will be able to study the full national curriculum. The SEN Code of Practice includes advice on approaches to identification of need which can support this. A minority of pupils will need access to specialist equipment and different approaches. The SEN Code of Practice outlines what needs to be done for them. (Section 4.3)

The key phrase in that section is 'no barriers to every pupil achieving', and it is the responsibility of teachers of reading to identify those barriers within their classrooms and pedagogical practice to do all they can to remove them. This also implies that teachers of reading know their children well and are able to identify their individual needs.

The Code of Practice for Special Educational Needs lays out the responsibilities and duties for the school, giving schools a legal responsibility to assess and provide for individual needs; this provision is identified in an individual education plan (IEP). All schools will have a Special Educational Needs Co-ordinator (SENCo) who is usually a senior member of staff. Teachers should turn to them for support and advice and work closely with them.

This chapter serves only as an introduction to some of the needs in relation to reading that teachers of reading are likely to encounter. It serves as a starting point for further reading and research.

Gifted and talented children

In 2008 the DCSF defined gifted and talented children as 'those children ... with one or more abilities developed to a level significantly ahead of their year group'. Terms such as 'gifted', 'talented', 'able' are used a lot in schools and definitions are not always precise. Normally, 'gifted' is used for children who excel academically in one or more subjects and 'talented' for those who excel in practical skills, for example sport, music, organisation. All schools are required to identify gifted and talented children and to have a policy for meeting their needs. These children need to be identified from a range of sources and experiences, not just from test scores, and it is important to remember that gifted children may not always be high achievers or the most mature within the class. Porter said that 'it is the ability to think creatively that distinguishes giftedness from precociousness' (1999: 28).

Most who write about giftedness in English write about exceptional talent in writing, and there are numerous examples to be found of primary-aged children who write creatively and to great effect. There is very little mention of children who are gifted readers. However, a sweep of the discussion board on Mumsnet (www.mumsnet.com) reveals that this is a common concern with parents; they talk of children who start school able to read fluently and are not easily accommodated by provision in school. It might be that a systematic approach to teaching, while being good for the majority of children, makes it difficult to accommodate those who do not conform to expected patterns of development and progression. Many years ago when I was teaching in an urban multicultural school in a challenging inner city area, David entered the reception class as a fluent reader. This was very unusual for this school and the reception class teacher did not really believe it! She asked for my help and I spent a wonderful half hour with David talking about what he liked to read, reading books with him and discussing his own view on them. When I reported back that David was indeed a very capable and experienced reader and suggested that we needed to look at an individualised programme for him as he probably did not need to work his way through the phonic scheme, the teacher exclaimed, 'But he'll miss out on the basics!'. For all the research that is done about the process of learning to read, there are always some children who just seem to know how to read without any explicit instruction.

In 1976 Margaret Clark reported the result of her study of 32 children who had learned to read before starting school. Clark gave these children a battery of tests for reading, intelligence, auditory discrimination, memory, visual awareness and other factors and it appeared that there was nothing to signify huge differences in these children as a group from others who had not learned to read. The number of books in the home was not a factor either, and although they all had parents who took an interest in their education, many had siblings who were not young fluent readers. The only feature which Clark identified as significant was that these children had strong auditory discrimination of phonological contrasts.

Clark identified lessons for teachers from the findings of her research and it is important for teachers of reading to note these. First is the significance of dialogue with at least one adult; second the role of libraries to their reading through the availability of a range of books and the expertise of the librarian and third, the children's growing sensitivity to the functions and features of written English through reading and book talk. It was also apparent that their ability to read had enabled them to engage in a wide range of other interests. Many were fascinated by a variety of printed material, which often was not the type or level of reading material enjoyed by children of that age.

Many other studies have been made of so-called 'precocious' readers. Olson et al. (2006) carried out a review of the findings of all these studies and came to the following conclusion:

Precocious readers represent a small portion of children who enter school each year. Researchers have investigated the environmental characteristics, acquisition process, psycholinguistic and neuropsychological characteristics, and academic skills of these children. Despite the research findings in the area, researchers and clinicians are still unable to predict who these children will be, describe how precocious readers fit into our current theories of emergent literacy and reading development, and confidently state whether this knowledge could be generalized beyond the precocious reader to the typically reading child. (2006: 205)

Stainthorp and Hughes (2004) followed up a group of precocious readers at the age of 11 and found that they maintained their advantage in relation to reading over other children in their year group. However, the authors argue that these children would have benefited even more from sustained individualised support in school. How then should teachers support gifted readers and what sort of support is appropriate?

Evans and Goodhew (1997) describe some of the characteristics of gifted readers: they are able to identify irony, humour, absurdity and implied meaning; they are able to select, extract and synthesise facts from a passage of writing; they are able to sustain reading from a wider range of material. These characteristics give teachers some idea of how they can both support and challenge gifted readers. In considering this there are two important principles to remember which I hope have been clear throughout this book. The first is the importance of talk and the second is the importance of teachers' knowledge of children's books.

For some children the conversations held about the books are what will challenge and stimulate to more advanced thinking. In an earlier chapter I described how Jamie responded when I read *Don't Let the Pigeon Drive the Bus* by Mo Willems to him. The first time he joined in with a loud 'No' as most children do. He quickly realised that it was more fun to break the rules and play with the story and the role of the reader in relation to the pigeon and driver. The second time he answered 'Yes!'. Jamie is just three years old and is a very able child; he was certainly demonstrating Evans and Goodhew's first characteristic. How could a teacher follow that up? It might be that a conversation about how the story would change if the pigeon did drive the bus would challenge Jamie to reflect on his role as a reader in making the meaning of the story. What might happen? How would the driver feel if he came back and found you had not done as he had asked? This could be followed on by sharing other books where the role of the reader is clear, for example *Open Very Carefully* by Nick Bromley. This could develop into looking at books where the message is not completely conveyed through the written text, for example, *Come Away from the Water Shirley* by John Burningham. In this book identifying the parallel stories and deciding which is the truth (if there is such a thing!) requires advanced comprehension skills. With children as young as Jamie however, it is important to remember that the content and theme of the books need to be appropriate to their interest and emotional developmental stage. Jamie is still only just three. It would be tempting to choose a book like *The Conquerors* by David McKee, but although apparently simple in design and layout, the underlying theme and message of the book is not appropriate for a three year old.

For slightly older children it can be challenging to look at different versions of the same story and compare and contrast them. You could explore the traditional story of the three little pigs and then look at *The True Story of the Three Little Pigs* by Jon Scieszka and *The Three Little Wolves and the Big Bad Pig* by Eugene Trivizas. This gives opportunity to explore character, setting, mood, the narrative voice and narrative structure.

For older children, offering them the opportunity to read series of books such as *His Dark Materials* by Philip Pullman or different books which explore a similar theme. If the class theme is the Second World War there are some books which would challenge the more able to think about things from a slightly different per-spective. For example, *Auslander* by Paul Dowswell explores life in Berlin during the Second World War; *Code Name Verity* by Elisabeth Wein is a story of friendship between two girls, espionage and war; *The Boy in the Striped Pyjamas* by John Boyne is the story of a young German boy and his experiences of a concentration camp. As with any choice of book, teachers of reading must know the child and the book really well. Never offer a book to a child that you have not read yourself.

It is clear that these activities are not essentially different from anything a teacher might do with any child, perhaps with slightly older children. The challenge offered to the able children will be through the conversations that are held and the ques-tions that are asked. The section on guided reading in Chapter 9 will offer some indication of how teacher questions can be refined to offer challenge.

Planning to include children who are gifted in reading should show:

- breadth (enrichment through a wider range of content, activities and resources)
- depth (increased complexity of tasks, resources or dialogue)
- pace (accelerated progress through objectives and curriculum programmes of study).

Remember always that gifted children are not always advanced socially and emo-tionally and are not always high achievers. Increase the cognitive challenge but be careful about maintaining the interest level. Do not make able children work through something which is easy for them as that will increase boredom and decrease motivation and engagement. As with effective teaching for all children, keep the needs of the individual child in mind.

Those who can read but don't

For those of us who love reading, for whom pleasure is nothing less than a long period of uninterrupted time to curl up with a favourite book, who go into book-shops and libraries and sigh with the feeling that there is just not enough time to do justice to all that is contained there, who always carry a book in their bag and have a pile by the side of the bed, who love talking about books with friends and read book reviews, who would like to take seven books to a desert island and that would not be enough – for those people it is really difficult to imagine not wanting to read. There is a strong sense of elitism about reading; somehow it is better to read through the Man Booker prize shortlist than to read a magazine or a graphic novel. Why is that? It is true that things are changing; there is now a recognition that picture books are not just for young children and are something to grow out of. Graphic novels are now an acclaimed genre in their own right and some books, for example the *Alex Rider* series by Anthony Horowitz, are published as an ordinary paperback and a graphic novel. Books such as *Ernest and Ethel* by Raymond Briggs are adult novels written in comic book form.

Non-fiction books have changed enormously and become much more accessible. Authors such as Marcia Williams and Nicola Davies challenge our stereotypical views of what certain types of book should look like. However, for many people today the printed word is no longer their first port of call. My nineteen-year-old son will turn to YouTube to find demonstrations and instructions or information; it does not enter his head to look for a book and neither does he look for a print-based text on the Internet. He is not alone among his peers. He listens to discussions, talks and explanations through earphones from his phone. He reflects on these, discusses them, argues with them and puts forward different points of view – behaving just as a critical reader does with a printed text. For him, reading is too slow and cannot be done on the move.

Does this matter? McMaster, in a paper entitled, 'Why read?', justifies reading in this way:

> Literature then, in addition to the intellectual excitement it provides in the inherent structures and textures of individual works, bestows an intellectual benefit in satisfying curiosity about other minds and cultures and about our own. And, because of the intricate criss-crossing of life and literature, it encourages a critical assessment of our personal and social values. (2013: 50)

There is no doubt that other media can offer much of what McMaster describes but not all; it must also be the case that in the twenty-first century we need to broaden our concept of reading and ensure that the new literacies are given as much value and recognition as the old.

The evidence seems to indicate that most reluctant readers are boys. In 2012 the Boys' Reading Commission was published by the National Literacy Trust. A survey of the research (Clark, 2012) confirmed that girls outperform boys on all National Curriculum reading tests, that girls enjoy reading more, read more than boys and have more positive attitudes to reading than boys. The commission asked why this was and uncovered several reasons. The effect of peer pressure is strong – reading is perceived as being 'not cool'; texts commonly used within schools engage more with girls' interests; there is a lack of male reading models and the workforce in most primary schools is largely female; boys prefer to be more active and do not maintain concentration for more sustained reading.

How can schools and teachers of reading address these issues? Let us first consider the issue of books not addressing the interests of boys and again, this comes down to the teacher's knowledge of the range of books available. Teachers tend to stick to well-loved texts for their teaching and often these are ones which they themselves enjoy. Goodwin (1995) in a small-scale study of reluctant readers found that one of their complaints was that there was not a wide enough range of books to choose from in classrooms and those books that were available tended to be fiction and not non-fiction, which they preferred. How ironic it is that often comics and magazines are only allowed out to be read during wet playtimes. Why do you think schools think the reading of those is not as worthy as the reading of books?

Reflective activity

Go into a classroom and look in the reading corner at the types of reading materials that are on offer. Can you see anything that would entice a reluctant reader?

Powling (2000) describes the book which got him hooked onto reading. Between the ages of 9 and 11 he re-read it 22 times, although his teacher did not completely approve as it was the biography of a boxer and the quality of the writing was, according to Powling, 'both plodding and over-excited' (2000: 14). It was only when he re-read the book in adulthood that he realised the parallels between the protagonist's childhood and his own. Pennac (1994) believed that the emphasis on teaching led to a lack of this personal identification with the texts used in school by pupils. He talks of how we stifle the imagination and the possibility of submersion in the text by endless questions and focus on the detail:

> Where then are all those magical creatures hiding ... can they possibly bear any relation to the brutally squashed traces of ink called letters? ... Can a book have become such an object? The opposite of magic, his heroes stifled by books and their dumbfounding impenetrability ... Are these the same parents who would never, never have thought to worry, when reading him a book, about whether he had properly understood ... that Snow White was asleep because she had bitten into an apple? ... I'm asking you again, what happened to the prince when his father drove him out of the castle? ... We used to be his story-teller; now we're his accountant. (Pennac, 1994: 43–4)

For both Pennac and Powling the solution is to read to children out loud. Reading aloud to children in order to re-inspire and to find again that enthusiasm for reading is the way to engage children with the power of the written word. That means, at the risk of repeating myself, that teachers of reading need to know those books which will inspire and rekindle enthusiasm.

Many boys are enthusiastic about football. If they are supporters of a local team, teachers could have copies of the programmes from each match in the reading corner in the classroom and collect several newspaper reports of the matches from different newspapers and read them to look for evidence of bias. Record commentaries and post-match discussions and consider how they use language to make the match real. Use the team's website as a shared reading activity. Read Terence Blacker's *Hotshots* series about a girl football team. Make sure your book corner contains some football books such as: *Keeper* by Mal Peet, *Extra Time* by Morris Gleitzman, *Death Match* by Andy Croft, *Foul Play* by Tom Palmer, *Zero to Hero* by Rob Childs, *Man of the Match* by Sophie Smiley, *Wonder Goal* by Michael Foreman, *Dino F.C.: The Great Kit Catastrophe* by Keith Brumpton or even *Friendly Matches*, a collection of football poems by Allan Ahlberg. As Goodwin (1995: 2) argues, 'The opposite of reluctance is not ability but enthusiasm. It is possible to argue that it is as important to teach readerly behaviours such as enthusiasm for books as it is to teach skills such as word recognition'.

Clarke and Burke (2012) also suggest that work needs to be done to create more 'cool' reading models for boys. The National Literacy Trust website (www.literacytrust. org.uk) gives details of many such projects with which teachers and schools can engage. These include things like 'Premier League Reading Stars' and the Young Readers Project. Places like the Roald Dahl Museum and Story Centre (www.roalddahl. com/museum) offer workshops and ideas and the websites of many children's authors offer ways to involve children more, for example Tom Palmer (www.tompalmer.co.uk). Finally, The Story Museum in Oxford (www.storymuseum.org.uk) offers all sorts of opportunities. Those are just a few of the available resources to enthuse children, but teachers of reading need to remember that a resource is only effective if it matches the enthusiasms of both the children and the teacher. Teachers need to choose carefully.

Clarke and Burke (2012) also talk about the need to incorporate information technology (IT) much more into the reading curriculum. The school library needs to be designed so that IT is at its heart – not only for cataloguing and reviewing but for reading websites, games and other materials. Children need to be taught explicitly how to choose a book and be given the freedom to reject a book if they start it and then change their minds. E-readers and tablets need to be available for electronic reading and even some computer games offer good reading material. It offers a very different approach to reading and one I would not normally recom-mend but for some children, boys in particular, a structured IT programme such as Lexia (www.lexialearning.com) works well.

Reading does not always have to be something where children are sitting down quietly. Use the outdoor environment to create opportunities for reading: a treasure hunt with clues written down and hidden, letters hanging in the tree to collect and make into words, chapters of a book in different places around the outdoor space, information notices around the building or asking the children to match labels to places. You can also create role plays based on popular computer games; create roles and scenarios written on cards and each child in a group chooses a role, then the group chooses a scenario card and they have to role play that scenario.

As Goodwin (1995) said, the aim, when working with reluctant readers whether boys or girls, is to generate within them an enthusiasm for reading by finding the texts which engage and relate to them.

Children who have English as an Additional Language (eal)

When working with EAL children it is very important to remember that their difficulty is with the language, not with cognitive understanding. I was once visiting some primary schools in Paris; my French was fine for general conversation with the teachers and the children and I felt quite pleased with myself at how well I was doing. Then one teacher said he would be very interested to have a talk with me about social constructivism and how that related to teaching and learning in the classroom. If that conversation had been in English I would have loved it and would have enjoyed sharing ideas; however, I soon discovered that my French was not really up to such a topic of conversation and found myself uttering very simplistic comments and repeating and agreeing with what my colleague was saying. I felt he must be thinking that these English academics are not really very bright! My experience is very similar to what school is like for children who have EAL. Many of them have good conversational English but struggle to express complex ideas and concepts; that does not mean they do not understand them – it means they do not have the English to express them.

Collier and Thomas (2001) found that it can take between 10 and 12 years for children who are new to English to become competent in 'academic' English. They can become competent in conversational language or playground English in between two and four years. This is where difficulties can often arise, as teachers assume that because a child is conversationally fluent they can understand the language of the classroom lessons. Cummins (2000) distinguished these two language competencies as Basic Interpersonal Communicative Skills (BICS) and Cognitive Academic Language Proficiency (CALP). The gap between these two accounts for the under-achievement of many children. Incidentally, it is not only children who have EAL who suffer from this competency gap.

Children with EAL are not a homogeneous group. There are more than a million children between 5 and 16 years old in UK schools who speak in excess of 360 languages between them in addition to English. Similar figures from 2005 indicated that there were 687,000 children in UK schools who spoke 200 languages. Since 1997 the figures have doubled. It is clear that both the number of children and the number of languages is rapidly increasing. so it is important that teachers know how best to help these children. In January 2013 one in six primary school pupils in England had EAL. The percentage varies from school to school, but in March 2012 it was thought that there were 1,363 primary schools where more than half the pupils had EAL. Most are to be found in large urban areas but some of these schools were in places such as Brighton, Gloucestershire, Milton Keynes, Southampton, Surrey, Scunthorpe, Skipton, Windsor and Maidenhead. A huge number of different languages are spoken; in 2012 there were 18 languages which were spoken by more than 10,000 pupils. The languages spoken in primary schools included Punjabi, Urdu, Bengali, Polish, Somali, Gujarati, Arabic, Portuguese, Tamil, French, Chinese, Turkish, Yoruba, Spanish, Pashto, Lithuanian and Albanian. These statistics, and those that follow, were taken from the National Association for Language Development in the Curriculum (NALDIC) website (www.naldic.org.uk).

Reflective activity

Find an example of the written form of some or all of those languages. Think about what the challenges of learning English would be for pupils for whom this is their home language.

These children have a lot to achieve in school. They are not able to focus solely on learning English but have to address all the requirements of the National Curriculum at the same time. As well as this they are learning a new culture with its attendant values, expectations and social skills. In 2013, a lower percentage of bilingual pupils achieved the expected level (level 2) in reading, writing, mathematics and science at Key Stage 1 compared to pupils whose first language is English. Of pupils whose first language is English, 90 per cent achieved the expected level in speaking and listening; 83 per cent of those pupils whose first language is not English achieved the expected level. Interestingly, the results of the phonics screening check showed hardly any difference between the decoding ability of bilingual learners and mother tongue English learners: 69 per cent of both bilingual and mother tongue English learners were able to decode 32 or more of the words. Of EAL and bilingual pupils, 73 per cent achieved the expected level (level 4) in reading, writing and mathematics at the end of Key Stage 2 compared to 76 per cent of pupils whose first language is English. Bilingual pupils slightly outperformed monolingual pupils in the grammar, spelling and punctuation task: 66 per cent attained a 4b or above in this task compared to 64 per cent of monolingual pupils.

Much of what is helpful for EAL children is also good practice for all children, so teachers of reading do well to adopt these practices generally. Learning opportunities need to be embedded in a recognisable context so that there are lots of other cues to help with the language. Practical activities are better as children with EAL can grasp the concept even if the language is still uncertain. Activity needs to be accompanied by lots of oral interactions, where the language is modelled, used and repeated. Remember that children not only need to learn the new vocabulary but also the language structures.

In relation to the teaching of reading, telling, reading aloud and re-telling stories is a wonderful way of learning the patterns and rhythms of language. For EAL children stories can be accompanied by physical gestures, props and/or visual aids. All these will aid understanding. The stories need strong plots and predictable repetitive language. Remember that some children will need to learn new book-handling skills; they might be used to books which are read from right to left or from top to bottom. They might be used to seeing books written in a completely different script, which may be non-alphabetic.

Try to have as much of the children's home languages around in classroom display as possible. This will not only help the children but also their parents. Make sure there are books in the home languages in the book corner, and you may want to include some dual-language texts. It can be good to ask some parents to record stories in their home languages so children can listen to these when in school. Use traditional stories from the children's home country but remember that while some children with EAL might be newly arrived, some may have been born in England and lived here all their lives. Talk about the languages children know and share them with the whole class. For example, it can be fun to collect different ways of greeting in as many languages as possible.

NALDIC is a wonderful source of information and ideas for working with children with EAL. Explore their website (www.naldic.org.uk) to find ideas for school and for your own subject knowledge.

Children with dyslexia

Definitions of dyslexia have been many and varied over the years. In 2009 Rose produced a report on identifying and teaching pupils with dyslexia and used the following definition as the basis for the report:

- Dyslexia is a learning difficulty that primarily affects the skills involved in accurate and fluent word reading and spelling.

- Characteristic features of dyslexia are difficulties in phonological awareness, verbal memory and verbal processing speed.

- Dyslexia occurs across the range of intellectual abilities.

- It is best thought of as a continuum, not a distinct category, and there are no clear cut-off points.

- Co-occurring difficulties may be seen in aspects of language, motor co-ordination, mental calculation, concentration and personal organisation, but these are not, by themselves, markers of dyslexia.

- A good indication of the severity and persistence of dyslexic difficulties can be gained by examining how the individual responds or has responded to well founded intervention.

(Rose, 2009: 10)

Dyslexia was first defined in November 1896 by Pringle Morgan, who described it as 'congenital word blindness'. The word dyslexia actually comes from the Greek where 'dys' means difficulty and 'lexis' means the written word. There are lots of variations of opinions and definitions of dyslexia, but generally it means a language-based difficulty. It is thought to affect about 10 per cent of the population and tends to run in families. It was once thought to be more common in males than females but more recent evidence suggests that is no longer the case. It is not a disease and so cannot be cured. Thinking of dyslexia as a continuum means that there are varying degrees of the condition which manifest in varying levels of difficulty with reading. Imagine the four quadrants of the simple view of reading; people with dyslexia would tend to populate the top left quadrant with good comprehension skills but poor decoding skills. People who just struggle with reading would probably be in the bottom right quadrant with both poor comprehension skills and poor decoding skills.

Much of the research on dyslexia has been carried out by cognitive psychologists and so the emphasis has been on word reading skills. Research has identified three main areas of difficulty:

- Visual processing – people with dyslexia have problems in copying, particularly from a board on the wall; they have difficulty in following text and often say that the words move around or 'jump off the page'. They will frequently confuse words such as 'saw' and 'was' or letters such as 'b' and 'd'.
- Automaticity – people with dyslexia have difficulties with motor timing which means that skills of word decoding, retrieval of words from memory and speech processing are not automatic.
- Phonological – people with dyslexia have poor phonological awareness which leads to poor reading.

Stein and Walsh (1997) suggested that these three areas work together so that the visual processing and the phonological difficulties may be regulated by motor timing. Motor timing is controlled by the cerebellum in the base of the brain. The British Dyslexia Association (BDA) claims that between 30 to 40 per cent of people with dyslexia suffer with visual stress difficulty, which means that the text appears to move around on the page or look distorted. The BDA recommends using coloured filters which can make the text clearer and easier to see.

The BDA gives some signs which might indicate that dyslexia is present. General indications are obvious good or bad days but with no clear reason, confusion between directional words and a family history of dyslexia. For pre-school children some of the signs are jumbling words, difficulty with learning nursery rhymes, later speech development, no crawling but bottom wriggling before walking, difficulty in dressing, often accused of not listening or paying attention, difficulty in catching, kicking and throwing, often bumping into things and falling over, unable to clap a simple rhythm. For primary children some of the common signs are problems with reading and spelling, letters and figures written the wrong way round, the need to use fingers to help with simple calculations, difficulty with shoelaces and dressing, written work takes a long time, poor sense of direction, poor self-image. It must be understood that these are indications, and if a child possesses these characteristics it must not be necessarily assumed that they have dyslexia.

How can teachers of reading support children with dyslexia in the classroom? The BDA gives ten top tips and many of these are completely appropriate for all children. It is often the case that just a slight change in resources or practice can make life so much easier for children with dyslexia.

1. Praise all successes not just academic achievements, ensuring that every child knows that their strengths are recognised.
2. Use visual aids in every lesson and try to ensure that resources are multisensory. One simple tip which supports those with dyslexia is to display the alphabet in an arc rather than in a straight line.
3. Teach study skills, for example note-taking, explicitly.
4. Vary methods of conveying information using discussion, multimedia, audio tapes. Explain your teaching point in several different ways especially if it is not understood first time round.
5. Have a clear lesson structure and display it visually. Avoid long instructions.
6. Have lists of high-frequency words and subject-specific words available on tables.
7. Have a large range of books available for each reading ability.
8. Encourage different ways of recording, for example large sheets of paper, recording, writing frames.
9. Label classroom resources clearly and avoid clutter.
10. Avoid activities which draw attention to difficulties; avoid copying from the board, reciting times tables, reading aloud, undifferentiated spelling tests.

There are ways of presenting written resources which can help children with dyslexia in very simple ways:

- use matt paper which is thick enough so it cannot be seen through and is cream or a soft pastel colour but not white
- use a plain even sans serif font in 12 to 14 font size with dark text on a light background. **Comic Sans** or **Arial** are good fonts to use

- avoid underlining or italics but use **bold** for emphasis
- avoid text which is all in UPPER CASE
- use boxes and borders to highlight important bits of a text
- left-justify text but leave the right-hand side ragged
- use 1.5 line spacing
- use bullet points rather than a long passage of continuous prose
- use flow charts, pictograms and graphics as much as possible.

It is also helpful to create a quiet area in the classroom, where children with dyslexia can go when they feel stressed, and also an area where they can work if they choose with less noise to distract. This need not necessarily be just for those who have dyslexia!

It is important to have the right resources for children with dyslexia and to have a range of books available for them to choose which they are able to read and enjoy independently. Barrington Stoke (www.barringtonstoke.co.uk/) is an independent publisher committed to breaking down the barriers which prevent children from becoming enthusiastic readers. This includes what they describe as 'dyslexia-friendly' books. These books fulfil many of the criteria for written resources outlined above in the way they are printed, more especially they have a reading level which is much less demanding but are about topics which would be of interest to older children. Books are advertised by their reading age and interest age which makes it easier to find books which are suitable.

How can teachers of reading help children with dyslexia to become readers? There is no way I can do justice to all the possible ideas in response to this question, but there are some important principles which can continually be borne in mind. Svensson (2008) gives two case studies of children with dyslexia and from these can be drawn key factors to be borne in mind by teachers of reading:

- Separate the decoding and comprehension elements of reading so that each can be supported at different levels (2008: 168)
- Ensure texts are differentiated for decoding but are conceptually challenging (2008: 171)
- Use audio books, IT and reading aloud to maintain interest in reading
- Maintain a clear and explicit structure to the pattern of the day and also to resources
- Employ strategies which support success in classroom activities, for example if needing to copy or refer to text on the board, write each line in a different colour.

If as a teacher of reading you are concerned about the reading progress of a child in your class and you have attempted a variety of strategies and methods without success, it is important to liaise with the school SENCO and with the child's parents. Children with specific learning difficulties will need to be referred to an educational psychologist for diagnosis and an IEP will be drawn up, but children who are struggling with reading will need extra support within the classroom.

There are many interventions available to support struggling readers and it is sometimes difficult for teachers of reading to decide which is best for a particular child. There is a very helpful website, *Interventions for Literacy* (www.gov.uk/government/uploads/system/uploads/attachment_data/file/273877/special_educational_needs_code_of_practice.pdf) which lists all the interventions available and is designed to help teachers select the most appropriate one. This is based on the work of Greg Brooks (2013), who looked at 48 different schemes and the evaluations of them. In this chapter we briefly consider just one of these, but teachers of reading who need to choose an intervention strategy for a particular child are advised to look at Brooks' report in more detail.

Reading Recovery

Reading Recovery is designed for children who are falling behind in reading; these children will be in the bottom 20 per cent of the country after one year in school. Over a period of about 20 weeks children receive individual daily lessons of half an hour out of the classroom from a Reading Recovery-trained teacher. The individual lessons finish when the child's reading reaches the level of the average children in the class and they can cope unsupported with the class work.

The programme arose from the work of Marie Clay (1985) in New Zealand and was first introduced into England in 1990. In the early 1990s local authorities received government funding to implement Reading Recovery, but that funding stopped in 1995 despite the programme's success. In 2005 funding from charitable trusts, business and the government was raised for a Reading Recovery revival called Every Child a Reader.

Hurry and Sylva (2007) carried out a detailed evaluation of Reading Recovery in London and Surrey. They found that children undertaking Reading Recovery made significant gains in both reading accuracy and comprehension. After three years the gains were maintained but the children were still behind national norms. The researchers also found that Reading Recovery was more effective with those children who were non-readers at age six rather than those who were struggling readers at the same age.

The training of Reading Recovery teachers is very stringent and intensive and teachers are required to go through the training before they can teach on the programme. There is a high expectation of success and the underlying philosophy is that reading is a meaning-making process. Children taking part in Reading Recovery show increased confidence and enthusiasm for reading; they have gained a wider range of reading strategies and are more independent as readers.

A typical Reading Recovery session follows basically the same pattern each day, although recently it has been revised to include more of a phonic element. There are seven key stages:

- re-reading of known books, usually those which have been worked on in recent sessions
- letter identification using magnetic letters
- shared writing with the teacher of a story which is used for reading practice
- rearranging the parts of a story which have been cut up
- practice in blending and segmenting
- introduction to a new book with the teacher teaching new vocabulary and the child attempting to read it
- practice of specific strategies according to individual needs.

Burroughs-Lange (2006) found that having a trained Reading Recovery teacher in the school with an expertise in literacy improved literacy teaching and learning throughout the whole school. Teachers of reading might like to consider those elements of Reading Recovery which are easily translatable into general classroom practice and which support all those learning to read as much as those who are struggling. Those principles are:

- a wide range of texts available for reading
- many opportunities for reading, giving frequent regular practice
- learners writing texts which were then used for reading practice
- very explicit teaching of reading strategies
- an emphasis on what is known and teaching which builds on that.

Conclusion

Meek once said that if a child has failed to learn from one particular type of teaching the solution is not to give them a more intensive experience of the same strategy but to try other approaches. Teachers have to remember that what is important is that every child receives 'quality first teaching' (TDA, 2008); it is after every possible support has been given within the classroom and the school that additional external help is needed. However, if specific problems are apparent, teachers should not delay in talking to the school SENCO.

It is the knowledge of the teacher of reading about the children, about the expected progression in learning to read, about a variety of teaching strategies and approaches and about a wide range of different children's books which will ensure that every child receives the best opportunities possible to become a reader.

The key messages of this chapter are:

- teachers of reading need to adapt their teaching to the needs of individual children
- teachers need to know and provide access to a wide range of children's books and reading materials to address individual needs and interests
- teachers of reading need to be flexible in their teaching approaches.

Further reading

Martin, T. (1989) *The Strugglers: Working with Children who Fail to Learn to Read.* Buckingham: Open University Press.
I think this is an important book for every teacher of reading to read because it reminds us of the lasting impact of what we do in the classroom, both emotionally and cognitively, on pupils.

Goepel, J. and Sharpe, S.E. (2014) *Inclusive Primary Teaching: A Critical Approach.* Northwich: Critical Publishing Ltd.
This is a book which puts inclusion into the current educational climate of raising standards and accountability and explores how teachers can effectively address individual needs.

CHAPTER 12

BECOMING AN OUTSTANDING TEACHER OF READING

Chapter objectives

At the end of this chapter you should:

- know what Ofsted regards as good practice in the teaching of reading
- be able to relate the requirements of the *Teachers' Standards* (DfE, 2011a) to the teaching of reading
- be aware of sources of support and development for teachers of reading.

Introduction

Over 15 years ago Jane Medwell and her colleagues carried out some research, sponsored by the then Teacher Training Agency, to discover the characteristics of effective teachers of literacy. They identified eight key elements which made a teacher really effective:

1. The emphasis in all teaching and learning was on meaning-making.
2. Teaching was done through the use of shared texts – these might be books which a class read and discussed together or it might be a text written together and then used for reading.
3. Decoding was taught in a clear systematic fashion.
4. In all teaching the functions and purposes of literacy were made explicit.
5. Effective teachers had a strong personal philosophy of literacy and a grasp of underpinning theories.
6. Children's progress was carefully and systematically monitored.
7. Teachers had a strong subject knowledge but this was in relation to pedagogy and not necessarily in isolation.
8. Teachers saw themselves as learners and took every opportunity to develop their own knowledge and understanding.

This was published many years ago, yet when looking at recent Ofsted reports and considering the requirements of the *Teachers' Standards* (DfE, 2011a) not much has changed.

This chapter begins by considering what three recent Ofsted reports have said about outstanding teaching of reading and then looks at how the teaching of reading relates to the eight standards for teachers. This will include consideration of how planning for reading is incorporated both into English planning and other subjects of the curriculum. Finally, professional associations and resources to support teachers of reading both in subject knowledge and pedagogy are described.

Ofsted and the teaching of reading

There have been three Ofsted reports in recent years on reading in particular and English in general, and we will look at what each of them says in turn. Firstly, we explore *Reading by Six: How the Best Schools Do It* (2010). This looked at a sample of 12 schools (some primary schools and some infant schools) whose children were achieving good results in reading at the age of six. The 12 schools were located all over England; they were all judged to be outstanding and achieved above average results in reading at Key Stage 1. The schools also represented a range of socio-economic and ethnically mixed settings. All said they had reviewed their teaching of reading when the teaching of phonics became a requirement, and in the pen portraits of the schools only one mentions reading for pleasure. Seven out of the 12 schools used Read Write Inc. – a phonics scheme devised and published by Ruth Miskin, who has acted in an advisory role to the government about the teaching of systematic synthetic phonics.

The summary of this report says that:

> The schools in this survey have two things in common: the belief that every child can learn to read and the strategies to make this happen. 'The most important gift our school can give a child is the power to read,' said one headteacher, a sentiment echoed by others. But it is not just rhetoric; the best primary schools do teach every child to read and nearly every child to read well. (Ofsted, 2010: 6)

What does Ofsted believe are those strategies which make it happen? Five common features across all the schools are identified. These were:

- In every school there was a determination that every child will learn to read which led to a clarity and purpose in policy, planning and pedagogy. Everybody was united in working towards this aim.
- Teachers had a firm grasp and understanding of what it is that helps children to learn to read. They knew about the process of reading, progression in reading and strategies for teaching reading.
- In every school there was a 'programme of rigorous systematic phonics work as the prime approach to decoding print'. As indicated above the majority used Read Write Inc. but others used Jolly Phonics or Letters and Sounds.
- Teaching was consistently of a very high quality and teachers were effective in monitoring children's progress and adapting their teaching to cater for individual needs.
- Leadership and management within the school put a high priority on the teaching of reading with a resultant emphasis on resources and training of teachers and support staff. For example, one school had a 'reading manager' who during the time when the whole school taught phonics was free to monitor teaching and to provide training as and when necessary.

In addition, these schools gave children the opportunity to apply what they had learned, that is there were opportunities for reading both independently and aloud to adults. The report does warn that using only decodable books could set an artificial ceiling to pupils' learning and advises the use of a wide range of books to maintain pleasure and enjoyment in reading. The report states that schools have a 'moral imperative' to ensure that all children learn to read – a strong sentiment.

The second Ofsted report on the teaching of English came out just a year later in 2011 and was called *Excellence in English* (Ofsted, 2011a). Again, this report looked at 12 outstanding schools but a mixture of primary and secondary schools; all their pupils demonstrated outstanding achievement. The purpose of this report was to support schools in moving towards outstanding status.

This report is aware that it came soon after *Reading by Six* and so does not place so much emphasis on phonics teaching. It makes ten key points about these outstanding schools:

- The curriculum was innovative and creative and was designed around the needs of the children. The writers of the report stress that a dull curriculum does not engage pupils and so does not result in high standards. This is a really important point and it is good to see Ofsted recognising that exciting curriculum and teaching are essential prerequisites for success. The outstanding teacher of reading does not play safe.
- Each school had a clear vision for what the teaching of English involved. There had been debate among staff about this, and the purpose of English for the pupils in that particular school was understood and clearly communicated. This led to clearly articulated aims for teaching within the whole school.
- Teachers worked as a team; they shared practice, observed and team taught; they discussed methodology and resources in meetings. This led to a strong team where there was a consistency of approach.
- Teaching was adapted to meet the needs of individual pupils; all pupils had access to the same curriculum but methodologies and resources were adapted to address needs. There was a flexibility based on a strong knowledge of pupil needs.
- Motivation and enthusiasm for learning by the pupils was a high priority for teachers and they gave pupils a 'voice' about the curriculum. Lessons were challenging and there were high expectations but pupils were engaged.
- Opportunities were created for English outside the classroom – visits, reading groups and reading with expert visitors. Reading experiences were authentic, embedded in real contexts.
- Teachers saw themselves as learners and were continually seeking to improve their practice. They monitored and reviewed their own practice and there was a culture of mutual support.
- There was no difference between the achievements of boys and girls. It is likely that this was related to the authentic and creative curricular opportunities.
- There was a strong emphasis on oral work and this was planned carefully into the curriculum.
- Reading for pleasure was given a high profile. As the report says, 'Schools that take the business of reading for pleasure seriously, where teachers read, talk with enthusiasm and recommend books, and where provision for reading is planned carefully, are more likely to succeed with their pupils' reading' (Ofsted, 2011a: 8).

At the end of the report, inspectors considered why reading standards were not higher generally. They emphasised the importance of teachers' subject knowledge both in relation to their knowledge of English as a subject and their knowledge of a range of children's books. In relation to the former, inspectors lament the fact that few primary teachers have a degree or even an A level in English. I am absolutely convinced of the importance of teachers' subject knowledge but am not sure that the content of most English degrees or A level courses would necessarily give teachers the relevant knowledge and understanding to be an effective teacher of English in the primary school. I wholeheartedly agree, however, that teachers' knowledge of children's books needs both extending and deepening (Cremin et al., 2009).

In 2012 Ofsted produced a report entitled *Moving English Forward*. In the introduction the importance of English is stated; it is the most important subject of the curriculum and is at the heart of our culture. The focus of this report is, 'How can attainment be raised in order to move English forward in schools?'. By 'moving English forward', it seems that inspectors are referring to raising standards of achievement and quality of teaching. Part A of the report identified key features of outstanding practice; it has to be said that there is nothing significantly different from the key features emerging from the previous two reports and so, in this chapter, we will focus on Part B which identifies actions to raise the standards of English in schools. The report states that all schools should:

- have a policy for reading for enjoyment
- ensure that preparation for tests does not lead to a stifling of creativity in the curriculum
- improve transition between Key Stage 2 and Key Stage 3
- simplify lesson plans so that the focus is on the learning objectives and teachers can be flexible during lessons.

In addition, primary schools should emphasise oral skills in Foundation and Key Stage 1 and make sure that pupils' reading skills are secure by the end of Key Stage 1. The report does not clarify what is meant by reading skills. It seems ironic in the light of the second bullet point above that the introduction of the phonic screening text has lead to a greater emphasis on 'teaching to the test' in Key Stage 1 classes.

It appears that in these three recent Ofsted reports there is a fairly consistent view of what constitutes outstanding teaching in English and that it is to do with the attainment of pupils. However, as mentioned in Chapter 10, one must be aware of what is being measured in terms of attainment and remember that being a reader involves much more than that which is measurable. There is an encouraging emphasis on creativity within the curriculum and on reading for pleasure, and teachers are reminded of the importance of their own subject knowledge. There is a real tension for teachers in maintaining high levels of achievement and also introducing creativity and flexibility into the curriculum. The consequences of not achieving high standards can be serious for a school, so one cannot blame headteachers for a cautious approach. One headteacher who achieves extremely high standards in his school within a highly innovative curriculum told me that if you 'play it safe' and achieve high standards you have no story to tell when Ofsted visit, but if you adopt a risk-taking approach to teaching and learning you have to create a valid and convincing story even though standards are high. I know of many outstanding schools that are so anxious to maintain this status that they worry about anything which might disrupt pupils' progress as set out in the school planning. For me, that is sad and not truly 'outstanding' in the widest sense of the word.

Ofsted (2014) in the latest *School Inspection Handbook* describes outstanding teaching as first ensuring that pupils make sustained progress. This leads on to further descriptions of outstanding teaching: it has high expectations, systematically and effectively checks pupils' understanding, has cohesive planning and authoritative subject knowledge and uses well-judged teaching strategies which match pupils' needs. How do trainee teachers move towards that as they seek to address the Teachers' Standards during their training programme?

It is interesting to note that in all these reports outstanding teaching is synonymous with above-average achievement by pupils but that this is measured only by what is assessed. There is surely much more to outstanding teaching of reading than producing pupils who achieve highly in statutory summative assessments.

 Reflective activity

Think back over teaching of reading that you have observed. Would you say it was outstanding? How would you make that decision based on what Ofsted says? How would you describe outstanding teaching of reading?

Do you think teaching can ever be outstanding if pupils' achievements are not high? Think out your own viewpoint with a justification for it and then share views with a friend. Do you both agree?

Teachers' Standards

The Teachers' Standards came into effect in England from September 2012 and are for all teachers from the point of award of Qualified Teacher Status. People training to be teachers are required to address these standards at a minimum level.

> As their careers progress, teachers will be expected to extend the depth and breadth of knowledge, skill and understanding that they demonstrate in meeting the standards, as is judged to be appropriate to the role they are fulfilling and the context in which they are working. (DfE, 2011a: 7)

That is not the easiest thing to do and there is much debate as to what it means to be performing 'appropriate to the role'. The Universities' Council for the Education of Teachers (UCET) together with the National Association of School-based Initial Teacher Training (NASBITT) produced some guidance for providers of initial teacher training (www.ucet.ac.uk/3912), showing progression towards the standards for trainee teachers. It is not unproblematic and it can be too easy for those making judgments of trainee or newly qualified teachers to have the same expectations of them as of experienced teachers. Let us look at the standards specifically in relation to the teaching and learning of reading. Under each standard I will give several examples from the teaching of reading which could act as evidence for that standard. Trainee teachers and their tutors will be able to think of many more.

Standard 1: A teacher must set high expectations which inspire, motivate and challenge pupils

- Create a physical environment which demonstrates many different purposes and functions of reading and incorporate them into your teaching for example in the role play area or instructions for classroom activities.
- Make sure the emotional environment of the classroom feels safe for children so that they are able to take risks in their learning.
- Be sure that the reading corner contains a wide variety of all sorts of books and texts which appeal to all interests and abilities within the class.
- Use Bloom's taxonomy to plan questions in guided reading which challenge and extend thinking.
- In guided reading use a dialogic approach to discussion so that children are able to express and justify their own opinions.
- Encourage children to respond to their reading in a variety of ways.
- Make sure that the reading curriculum reflects the reading practices of the local community.
- Build time for independent reading into the timetable.
- During planned read aloud sessions, read texts which the children would not be able to read aloud and which challenge them.

Standard 2: Promote good progress and outcomes by pupils

- Know about children's experiences of reading at home and in the community and relate teaching and learning to prior experiences and existing knowledge.
- Choose books which are at an instructional level for a child so they are not too difficult to discourage but are not too easy so nothing is learned.
- Be familiar with expected progression in reading and how to provide deeper experiences and more challenging texts.
- Use dialogue and questioning to develop children's comprehension skills.
- Give the children opportunities to assess themselves as readers.
- Track pupils' phonic knowledge carefully and systematically and use that information to group children for phonic teaching.

Standard 3: demonstrate good subject and curriculum knowledge

- Know a range of children's books and other texts and continually keep that knowledge up to date.
- Be confident in your knowledge of teaching strategies for reading – reading aloud, shared reading, guided reading, discrete phonics, independent reading.
- Know how to use questioning to enable children to respond personally to their reading.
- Know how to teach GPCs, blending and segmenting.
- Know where to find out further information about the teaching of reading.

Standard 4: plan and teach well-structured lessons

- Be able to plan for reading aloud, shared reading, guided reading, discrete phonics and independent reading.
- Plan clear learning outcomes for each lesson but be flexible enough to adapt according to the children's response.
- Ensure that meaning-making is at the heart of your planning.
- Include opportunities for assessment in your planning.
- Create authentic problem-solving activities.
- Plan carefully for reading in all areas of the curriculum, being aware of the reading demands of all texts used.
- Involve outside experts in your teaching of reading – authors, poets, storytellers.

Standard 5: adapt teaching to respond to the strengths and needs of all pupils

- Ensure that all reading materials used reflect the interests of the children.
- Have books with an interest level for older children but which are at a less demanding level for decoding.
- Have reading materials in the classroom which reflect the home languages of the children, including dual language texts.
- Make sure that all written resources and your teaching approach is as supportive as possible for children with specific learning difficulties.
- In discussion about books, differentiate by the questions you ask.

Standard 6: make accurate and productive use of assessment

- Know how to gain information about children as readers through, for example, miscue analysis, observation and reading conferences.

- Track children's phonic knowledge systematically and in detail.
- Regularly change groups for guided reading and phonic teaching so that they are as compatible as possible with ability levels.
- Inform children of what it means to be an effective reader and give them opportunities to behave as readers in school.
- In reading conferences talk to children about their reading and make suggestions about reading materials that will challenge them.

Standard 7: manage behaviour effectively to ensure a good and safe learning environment

- Plan exciting and engaging lessons so that children are motivated and involved, eager to learn.
- Make sure that reading resources reflect the interests and abilities of the children.
- Make the purposes and functions of reading explicit to the children and create authentic learning activities.
- Read aloud to children from texts which they could not read independently but engage them.
- Allow children to behave as real readers, giving them opportunities to browse and to stop reading when they are not enjoying a book.
- Validate the reading of comics, magazines, graphic novels, picture books and newspapers within the classroom in reading lessons.
- Use the outdoor environment and the community to extend experiences and understandings of reading.

Standard 8: fulfil wider professional responsibilities

- Establish a time when everybody in the school reads.
- Make the school a reading active school.
- Have a reading club for children.
- Have a reading club for parents and children.
- Make the school library a place which is exciting and inviting to be and which reflects reading in the twenty-first century.
- Establish links with the local community library.
- Invite authors, poets, storytellers and book makers to visit as often as possible.
- Encourage parents to read with and to their children.
- Inform parents about what is important in the teaching of reading.

There are many more examples that could have been given; the key issue is that teachers of reading understand the reading process, are readers themselves and so do all they can to share the enjoyment and purpose of reading with children.

Planning for reading

We have talked a lot about planning for explicit reading lessons – shared reading, guided reading etcetera. Reading, however, is a part of every lesson and sometimes teachers forget what they know about progression in reading when they are planning for history or science.

All the principles of teaching reading which have been identified in this book apply to every lesson where there is a requirement for children to read something. Sometimes, the learning outcome of the lesson will be related to the teaching of reading but the text used for the shared reading will be a history text. This can be a powerful way of sourcing information and the shared reading lesson can be used to model the process: identifying what is already known about the topic, articulating questions to be asked, using the contents page and index to find the appropriate part of the text, looking for key words in the text, making notes from the text to answer the questions. In this way, children are learning to use information texts; that is the focus of the reading lesson and the content of the reading, be it history, science or geography, is almost irrelevant.

In other lessons, the learning outcome is related to the content of the subject and reading is a vehicle to access that content. However, teachers still need to be aware of the reading demands of the texts they are using in relation to the reading abilities of each pupil in the class and provide scaffolding to support those who need it. Teachers also need to consider the variety of texts and the different types of texts and the experience of reading these text types that their children have had. For some texts it is useful to introduce the children to the text, talking them through it and introducing key words, much as one would in a guided reading or Reading Recovery lesson, before the children are asked to read independently. It may also be that some children whose level of decoding ability is not as high would benefit from having the text read to them, either by an adult or on an audio tape, so they can concentrate on comprehension of the content.

When planning a sequence of lessons or a unit of work in English, the outcome of that unit is often a piece of writing. Teachers need to be very aware of the relationship between reading and writing and the need to make that connection explicit in teaching. It is true that experience of reading can increase vocabulary, broaden the use of language and give an understanding of how different types of text work. However, that knowledge is often implicit and deeply embedded and children do not always draw on it spontaneously when writing. Barrs and Cork (2001) looked at this relationship between reading and writing to see if the study of challenging texts in the classroom had any impact on the children's writing. They looked at Year 5 children, aged between nine and ten years. They found that reading aloud to children was highly significant as it enabled them to 'hear' the voice of the author in the text and to appreciate style and use of language. When they were writing, teachers reading the children's writing aloud also helped the children to hear what their own texts sounded like.

In order to write effectively, children need experience, not only of reading examples of that type of text but also of talking about how authors have made their texts effective both in terms of structure and language use. The beginning of any sequence of lessons in English should include lots of opportunities to read examples of the type of text children are going to write; these opportunities will be in browsing, reading aloud time, shared reading and guided reading. There will be a focus in the book corner with a display of books and texts of that type. Discussion around the text will be about how the author creates that particular effect – choice of words, language structures, illustrations, construction and layout of the book, etcetera. It is only after this input that children will begin to have the knowledge and understanding to be effective writers.

It is evident that outstanding teachers of reading are always thinking about reading and the reading needs of the children in their class. They are aware of the experiences needed and provide time, input and resources to supply those experiences. They also have the subject knowledge to explicitly draw out what it is that children need to know and to be able to make the connection between that knowledge and the required outcome of the lesson. In this way, will standards rise.

How do teachers of reading ensure that their personal knowledge and experiences of reading keeps developing? How do they know about children's books as they are published and how do they become aware of recent research and how it impacts on their teaching? How do teachers of reading become critically reflective practitioners who can make their own professional, informed decisions and not just do 'what they are told to do'? There are many sources of information and areas of support, and the next section of this chapter outlines where those can be found and how they can help.

Professional organisations

UKLA (www.ukla.org)

The website states that:

> The United Kingdom Literacy Association (UKLA) is a registered charity, which has as its sole object *the advancement of education in literacy*. UKLA is concerned with literacy education in school and out-of-school settings in all phases of education and members include classroom teachers, teaching assistants, school literacy co-ordinators, LEA literacy consultants, teacher educators, researchers, inspectors, advisors, publishers and librarians.

I joined UKLA when I was a newly qualified teacher many many years ago; I have attended conferences and read publications and made many friends and contacts through it. It has had a huge impact on me and my professional development. Membership gives you journals and magazines and access to blogs, discussion forums and local groups. UKLA also makes responses to government consultations and is involved in policy development; it is a good way of keeping on top of developments. The UKLA also makes annual book awards and these are becoming more prestigious within the field of children's literature.

National Association for the Teaching of English (NATE) (www.nate.org.uk)

On its website NATE says:

The National Association for the Teaching of English will work to:

- Promote standards of excellence in the teaching of English from Early Years to University
- Promote innovative and original ideas that have practical classroom outcomes
- Support teachers' own professional development through:
  - access to current research
  - publications
  - national and regional conferences
- Provide an informed national voice on matters concerning the teaching of English and its related subjects
- Encourage sharing and collaboration between teachers and learners of English and its related subjects.

It is probably true to say that NATE falls more easily within a secondary perspective but certainly not exclusively so, and it has much to offer primary teachers of reading. It also has an annual conference, lots of publications and resources and focused support for trainee and newly qualified teachers.

National centres which offer support and information

Seven Stories: National Centre for Children's Books (www.sevenstories.org.uk)

Seven Stories is the National Centre for Children's Books. Its mission is to champion children's books as an essential part of our childhood, our national heritage and our culture. It wants to inspire a love of reading across generations. The website says:

> Seven Stories is the only place in the UK dedicated to the art of children's books, and one of just a few such places in the world. We welcome over 70,000 visitors a year and there is something to enjoy 360 days a year. Everything we do inspires children and grownups to choose, share, read and enjoy the best children's literature. We attract some of the biggest names in children's literature to work with us to stage exhibitions and to take part in events.

If you are ever in Newcastle upon Tyne it is well worth a visit and the website is worth exploring too.

The Story Museum (www.storymuseum.org.uk)

The Story Museum is based in Oxford and is for lovers of story and literature of all ages. The website says, 'People love stories and they're a great way to learn. We hope you'll visit our most unusual museum, shop and café, and enjoy what's on. Maybe get involved. But that's enough about us. What's your story?'

Centre for Language in Primary Education (www.clpe.org.uk)

CLPE is based in London and offers training courses and research-based publications. Its website says:

> The Centre for Literacy in Primary Education (CLPE) is an independent UK charity that promotes the effective teaching of children's literacy. We are a well-established and highly renowned organisation with a nationally and internationally recognised reputation and research background. Our work emphasises the importance of children's literature in enabling children to become confident and enthusiastic readers and writers with all the benefits this brings. We believe in:

- A child's right to be literate and to enjoy literature
- The importance of texts that engage children and support developing literacy
- Practice that is underpinned and supported by robust classroom-based research.

Sources of information about research in reading

National Literacy Trust (www.literacytrust.org.uk)

Its website says:

> We work to improve the reading, writing, speaking and listening skills in the UK's most disadvantaged communities, where up to 40 per cent of people have literacy problems.

Our research and analysis make us the leading authority on literacy and drive our interventions. Because low literacy is intergenerational, we focus our work on families, young people and children.

- We establish literacy projects in the poorest communities
- We campaign to make literacy a priority for politicians and parents
- We support schools.

Sources of information about teaching ideas

Many of the websites already mentioned will give ideas for teaching and there are many more. The two specified below are ones which I have found useful at the time of writing.

The Literacy Shed (www.literacyshed.com)

The website says:

The Literacy Shed is home to a wealth of visual resources that I have collected over my 10 year career as a primary school teacher. I trawl YouTube, vimeo and other sites looking for suitable resources to use in the sheds. The sheds are broadly thematic but sometimes a resource could go in 2 or more sheds, I slot it in where I think it works best.

Most of the resources can be used in KS1 and KS2 but some do lend themselves to the upper age group and above. The aim is to provide high quality resources that can be used in stand alone literacy lessons, can form the basis for a whole Literacy unit or can support literacy units that you already have in place. With the many book based activities I would advocate using the book alongside the digital resource.

The site is well worth exploring as it is a useful store of ideas – particularly of videos and e-resources.

Key Stage 2 Literacy (www.keystage2literacy.co.uk)

The website says:

'keystage2literacy.co.uk...' is a webpage dedicated to all those hints and tips taught and learnt in the classroom, with a particular focus on Literacy and the Upper Key Stage 2 curriculum. This site is aimed at new and existing teachers who would like to brush up on their subject knowledge or find some new ideas for use in their classroom. This site is also ideal for parents to find out what their children are doing in class, and for children to explain to them. The process of learning should be one that is shared between a teacher, a parent and a child – this site hopes to deliver you a mutual ground upon which everyone can understand what is expected in the 21st century classroom.

Unfortunately, I have not been able to track down a site for Key Stage 1!

Sources for finding out about children's books

Booktrust (www.booktrust.org.uk)

The website says:

> Booktrust has a vision of a society where nobody misses out on the life-changing benefits that reading can bring. We recognise that to engage people with reading we need to adopt multi-stranded approaches – that might include reading aloud, writing about reading experiences, providing other learning resources – in order to effect social change. Through our programmes we aim to create a society of people who are motivated to read and who see themselves as readers whatever level that might be.

Booktrust is involved in the Bookstart project which gives away free packs of books to every child in England. The website has a brilliant book finder resource which will suggest books according to genre, age, theme or almost whatever you suggest. I use it almost every day!

Reading Zone (www.readingzone.com)

Reading Zone claims to contain 'Everything you need to know about children's books and authors, including new books, extracts, reviews, interviews, and competitions'. There are dedicated areas for *schools*, *families*, *children* and *young adults*. While being a useful resource for teachers of reading, it is also suitable to have available for children in the classroom.

Books for Keeps (www.booksforkeeps.co.uk)

The website says:

> Books for Keeps is the UK's leading, independent children's book magazine. It was launched in 1980 and ever since has been reviewing hundreds of new children's books each year and publishing articles on every aspect of writing for children. There are over 12,500 reviews on our new website and more than 2,000 articles including interviews with the top children's authors and illustrators.

UNIVERSITY OF WINCHESTER
LIBRARY

> The best scholars, reviewers, authors and critics write for Books for Keeps. We hold a mirror up to the children's book world and reflects back its output, issues and preoccupations with intelligence, scholarship and wit.

This my first port of call if I am looking for a particular book or want to find out what a book is like and am not able to access a hard copy. The reviews here can be relied upon to be accurate and fair. It also contains interesting articles about children's books and authors.

The sites I have described above are well-established and I personally use them. There are many many more and there is no space to list them here. When looking at the Internet for information be sure to examine the credentials of any website and try to identify the underlying view of the reading process.

Conclusion

This chapter has attempted to define what it is that makes an outstanding teacher of reading. In so doing it has attempted to find a path through the requirements of government and externally imposed assessment requirements and teaching policies and approaches and views that are grounded in research. Sometimes, the two are the same, but not always. Outstanding teachers of reading are able to find their individual path because they have a clearly defined philosophy of teaching and learning and understand what the reading process is and how it can impact on classroom experiences.

Following the publication of the National Curriculum and its implementation in schools in September 2014, expert groups were set up to create support for practising teachers. The English expert group was set up in September 2012 and published an *English Curriculum Review and Planning Tool*. This is available at www.literacytrust.org.uk/curriculum and is designed to support ITT providers, teachers, schools and trainee teachers. It takes the form of audits of practice and understanding. In each section there are five columns: principles based on the content of the National Curriculum, curriculum prompts, pedagogy prompts, assessment and outcomes for children prompts and finally outcomes for trainees. For example, the first principle quotes from the introduction to the National Curriculum for English that has already been quoted in this book, 'Reading feeds the imagination and opens up a treasure house of wonder and joy for curious young minds'.

The curriculum prompt is: How do your staff/trainees show awareness that reading widely and for enjoyment has to be developed from the earliest years? How do they develop children's positive attitudes and commitment to reading?

The pedagogy prompt is, 'How do your staff/trainees create a classroom environment that will encourage pupils to read widely and for enjoyment?'.

The assessment and outcomes prompt for children is, 'How do your staff and trainees use formative assessment to move learning forward?'.

The prompt for trainee outcomes is that, 'Trainees develop their own reading for pleasure, including expanding their knowledge of a range of books for children'.

It can be seen that these prompts, and there are many more, support a reflective evaluation of practice and understanding and can thus serve to make the teaching of reading outstanding.

The key messages of this chapter are:

- outstanding teachers of reading put meaning and texts at the centre of their teaching
- Ofsted sees outstanding teaching as being inextricably linked to the high achievements by pupils
- reading for pleasure needs to be at the heart of outstanding teaching
- much evidence can be found for the Teachers' Standards in outstanding teaching of reading
- planning for all subjects needs to include consideration of reading
- there are many sources of support and guidance available for teachers of reading
- critical reflection is the key way of becoming an outstanding teacher of reading.

Further reading

Medwell, J., Wray, D., Poulson, L. and Fox, R. (1998) *Effective Teachers of Literacy: A Report of a Research Project Commissioned by the Teacher Training Agency.* Exeter: University of Exeter.
This is an old but still meaningful study of what it is that makes teachers of literacy outstanding.
DfE (2011a) *Teachers' Standards*, https://www.gov.uk/government/uploads/system/uploads/attachment_data/file/301107/Teachers__Standards.pdf, accessed 2 August 2014.

Grigg, R. (2010) *Becoming an Outstanding Primary School Teacher.* Harlow: Pearson Education.
This is not about the teaching of reading but looks at what it means to be an 'outstanding' teacher and is written with trainee teachers in mind. At times it can feel a bit overwhelming, but there are some helpful activities and ideas in it.

CONCLUSION: READING

One of my favourite books at the moment is *I want my hat back* by Jon Klassen (2012). It tells of a bear who has lost his hat and wants it back. He wanders around disconsolately asking every animal he meets if they have seen his hat. Nobody has seen his hat and the rather sad bear politely replies, 'OK. Thank you anyway.' and goes on his way. He lies down on the floor in despair:

> Nobody has seen my hat. What if I never see it again? What if nobody ever finds it? My poor hat. I miss it so much. (2012: 12–13)

He begins to describe it to somebody and then the light dawns. The bear remembers that he has just seen his hat. The writing is all in upper case and the page is bright red. What does that tell the reader about how the bear is feeling? He runs back past all the animals to the rabbit, who was wearing his hat all along. The bear shouts at the rabbit and reclaims his hat. We see him sitting, happily wearing his hat. Then along comes another animal asking if he has seen a rabbit wearing a hat.

> No. Why are you asking me. I haven't seen him. I haven't seen any rabbits anywhere. I would not eat a rabbit. Don't ask me any more questions. (2012: 24)

What is the reader to make of that? The ending is both shocking and funny at the same time. I love it that Klassen teases the reader – we flick back to the pages and see that yes, the rabbit was wearing the hat all along – how did I miss that? Wow! The bear is so angry – look at those loud words and the red page. Where is the rabbit now? He hasn't, has he? Oh yes – he has!

For me, reading this book sums up what reading is all about. It is about joining in with the author to create the story; it's about identifying with the feeling of having lost something precious; it's about understanding the rage when it is realised that the rabbit took the hat and it's about not knowing whether to laugh, cry or be shocked at the ending. Probably a mixture of all three is about right!

I have shared this book with readers of all ages and every single one has laughed out loud and gasped at the end. Young readers have wanted to hear it over and over again and have taken the book from me to look carefully at the illustrations. One young reader listened to it twice and then read it to me all on his own. Of course, he was not decoding, he was remembering – but he was behaving as a reader and enjoying the experience of sharing a text.

There are times in the current climate when I feel a little like that bear. I go round looking for 'reading'. I see lots of excellent discrete phonics teaching; I see guided reading where children talk about the use of adjectives in the extract they are studying; I see lessons where whole classes repeat by heart stories with the accompanying actions and I see children silently reading in the ten minutes just after lunch. All these things are good and there are many superb teachers who achieve excellent results. I am looking though for that special hat that stands out from the crowd because it is red and pointy. Sometimes I want to talk in capital letters because I feel red inside at the missed opportunities.

There are however many schools and there are many teachers where the hat is firmly still in place. I have seen children laughing over books and wanting to share them with everybody who comes into the classroom; I have seen children reading to each other and discovering new texts; I have seen children sitting in front of a computer and navigating around a website to answer a question they posed; I have seen children listening to a story being read to them and crying because it made them feel so sad.

I want reading to come back. I want teachers of reading to experience and understand what reading has to offer and to share that with children. I want reading to be liberated from being just something to be decoded, something which must be simple so it can be read independently and something through which I progress as quickly as I can. To me, reading is not a race track along which children must race as fast as possible.

There is much that is missing from this book. It makes no claims to be an exhaustive account of everything to do with the teaching of reading. I could have talked much more about non-fiction and electronic texts; I could have included the use of storytelling and story sacks as part of learning to read; I could have explored the link between reading and writing in more depth. I hope that I have achieved what I hoped to achieve, and that is to ask teachers of reading to truly reflect on what reading is. If we are to call ourselves teachers of reading we need to know what it is we are teaching. Once we know what it is we are teaching, then we can begin to consider how we share that understanding with children so that they too can fully exploit all that reading has to offer.

Pennac's (1994) rights of the reader apply to us all, including the children we teach. Not all of them will be as passionate about reading as I am, neither will all teachers. It is important though that children are able to make the decision not to read, if they so do, from a position of knowing what it has to offer. That is the responsibility of the teacher of reading. As Pennac (1994, 151–2) says:

> As for the duty to educate, it consists fundamentally in teaching children to read, in initiating them in literature, and in giving them the means to judge freely whether or not they experience the 'need for books'. For, while it may be perfectly admissible that someone should reject reading, it's intolerable that he should be rejected – or think himself rejected – by it.

Being a teacher of reading is about showing children what reading can offer them – pleasure, power and purpose – and then enabling them to use reading to enrich and empower their lives. What a privilege.

REFERENCES

Adams, M.J. (1990) *Beginning to Read: Thinking and Learning about Print*. Cambridge, MA: MIT Press.

Afflerbach, P. (2005) National Reading Conference Policy Brief: High Stakes Testing and Reading. *Assessment Journal of Literacy Research*, 37 (2): 151–62.

Alexander, A. (2004) *Towards Dialogic Teaching: Rethinking Classroom Talk*. Cambridge: Dialogos.

Alexander, P.A. and Fox, E. (2004) A historical perspective on reading research and practice, in R.B. Ruddell and N.J. Unrau (eds), *Theoretical Models and Processes of Reading*, 5th edn, pp. 33–68. Newark, DE: International Reading Association.

Alexander, R. (2007) Where there is no vision … *Forum*, 49 (1): 187–99.

All Party Parliamentary Group (2011) *Overcoming the Barriers to Literacy*. www.educationengland.org.uk/documents/pdfs/2011-appge-literacy-report.pdf, accessed 16 July 2014.

Allan, J., Ellis, S. and Pearson, C. (2005) *Literature Circles, Gender and Reading for Enjoyment: Report for the Scottish Executive Education Department*. www.scotland.gov.uk/Publications/2005/11/SRLitCir, accessed 28 July 2014.

Applegate, A.J. and Applegate, M.D. (2004) The Peter effect: reading habits and attitudes of preservice teachers. *Reading Teacher*, 57 (6): 554–63.

Arrow, A.W. and Finch, B.T. (2013) Mulitmedia literacy practices in beginning classrooms and at home: the differences in practices and beliefs. *Literacy,* 47 (3): 131–41.

Atherton, F. and Nutbrown, C. (2013) *Understanding Schemas and Young Children: From Birth to Three.* London: Sage.

Au, K. (1997) A sociocultural model of reading instruction: the Kamehameha Elementary Education Program, in S.A. Stahl, *Instructional Models in Reading,* pp. 181–202. Hillsdale, NJ: Erlbaum.

Auerbach, B. (2006) Strangers in a strange land: read-alouds give us insight into others' struggles. *School Library Journal,* 52 (10): 18–21.

Bahktin, M.M. (1981) *The Dialogic Imagination.* Austin, TX: University of Texas Press.

Barker, I. (2010) Don't worry, be APPy: but onslaught of new assessment regime causes woe. *Times Educational Supplement,* 14 May, www.tes.co.uk/article.aspx?storycode=6043711, accessed 30 July 2014.

Barrs, M. and Cork, V. (2001) *The Reader in the Writer.* London: CLPE.

Barthes, R. (1993) *Mythologies.* London: Vintage Classics.

Barton, D. and Hamilton, M. (eds) (2000) *Situated Literacies: Reading and Writing in Context.* London: Routledge.

Beech, J.R. (2005) Ehri's model of phases of learning to read: a brief critique. *Journal of Research in Reading,* 28 (1): 50–58

Bell, D. (2005) Speech for World Book Day, 2 March, available at www.ofsted.gov.uk

Bennett, N., Desforges, C., Cockburn, A. and Wilkinson, B. (1984) *The Quality of Pupil Learning Experiences.* London: Lawrence Erlbaum Associates.

Bew, P. (2011) *Independent Review of Key Stage 2 Testing, Assessment and Accountability.* www.educationengland.org.uk/documents/pdfs/2011-bew-report-ks2tests.pdf, accessed 30 July 2014.

Bhabha, H.K. (1994) *The Location of Culture.* New York: Routledge.

Black, B., Harrison, C., Marshall, B. and William, D. (2002) *Working Inside the Black Box: Assessment for Learning in the Classroom.* London: GL Assessment.

Bloom, D. (1993) Necessary indeterminacy and the microethnographic study of reading as a social practice. *Journal of Research in Reading,* 16 (2): 98–111.

Bond, G.K. and Dykstra, R. (1967) The cooperative research program in first grade reading. *Reading Research Quarterly,* 32 (4): 348–427.

Booth, D. (2006) *Reading Doesn't Matter Anymore: Shattering the Myths of Literacy.* Markham, Ontario: Pembroke Publishers.

Bourdieu, P. (1993) *Language and Symbolic Power.* Cambridge, MA: Harvard University Press.

Brill, F. and Twist, L. (2013) *Where Have all the Levels Gone? The Importance of a Shared Understanding of Assessment at a Time of Major Policy Change.* NFER Thinks: What the Evidence Tells Us. Slough: NFER.

Bromley, H. (1996) Madam, read the scary book, Madam – the emergent bilingual reader, in V. Watson and M. Styles (eds), *Talking Pictures: Pictorial Texts and Young Readers.* London: Hodder.

Brooks, G. (2013) *What Works for Pupils with Literacy Difficulties? The Effectiveness of Intervention Schemes,* 3rd edn, http://webarchive.nationalarchives.gov.uk/20130401151715/ www.education.gov.uk/publications/eOrderingDownload/pri_lit_what_works0068807.pdf, accessed 3 August 2014.

Bruner, J. (1986) *Actual Minds, Possible Worlds.* Cambridge and London: Harvard University Press.

Bruner, J. (1990) *Acts of Meaning.* Cambridge, MA: Harvard University Press.

Bruner, J. (1996) *The Culture of Education.* Cambridge MA: Harvard University Press.

Bryant, P. (1993) Phonological aspects of learning to read, in R. Beard (ed.), *Teaching Literacy, Balancing Perspectives*, pp. 83–94. London: Hodder and Stoughton.

Burke, C. (1982) Redefining written language growth: the child as informant, paper presented at the 8th Australian Reading Association Conference, Adelaide.

Burkins, J.M. and Croft, M.M. (2010) *Preventing Misguided Reading: New Strategies for Guided Reading Teachers*. Newark, DE: International Reading Association.

Burnett, C. (2010) Technology and literacy in early childhood educational settings: a review of research. *Journal of Early Childhood Literacy,* 10 (3): 247–70.

Burroughs-Lange, S. (2006) *Evaluation of Reading Recovery in London Schools: Every Child a Reader 2005–2006*. London: Institute of Education, University of London.

Bussis, A., Chittenden, F., Amarel, M. and Klausner, E. (1985) *Inquiry into Meaning: An Investigation of Learning to Read*. Hillsdale, NJ: Erlbaum.

Cain, K. (2010) *Reading Development and Difficulties*. Chichester: Blackwell.

Capper, E. (2013) Children's perceptions of wider reading: to what extent do seven and eight year old children read beyond the scheme books? *Education 3–13,* 41 (1): 90–9.

Chall, J. (1983) *Stages of Reading Development*. New York: McGraw Hill.

Chambers, A. (1985) *Booktalk: Occasional Writing on Children and Literature*. London: Bodley Head.

Chambers, A. (1991) *The Reading Environment*. Stroud: Thimble Press.

Chambers, A. (2011) *Tell Me: Children, Reading and Talk with The Reading Environment*. Stroud: The Thimble Press.

Clark, C. (2013) *Children and Young People's Reading in 2012: Findings from the 2012 National Literacy Trust's Annual Survey*. London: National Literacy Trust.

Clark, C. and Burke, D. (2012) *Boys' Reading Commission 2012: A Review of Existing Research Conducted to Underpin the Commission*. London: National Literacy Trust.

Clark, C. and Rumbold, K. (2006) *Reading for Pleasure: A Research Overview*. London: National Literacy Trust.

Clark, M.M. (1976) *Young Fluent Readers*. London: Heinemann.

Clarke, S. (2008) *Active Learning through Formative Assessment*. London: Hodder Education.

Clay, M.M. (1985). *The Early Detection of Reading Difficulties: A Diagnostic Survey and Reading Recovery Procedures*. Auckland: Heinemann Educational Books.

Clay, M.M. (1991) *Becoming Literate: The Construction of Inner Control*. Auckland: Heinemann.

Cliff Hodges, G. (2010) Reasons for reading: why literature matters. *Literacy,* 44 (2): 60–68.

CLPE (1988) *The Primary Language Record: Handbook for Teachers*. London: CLPE.

Cole, M. (1990) Cognitive development and formal schooling, in L. Moll (ed.), *Vygotsky and Education,* pp. 89–110. New York, NY: Cambridge University Press.

Collier, V. and Thomas, W.P. (2001) *A National Study of School Effectiveness for Language Minority Students' Long-Term Academic Achievement*. Washington, DC: National Clearinghouse on Bilingual Education. www.usc.edu/dept/education/CMMR/CollierThomasComplete.pdf, accessed 1 August 2014.

Coltheart, M., Rastle, K., Perry, C. Langdon, R. and Ziegler, J.C. (2001) DRC: A dual-route cascade model of visual word recognition and reading aloud. *Psychological Review,* 6: 204–256.

Cook, M.A. (2005) 'A Place of Their Own': creating a classroom 'third space' to support a continuum of text construction between home and school, *Literacy,* 39 (2): 85–90.

Cowell, C. (2003) *How to Train Your Dragon*. London: Hodder.

Cox, B. (1998) *Literacy is Not Enough: Essays on the Importance of Reading*. Manchester: Manchester University Press.

Cremin, T. and Swann, J. (2012) *Report to Carnegie UK Trust and CILIP on a Two-stage Study of the Carnegie and Kate Greenaway Shadowing Scheme.* Milton Keynes: Open University.

Cremin, T., Bearne, E., Mottram, M. and Goodwin, P. (2008a) *Teachers as Readers: Phase 1 Research Report for UKLA.* Leicester: UKLA.

Cremin, T., Mottram, M., Bearne, E. and Goodwin, P. (2008b) Exploring teachers' knowledge of children's literature. *Cambridge Journal of Education,* 38 (4): 449–64.

Cremin, T., Mottram, M., Collins, F., Powell, S. and Safford, K. (2009) Teachers as readers: building communities of readers. *Literacy,* 43(1): 11–19.

Cronin, V., Farrell, D. and Delaney, M. (1999) Environmental print and word reading. *Journal of Research in Reading,* 22: 271–82.

Cummins, J. (2000) *Language, Power and Pedagogy: Bilingual Children in the Crossfire.* Clevedon: Multilingual Matters.

Davies, N. (2005) *Ice Bear.* London: Walker Books.

Davis, A. (2013) *To Read or Not to Read: Decoding Synthetic Phonics Impact No. 20.* Philosophy of Education Society of Great Britain. DOI: 10.1111/2048-416X.2013.12000.x.

DCSF (2008) *Effective Provision for Gifted and Talented Children in Primary Education,* http://webarchive.nationalarchives.gov.uk/20130401151715/www.education.gov.uk/publications/eOrderingDownload/GTPrimary.pdf, accessed 31 July 2014.

DES (1988) *National Curriculum Task Group on Assessment and Testing: A Report,* www.educationengland.org.uk/documents/pdfs/1988-TGAT-report.pdf, accessed 28 July 2014.

DES (2001) *Special Educational Needs Code of Practice,* https://www.gov.uk/government/uploads/system/uploads/attachment_data/file/273877/special_educational_needs_code_of_practice.pdf, accessed 3 August 2014.

DES (2006) *Primary Framework for Literacy and Mathematics.* London: Primary National Strategy.

DES (2007) *Letters and Sounds: Principles and Practice of High Quality Phonics.* London: Primary National Strategy.

Dewey, J. (1933) *How We Think: A Restatement of the Relation of Reflective Thinking to the Educative Process.* Chicago, IL: Henry Regency Co.

DfEE (1998) *The National Literacy Strategy: Framework for Teaching.* London: DfEE.

DfE (2010) *Phonics Teaching Materials: Core Criteria and Self-assessment,* https://www.gov.uk/government/publications/phonics-teaching-materials-core-criteria-and-self-assessment, accessed 18 July 2014.

DfE (2011a) *Teachers' Standards,* https://www.gov.uk/government/uploads/system/uploads/attachment_data/file/301107/Teachers__Standards.pdf, accessed 2 August 2014.

DfE (2011b) *The Early Years: Foundations for Life, Health and Learning – an Independent Report on the Early Years Foundation Stage to Her Majesty's Government.* London: DfE.

DfE (2013a) *English Programmes of Study: Key Stages 1 and 2,* https://www.gov.uk/government/uploads/system/uploads/attachment_data/file/335186/PRIMARY_national_curriculum_-_English_220714.pdf, accessed 30 June 2014.

DfE (2013b) *Assessing Without Levels,* http://webarchive.nationalarchives.gov.uk/20130904084116/https://www.education.gov.uk/schools/teachingandlearning/curriculum/nationalcurriculum2014/a00225864/assessing-without-levels, accessed 28 July 2014.

DfE (2013c) Reforming qualifications and the curriculum to better prepare pupils for life after school, available at www.gov.uk/government/policies/reforming-qualifications-and-the-curriculum-to-better-prepare-pupils-for-life-after-school/supporting-pages

DfE (2014) *National Curriculum in England: Framework for Key Stages 1–4,* www.gov.uk/government/publications/national-curriculum-in-england-framework-for-key-stages-1-to-4/the-national-curriculum-in-england-framework-for-key-stages-1-to-4, accessed 25 January 2015.

DfES (2001) *Progression in Phonics: Materials for Whole-class Teaching*. London: DfES.

DfES (2003) *Excellence and Enjoyment: A Strategy for Primary Schools*. London: DfES.

DfES (2005a) *Primary National Strategy. Understanding Reading Comprehension 1: What is Reading Comprehension?* London: DfES, https://bso.bradford.gov.uk/userfiles/file/Primary%20Literacy/Guided%20Reading/reading%20comprehension%201.pdf, accessed 24 July 2014.

DfES (2005b) *Primary National Strategy. Understanding Reading Comprehension 2: Strategies to Develop Reading Comprehension*. London: DfES, https://bso.bradford.gov.uk/userfiles/file/Primary%20Literacy/Guided%20Reading/reading%20comprehension%202.pdf, accessed 24 July 2014.

DfES (2005c) *Primary National Strategy. Understanding Reading Comprehension 3: Further Strategies Develop Reading Comprehension*. London: DfES, https://bso.bradford.gov.uk/userfiles/file/Primary%20Literacy/Guided%20Reading/reading%20comprehension3.pdf, accessed 24 July 2014.

DfES (2006a) *Primary National Strategy. Developing Reading Comprehension*, www.yarcsupport.co.uk/documents/devreadcomp.pdf, accessed 24 July 2014.

DfES (2006b) *Primary National Strategy. Primary Framework for Literacy*. London: DfES.

DfES (2007) *Letters and Sounds: Principles and Practice of High-quality Phonics*. Norwich: DfES.

Dombey, H. (1998) Changing literacy in the early years of school, in B. Cox (ed.), *Literacy is not Enough*, pp.125–32. Manchester: Manchester University Press and Book Trust.

Dombey, H. (2010) *Teaching Reading: What the Evidence Says*. Leicester: UKLA.

Dombey, H. and Moustafa, M. (1998) *Whole to Part Phonics: How Children Learn to Read and Spell*. London: CLPE.

Drummond, M.J. and Styles, M. (eds) (1993) *The Politics of Reading*, special issue, *Cambridge Journal of Education*.

Duke, N.K. (2000) For the rich it's richer: print experiences and environments offered to children in very low and very high socioeconomic status first-grade classrooms. *American Educational Research Journal*, 37 (2): 441–78.

Dyson, A.H. (1993) *Social Worlds of Children Learning to Write in an Urban Primary School*. New York: Teachers College Press.

Dyson, A.H. (2002) *Brothers and Sisters Learn to Write: Popular Literacies in Childhood and School Cultures*. New York: Teachers College Press.

Education Department of Western Australia (1997) *Reading Developmental Continuum*. Australia: Rigby.

Edwards, P.D. (1996) *Some Smug Slug*. London: Harper Collins.

Ehri, L.C. (1999) Phases of development in learning to read words, in J. Oakhill and R. Beard (eds), *Reading Development and the Teaching of Reading*, pp. 79–108. London: Blackwell.

Evans, L. and Goodhew, G. (1997) *Providing for Able Children: Activities for Staff in Primary and Secondary Schools*. Dunstable: Folens Publishers.

Fisher, R. (2002) *Inside the Literacy Hour: Learning from Classroom Experience*. London: Routledge/Palmer.

Fletcher, K.L. and Reese, E. (2005) Picture book reading with young children: a conceptual framework, *Developmental Review*, 25 (1): 64–103.

Flynn, N. and Stainthorp, R. (2006) *The Learning and Teaching of Reading and Writing*. Chichester: John Wiley and Sons.

Fountas, I.C. and Pinnell, G.S. (2012) Guided reading: the romance and the reality. *The Reading Teacher*, 66 (4): 268–84.

Francis, H. (1987) Hearing beginner readers read: problems of relating practice to theory in interpretation and evaluation. *British Journal of Educational Research*, 13 (3): 215–328.

Freebody, P. and Freiberg, J. (2001) Re-discovering practical reading activities in homes and schools. *Journal of Research in Reading,* 24 (3): 222–34.

Frith, U. (1985) Beneath the surface of developmental dyslexia, in K.E. Patterson, J.C. Marshall and M. Coltheart (eds), *Surface Dyslexia*, pp. 301–30. London: Lawrence Erlbaum.

Frith, U. (1986) A developmental framework for developmental dyslexia. *Annals of Dyslexia,* 36: 69–81.

Gaiman, N. (2008) *The Graveyard Book.* London: Bloomsbury.

Gamble, N. and Yates, S. (2008) *Exploring Children's Literature*, 2nd edn. London: Sage.

Gee, J.P. (1999) *An Introduction to Discourse Analysis: Theory and Method.* London: Routledge.

Geertz, Clifford. (1973) Thick description: toward an interpretive theory of culture, in C. Geertz, *The Interpretation of Cultures: Selected Essays*, pp. 3–30. New York: Basic Books.

Gerrig, R.J. (1998) *Experiencing Narrative Worlds: On the Psychological Activities of Reading.* New Haven, CT: Yale University Press.

Ghaye, T. (2010) *Teaching and Learning through Reflective Practice: A Practical Guide*, 2nd edn. London: Routledge.

Gilbert, R. and Gilbert, P. (1998) *Masculinity Goes to School.* London: Routledge.

Gleed, A. (2013) *Booktrust Reading Habits Survey 2013: A National Survey of Reading Habits and Attitudes to Books Amongst Adults in England.* London: Booktrust.

Goepel, J. and Sharpe, S.E. (2014) *Inclusive Primary Teaching: A Critical Approach.* Northwich: Critical Publishing Ltd.

Goodman, K.S. (1967) Reading: a psycholinguistic guessing game. *Journal of the Reading Specialist,* 4: 126–35.

Goodman, K.S. (1969) Analysis of oral reading miscues: applied psycholinguistics. *Reading Research Quarterly,* 5: 9–30.

Goodman, K.S. (1986) *What's Whole in Whole Language?* London: Heinemann Educational Books.

Goodman, K.S. (1992) Why whole language is today's agenda in education. *Language Arts,* 69: 354–63.

Goodwin, P. (1995) *Reluctant to Read.* Reading: Reading and Language Information Centre.

Goodwin, P. (2004) *Literacy Through Creativity.* London: David Fulton.

Goodwin, P. (2008) *Understanding Children's Books: A Guide for Educational Professionals.* London: Sage.

Goodwin, P. (2011) *The Literate Classroom*, 3rd edn. London: David Fulton.

Goouch, K. (2007) Understanding educational discourse: attending to multiple voices, in K. Goouch and A. Lambirth (eds), *Understanding Phonics and the Teaching of Reading: Critical Perspectives*, pp. 41–58. Maidenhead: Open University Press.

Goswami, U. (1986) Children's use of analogy in learning to read: a developmental study. *Journal of Experimental Psychology,* 42: 73–8.

Goswami, U. (1992) *Analogical Reasoning in Children.* Hove: Lawrence Erlbaum Associates.

Gough, P.B. and Tumner, W.E. (1986) Decoding, reading and reading disability. *Remedial and Special Education,* 7: 6–10.

Gough, P.B. and Juel, C. (1991) The first stages of word recognition, in L. Rieben and C.A. Perfetti (eds), *Learning to Read*, pp. 47–56. Hillsdale, NJ: Lawrence Erlbaum Associates.

Gough, P.B., Juel, C. and Griffith, P.L. (1992) Reading, spelling and the orthographic cipher, in P.B. Gough, L.C. Ehri and R. Treiman (eds), *Reading Acquisition*, pp. 35–47. Hillsdale, NJ: Erlbaum.

Graham, J. and Kelly, A. (2008) *Reading Under Control: Teaching Reading in the Primary School*, 3rd edn. London: Routledge.

Gregory, E. (1996) *Making Sense of a New World: Learning to Read in a Second Language.* London: Paul Chapman Educational Publishers.

Gregory, E. and Williams, A. (2000) *City Literacies: Learning to Read Across Generations and Cultures.* London: Routledge.

Grigg, R. (2010) *Becoming an Outstanding Primary School Teacher.* Harlow: Pearson Education.

Hall, N. (1987) *The Emergence of Literacy.* London: Hodder and Stoughton/UKRA.

Hall, K. (2003) *Listening to Stephen Read; Multiple Perspectives on Literacy.* Buckingham: Open University Press.

Hall, K. (2007) To codify pedagogy or enrich learning? A Wengerian perspective on early literacy policy in England, in K. Goouch and A. Lambirth (eds), *Understanding Phonics and the Teaching of Reading: Critical Perspectives*, pp. 88–100. Maidenhead: Open University Press.

Harding, D.W. (1977) Ways forward for the teacher (2): making way for the child's own 'feeling comprehension', in M. Meek, A. Warlow and G. Barton (eds), *The Cool Web*, pp. 379–92. London: Bodley Head.

Hardy, B. (1977) Narrative as a primary act of mind, in M. Meek, A. Warlow and G. Barton (eds), *The Cool Web: The Pattern of Children's Learning*, pp. 12–23. London: Bodley Head.

Harnett, P. (2010) Life history and narrative research revisited, in A. Bathmaker and P. Harnett (eds), *Exploring Learning, Identity and Power through Life History and Narrative Research*, pp. 25–36. London: Routledge.

Harrison, C. (2004) *Understanding Reading Development.* London: Sage.

Harste, J., Woodward, V. and Burke, C. (1984) *Language Stories and Literacy Lessons.* Portsmouth, NH: Heinemann.

Hattersley, R. (1998) Reading to make us glad, in B. Cox (ed.), *Literacy is Not Enough: Essays on the Importance of Reading*, pp. 50–52. Manchester: Manchester University Press.

Heath, S.B. (1983) *Ways with Words: Language, Life and Work in Communities and Classrooms.* Cambridge: Cambridge University Press.

Hilton, M. (2006) Measuring standards in primary English: issues of validity and accountability with respect to PIRLS and National Curriculum test scores. *British Educational Research Journal,* 32 (6): 817–37.

Hilton, M. (2007) A further brief response from Mary Hilton to 'Measuring Standards in Primary English: the validity of PIRLS' – a response to Mary Hilton by Chris Whetton, Liz Twist and Marion Sainsbury. *British Educational Research Journal,* 33 (6): 987–90.

Hobsbaum, A., Gamble, N. and Reedy, D. (2006) *Guided Reading*, 2nd edn. London: Institute of Education.

Holdaway, D. (1979) *The Foundations of Literacy.* Sydney: Ashton Scholastic.

Hollindale, P. (1988) *Ideology and Children's Books.* Stroud: Thimble Press.

House of Commons Education and Skills Committee (2005) *Teaching Children to Read.* London: The Stationery Office.

House of Commons Select Committee Report (2003) *Teaching Children to Read*, www. parliament.the-stationery-office.co.uk/pa/cm200405/cmselect/cmeduski/121/12103.htm, accessed 16 July 2014.

Hurry, J. and Sylva, K. (2007) Long-term outcomes of early reading intervention. *Journal of Research in Reading,* 30 (3): 227–48.

Iaquinta, A. (2006) Guided reading: a research-based response to the challenges of early reading instruction. *Early Childhood Education Journal,* 33 (6): 413–18.

Illeris, K. (2007) *How We Learn: Learning and Non-learning in School and Beyond.* London: Routledge.

Iser, W. (1978) *The Act of Reading: A Theory of Aesthetic Response*. Baltimore, MD: Johns Hopkins University Press.

Johnson, N.L. and Giorgis, C. (2003) Literature in the reading curriculum. *The Reading Teacher,* 56 (7): 704–12.

Johnston, R. and Watson, J. (2005) *The Effects of Synthetic Phonics Teaching on Reading and Spelling Attainment: A Seven-year Longitudinal Study*, www.scotland.gov.uk/Publications/2005/02/20688/52449, accessed 10 July 2014.

Johnston, R. and Watson, J. (2007) *Teaching Synthetic Phonics*. Exeter: Learning Matters.

Jolliffe, W. and Waugh, D. (2012) *Teaching Systematic Synthetic Phonics in Primary Schools*. London: Learning Matters.

Juel, C. (1991) Beginning reading, in R. Barr, M. Kamil, P. Mosenthal and D. Pearson (eds), *Handbook of Reading Research, Vol. 2*, pp. 759–88. New York, NY: Longman.

Justice, L.M. and Pence, K.L. (2005) *Scaffolding with Storybooks: A Guide for Enhancing Young Children's Language and Literacy Achievement*. Newark, DE: International Reading Association.

Kagan, S. (2005) *Rethinking Thinking – Does Bloom's Taxonomy Align with Brain Science?* San Clemente, CA: Kagan Publishing, www.KaganOnline.com, accessed 24 July 2014.

Kelly, C. (2004) Buzz Lightyear in the nursery, in E. Gregory, S. Long and D. Volk (eds), *Many Pathways to Literacy*. London: Routledge Falmer.

Kelly, R. (2005) Letter to Jim Rose from the Secretary of State, 22 June.

Kennedy, E., Dunphy, E., Dwyer, B., Hayes, G., McPhillips, T., Marsh, J., O'Connor, M. and Shiel, G. (2012) *Literacy in Early Childhood and Primary Education: Commissioned Research Report*. Dublin: National Council for Curriculum and Assessment.

King, C. and Briggs, J. (2005) *Literature Circles: Better Talking, More Ideas*, 2nd edn, Leicester: UKLA.

Kirby, J.R. and Savage, R.S. (2008) Can the simple view deal with the complexities of reading? *Literacy,* 42 (2): 75–82.

Kirtley, C., Bryant, P., MacLean, M. and Bradley, L. (1989) Rhyme, rime and the onset of reading. *Journal of Experimental Child Psychology,* 48: 224–45.

Kispal, A. (2008) *Effective Teaching of Inference Skills for Reading: Literature Review. DSCF Research Report 031*. London: DCSF.

Klassen, J. (2012) *I Want My Hat Back*. London: Walker Books.

Kucirkova, N., Messer, D., Sheehy, K. and Flewitt, R. (2013) Sharing personalised stories on iPads: a close look at one parent-child interaction. *Literacy,* 47 (3): 115–22.

Lancashire Primary Strategy (2006) *'I Can', Reading Statements*, www.dallas.lancsngfl.ac.uk/download/file/I%20can%20reading%20statements.pdf, accessed 30 July 2014.

Lane, H. and Wright, T. (2007) Maximising the effectiveness of reading aloud. *Reading Teacher,* 60 (7): 668–75.

Larrivee, B. (2000) Transforming teaching practice: becoming the critically reflective teacher. *Reflective Practice,* 1 (3): 293–307.

Larson, J. and Marsh, J. (eds) (2013) *Handbook of Early Childhood Literacy*, 2nd edn. London: Sage.

Lejeune, P. (1989) *On Autobiography*. Minneapolis, MN: University of Minnesota Press.

Lennox, S. (2012) Language, literature and literacy: authentic engagement in the early years. *Practically Primary,* 17 (2): 33–6.

Lesesne, T.S. (2006) Reading aloud: a worthwhile investment. *Voices from the Middle,* 13 (4): 50–54.

Lesser, W. (2014) *Why I Read: The Serious Pleasure of Books*. New York: Farrar, Strauss and Giroux.

Lessing, D. (1998) Love of reading, in Brian Cox (ed.), *Literacy is Not Enough: Essays on the Importance of Reading*, pp. 47–50. Manchester: Manchester University Press.

Levy, R. (2009) You have to understand words ... but not read them: young children becoming readers in a digital age. *Journal of Research in Reading*, 32: 75–91.

Levy, R. (2011) *Young Children Reading: At Home and At School*. London: Sage.

Lewis, M. and Tregenza, J. (2007) Beyond simple comprehension. *English 4–11*, 30: 11.

Liberman, I.Y. and Liberman, A.M. (1990) Whole language vs. code emphasis: underlying assumptions and their implications for reading instruction. *Bulletin of the Orton Society*, 40 (1): 51–76.

Lipman, P. (2010) *Can the Physical Environment have an Impact on the Learning Environment?* OECD: CELE Exchange.

Lockwood, M. (2008) *Promoting Reading for Pleasure in the Primary School*. London: Sage.

Loughland, T. and Kilpatrick, L. (2013) Formative assessment in primary science. *Education 3–13: International Journal of Primary, Elementary and Early Years Education*, published online www.tandfonline.com/doi/full/10.1080/03004279.2013.767850#tabModule, accessed 20 June 2014.

Lowe, V. (2007) *Stories, Pictures and Reality: Two Children Tell*. London: Routledge.

Luke, A., Carrington, V. and Kaptitzke, C. (2003) Textbooks and early childhood literacy, in N. Hall, J. Larson and J. Marsh (eds), *Handbook of Early Childhood Literacy*, pp. 249–57. London: Sage.

Mail Online (2014) 'Farah promises to stick with marathon after disappointing eighth on debut in London', 14 April 2014.

Malaguzzi, L. (1996) The right to the environment, in T. Filipini and V. Vecchi (eds), *The Hundred Languages of Children: The Exhibit*. Reggio Emilia: Reggio.

Marsh, J. (2000) Teletubby tales: popular culture in the early years language and literacy curriculum. *Contemporary Issues in Early Childhood*, 1 (2): 119–36.

Marsh, J. (2014) Purposes for literacy in children's use of the online virtual world Club Penguin. *Journal of Research in Reading*, 37 (2): 179–95.

Marsh, J., Brooks, G., Hughes, J., Ritchie, L., Roberts, S. and Wright, K. (2005) *Digital Beginnings: Young Children's use of Popular Culture, Media and New Technologies*. Sheffield: Literacy Research Centre.

Martin, T. (1989) *The Strugglers: Working with Children who Fail to Learn to Read*. Buckingham: Open University Press.

Martin, T. (2011) Readers making meaning: responding to narrative, in P. Goodwin (ed.), *The Literate Classroom*, 3rd edn, pp. 87–97. London: David Fulton.

Masonheimer, P.E., Drum, P.A. and Ehri, L.C. (1984) Does environmental print identification lead children into word reading? *Journal of Reading Behavior*, 16: 257–71.

McKee, D. (2004) *The Conquerors*. London: Anderson Press.

McMaster, R. (2013) Why read? *English Studies in Canada*, 38 (2–3): 43–61.

Medwell, J., Wray, D., Poulson, L. and Fox, R. (1998) *Effective Teachers of Literacy: A Report of a Research Project Commissioned by the Teacher Training Agency*. Exeter: University of Exeter.

Meehan, P. (1998) Beyond a chocolate crunch bar: a teacher examines her philosophy of teaching reading. *The Reading Teacher*, 51 (4): 314–24.

Meek, M. (1988) *How Texts Teach What Readers Learn*. Stroud: The Thimble Press.

Mercer, N. (2000) *Words and Minds: How we use Language to Think Together*. London: Routledge.

Merchant, G.H. (2010) *3D Virtual Worlds as Environments for Literacy Learning*, http://shura. shu.ac.uk/1206/1/Final_GM_Ed_Res.pdf, accessed 16 July 2014.

Millard, E. (2006) Transformative pedagogy: teachers creating a literacy of fusion, in K. Pahl and J. Rowsell (eds), *Travel Notes from the New Literacy Studies*. Clevedon: Multilingual Matters.

Milsom, S.F.C. (1969) *Historical Foundations of the Common Law*. London: Butterworth & Co. Ltd.

Minns, H. (1990) *Read It To Me Now: Learning at Home and School*. London: Virago.

Miskin, R. (1999) Fast track to reading: literacy. *TES Magazine* 22 January, www.tes.co.uk/ article.aspx?storycode=315580, accessed 18 June 2014.

Moje, E.B., Ciechanowski, K.M., Kramer, K., Ellis, L., Carrillo, R. and Collazo, T. (2004) Working towards third space in content area literacy: an examination of everyday funds of knowledge and discourse. *Reading Research Quarterly*, 39 (1): 40–70.

Moll, L.C. (2000) Inspired by Vygotsky: ethnographic experiments in education, in C.D. Lee and P. Smagorinsky (eds), *Vygotskian Perspectives on Literacy Research*, pp. 256–68. Cambridge: Cambridge University Press.

Montessori, M. (1966) *The Secret of Childhood*. New York: Random House.

Morgan, W. with Gilbert, P., Lankshear, C., Werba, S. and Williams, L. (1996) *Critical Literacy: Readings and Resources*. Norwood: Australian Association for the Teaching of English.

Morpurgo, M. (2012) *We are Failing too Many Boys in the Teaching of Reading*. www. theguardian.com/teacher-network/teacher-blog/2012/jul/02/michael-morpurgo-boys-reading, accessed 4 April 2014.

Morris, E. (2010) *School Libraries: A Plan for Improvement*. National Literacy Trust and Museums, Libraries and Archives.

Munton, G and Miskin, R. (2006) *Billy the Kid*, Read Write Inc phonics purple storybook. Oxford: Oxford University Press.

NAHT (2014) *Report of the NAHT Commission on Assessment*. Haywards Heath: NAHT.

Nation, K. and Angell, P. (2006) Learning to read and learning to comprehend. *London Review of Education*, 4 (1): 77–87.

National Reading Panel (2000) *Report of The National Reading Panel, Washington, DC*, www. nichd.nih.gov/research/supported/Pages/nrp.aspx/, accessed 24 July 2014.

Neumann, M.N., Hood, M. and Ford, F. (2013) Mother-child referencing of environmental print and its relationship with emergent literacy skills, *Early Education and Development*, 24 (8): 1175–93.

Newton, P. (2003) The defensibility of national curriculum assessment in England. *Research Papers in Education*, 18 (2): 101–27.

Newton, P. (2009) The reliability of results from national curriculum testing in England. *Educational Research*, 51 (2): 181–212.

NFER (2007) *Getting to Grips with Assessment: Primary*. Slough: NFER, www.nfer.ac.uk/ publications/99904/99904.pdf, accessed 28 July 2014.

Nicholson, C. (2004) Creative readers at KS2, in P. Goodwin (ed.), *Literacy Through Creativity*, pp. 65–72. London: David Fulton.

O'Sullivan, O. and McGonigle, S. (2010) Transforming readers: teachers and children in the Centre for Literacy in Primary Education Power of Reading Project. *Literacy*, 44 (2): 51–9.

Oatley, K. (1999) Why fiction may be twice as true as fact: fiction as cognitive and emotional simulation. *Review of General Psychology*, 3 (2): 101–17.

Ofsted (1996) *The Teaching of Reading in 45 Inner London Primary Schools: A Report of Her Majesty's Inspectors in Collaboration with the LEAs of Islington, Southwark and Tower Hamlets*. London: The Stationery Office.

Ofsted (2004) *Reading for Purpose and Pleasure: An Evaluation of the Teaching of Reading in Primary Schools.* London: Ofsted.

Ofsted (2005) English 2000–2005: A review of inspection evidence, www.ofsted.gov.uk, accessed 25 May 2014.

Ofsted (2010) *Reading by Six: How the Best Schools Do It.* Manchester: Ofsted.

Ofsted (2011a) *Excellence in English.* Manchester: Ofsted.

Ofsted (2011b) *The Impact of the 'Assessing Pupils' Progress' Initiative.* Manchester: Ofsted.

Ofsted (2012) *Moving English Forward.* Manchester: Ofsted.

Ofsted (2014) *School Inspection Handbook.* Manchester: Ofsted.

Olson, L.A., Evans, J.R. and Keckler, W.T. (2006) Precocious readers: past, present and future. *Journal for the Education for the Gifted,* 30 (2): 205–35.

Pardo, L. (2004) What every teacher needs to know about comprehension. *The Reading Teacher,* 58 (3): 272–9.

Paterson, K. (1978) *Bridge to Terabithia.* London: Victor Gollancz.

Paterson, C. and Chapman, J. (2013) Enhancing skills of critical reflection to evidence learning in professional practice. *Physical Therapy in Sport,* 14 (3): 133–8.

Pennac, D. (1994) *Reads Like a Novel.* London: Quartet Books.

Perera, K. (1987) *Understanding Language.* Worcester: NAAE.

Perfetti, C.K. and McCutchen, D. (1987) Schooled language competence: linguistic abilities in reading and writing, in S. Rosenberg (ed.), *Advances in Applied Psychlinguistics, Vol. 2,* pp. 105–41. Cambridge: Cambridge University Press.

Pollard, A. with J. Anderson, M. Maddock, S. Swaffield, J. Warin and P. Warwick (2014) *Reflective Teaching,* 4th edn. London: Continuum.

Porter, L. (1999) *Gifted Young Children.* Buckingham: Open University Press.

Powell, R., Chambers-Cantrell, S. and Adams, S. (2001) Saving Black Mountain: the promise of critical literacy in a multicultural democracy. *The Reading Teacher,* 54 (8): 772–81.

Powling, C. (2000) *Readers Who Don't … and How to Persuade Them Otherwise.* Reading: Reading and Language Information Centre.

Powling, C., Ashley, B., Pullman, P., Fine, A. and Gavin, J. (2003) *Meetings with the Minister: Five Children's Authors on the National Literacy Strategy.* Reading: National Centre for Language and Literacy.

Pressley, M. (2000) What should comprehension instruction be the instruction of?, in M. Kamil, P. Mosenthal, P. Pearson and R.Barr (eds), *Handbook of Reading Research,* pp. 545–561. Mahwah, NJ: Erlbaum.

Pringle Morgan, W. (1896) A Case of Congenital Word Blindness. *British Medical Journal,* 2: 1378.

Pullman, P. (1996) *Clockwork or all Wound Up.* London: Random House.

Qualifications and Curriculum Authority (2006) *Monitoring Pupils' Progress in English at Key Stage 3. Final Report of the 2003–05 Pilot.* London: QCA.

Raikes, H., Alexander, H., Luze, G., Tamis-LeMonda, C., Brooks-Gunn, J., Constantine, J., Tarulio, L. and Rodriguez, E. (2006) Mother–child bookreading in low-income families: correlates and outcomes during the first three years of life. *Child Development,* 77 (4): 924–53.

Ramus, F. (2004) The neural basis of reading acquisition, in M.S. Gazzaniga (ed.), *The Cognitive Neurosciences,* 3rd edn, pp. 815–24. Cambridge, MA: MIT Press.

Ranker, J. (2007) Using comic books as read-alouds: insights on reading instruction from an English as a second language classroom. *Reading Teacher,* 61 (4): 296–305.

Rayner, K. and Pollatsek, A. (1989) *The Psychology of Reading.* Englewood Cliffs, NJ: Prentice Hall International.

Reedy, D. (2011) Talk in guided reading sessions, in P. Goodwin (ed.), *The Literate Classroom,* 3rd edn, pp. 56–66. London: David Fulton.

Richards, C. (2006) This could be the end of teacher autonomy. *Educational Journal*, 94: 19–22.

Richmond, J. (2013) *Teaching Reading: How To*. Leicester: UKLA.

Riley, J. (1996) *The Teaching of Reading: The Development of Reading in the Early Years at School*. London: Sage.

Rolfe, G., Freshwater, D. and Jasper, M. (2001) *Critical Reflection for Nursing and the Helping Professionals*. Basingstoke: Palgrave.

Rose, F. (2011) *The Art of Immersion. Why do we Tell Stories?*, www.wired.com/2011/03/why-do-we-tell-stories/2/, accessed 11 May 2014.

Rose, J. (2006) *Independent Review of the Teaching of Early Reading, Final Report*. London: DES.

Rose, J. (2009) *Identifying and Teaching Young People with Dyslexia and Literacy Difficulties*, http://webarchive.nationalarchives.gov.uk/20130401151715/www.education.gov.uk/publications/eOrderingDownload/00659-2009DOM-EN.pdf, accessed 20 July 2014.

Rosenblatt, L.M. (1978) *The Reader, the Text, the Poem: The Transactional Theory of the Literary Work*. Carbondale and Edwardsville: Southern Illinois University Press.

Rumelhart, D.E. (1985) Toward an interactive model of reading, in R. Barr, M.L. Kamil, P. Mosenthal and P.D. Pearson (eds), *Theoretical Models and Processes of Reading*, 3rd edn. Newark, DE: International Reading Association.

Rutherford, G. (2012) *The Wyche Curriculum: Designing a Curriculum for the 21st Century*. Gloucester: Little Inky Fingers.

Ryan, A.M. and Patrick, H. (2001) The classroom social environment and changes in adolescents' motivation and engagement during middle school. *American Educational Research Journal*, 38 (2): 437–60.

Schön, D.A. (1983) *The Reflective Practitioner: How Professionals Think in Action*. New York: Basic Books.

Scribner, S. and Cole, M. (1981) *The Psychology of Literacy*. Cambridge: Cambridge University Press.

Sigman, A. (2005) *Remotely Controlled: How Television is Damaging our Lives*. London: Vermillion.

Simpson, A., Walsh, M. and Rowsell, J. (2013) The digital reading path: researching modes and multidirectionality with iPads. *Literacy*, 47 (3): 123–31.

Sinclair, J. and Coulthard, M. (1992) Towards an analysis of discourse, in M. Coulthard (ed.), *Advances in Spoken Discourse Analysis*, pp. 1–34. London: Routledge.

Smith, F. (1971) *Understanding Reading: A Psycholinguistic Analysis of Reading and Learning to Read*. New York, NY: Holt, Rinehart and Winston.

Smith, F. (1973) *Psycholinguistics and Reading*. New York, NY: Holt, Rinehart and Winston.

Smith, F. (1976) Learning to read by reading. *Language Arts*, 53: 297–99.

Smith, F. (1978) *Reading*. Cambridge: Cambridge University Press.

Smith, F. (1987) *Joining the Literacy Club: Further Essays into Education*. Portsmouth, NH: Heinemann Educational Books.

Smith, S. (2004) The non-fiction reading habits of young successful boy readers: forming connections between masculinity and reading. *Literacy*, 38 (1): 10–16.

Smith, V. (2008) Learning to be a reader: promoting good textual health, in P. Goodwin (ed.), *Understanding Children's Books*, pp. 33–42. London: Sage.

Solsken, J.W. (1993) *Literacy, Gender and Work in Families and School*. Norwood, NJ: Ablex.

Southgate, V., Arnold, H. and Johnson, S. (1981) *Extending Beginning Reading*. London: Heinemann.

Spooner, A.L.R., Baddeley, A.D. and Gathercole, S.E. (2004) Can reading accuracy and comprehension be separated in the Neale analysis of reading ability? *British Journal of Educational Psychology*, 74: 187–204.

Spufford, F. (2002) *The Child that Books Built: A Memoir of Childhood and Reading*. London: Faber and Faber.

Stahl, S. (1997) Instructional models in reading: an introduction, in S. Stahl and D.A. Hayes (eds), *Instructional Models in Reading*, pp. 1–29. Mahwah, NH: Erlbaum.

Stainthorp, R. and Hughes, D. (2004) What happens to precocious readers' performance at the age of eleven? *Journal of Research in Reading,* 27 (4): 357–72.

Standards and Testing Agency (2014a) *Key Stage 1 English Reading Test Framework (draft): National Curriculum Tests from 2016*, https://www.gov.uk/government/publications/key-stage-1-english-reading-test-framework, accessed 25 July 2014.

Standards and Testing Agency (2014b) *Key Stage 2 English Reading Test Framework (draft): National Curriculum Tests From 2016*, www.gov.uk/government/publications, accessed 30 July 2014.

Standing, E. (1998) *Maria Montessori: Her Life and Work*. Harmondsworth: Penguin Putnam Inc.

Stanovich, K.E. (1995) How research might inform the debate about early reading acquisition. *Journal of Research in Reading,* 18 (2): 87–105.

Stein, J. and Walsh, V. (1997) To see but not to read: the magnocellular theory of dyslexia. *Trends in Neurological Science,* 20 (4): 147–52.

Stephens, J. (1992) *Language and Ideology in Children's Fiction*. Harlow: Longman.

Stobart, G. (2009) Determining validity in national curriculum assessments. *Educational Research,* 51 (2): 161–79.

Stone, G. (2011) *The Digital Literacy Classroom*. Herts: UKLA Minibook.

Stuart, M. (2006) Learning to read: developing processes for recognizing, understanding and pronouncing written words. *London Review of Education,* 4 (1): 19–29.

Stuart, M., Stainthorp, R. and Snowling, M. (2008) Literacy as a complex activity: deconstructing the simple view of reading. *Literacy,* 42 (2): 59–65.

Sullivan, A. and Brown, M. (2013) *Social Inequalities in Cognitive Scores at Age 16: The Role of Reading*. CLS Working Paper 2013/10. London: Centre for Longitudinal Studies, Institute of Education.

Svensson, C. (2008) Dyslexia and Reading, in J. Graham and A. Kelly (eds), *Reading Under Control: Teaching Reading in the Primary School*, 3rd edn. London, David Fulton.

Swann, M., Peacock, A., Hart, S. and Drummond, M.J. (2012) *Creating Learning Without Limits*. Maidenhead: Open University Press.

TDA (2008) *Special Educational Needs and/or Disabilities: A Training Resource for Initial Teacher Training Providers: Primary Undergraduate Courses*. London: TDA.

Teale, W.H., Hoffman, J. and Paciga, K. (2014) What do children need to succeed in early literacy – and beyond?, in K. Goodman, R. Calfee, and Y. Goodman (eds), *Whose Knowledge Counts in Government Literacy Policies? Why Expertise Matters,* pp. 179–86. New York: Routledge.

Teale, W.H., Paciga, K.A. and Hoffman, J.L. (2010) What it takes in early schooling to have adolescents who are skilled and eager readers and writers, in K. Hall, U. Goswami, C. Harrison, S. Ellis and J. Soler (eds), *Interdisciplinary Perspectives on Learning to Read: Culture, Cognition and Pedagogy,* pp. 151–63. London: Routledge.

Treiman, R., Tincoff, R. and Richmond-Welty, E.D. (1998) Letter names help children to connect print and speech. *Developmental Psychology,* 32: 505–14.

Tucker, N. (1981) *The Child and the Book: A Psychological and Literary Exploration*. Cambridge: Cambridge University Press.

Turner, M. (1990) *Sponsored Reading Failure*. Surrey: IPSET Education Unit.

UKLA (2005) *Submission to the Review of Best Practice in the Teaching of Reading*. Herts: UKLA.

UKLA (2012) *Analysis of Schools' Response to the Year 1 Phonic Screening Test*, www.ukla.org/news/story/phonics_screening_check_fails_a_generation_of_able_readers/, accessed 16 July 2014.

UKLA (2013) *Response to the Consultation on Primary Assessment and Accountability Under the New National Curriculum*, www.ukla.org/news/story/respond_to_the_dfe_consultation_on_primary_assessment_and_accountability/, accessed 28 July 2014.

UKLA (2014) *Open Letter Concerning the Phonics Check for Six Year Olds*. Available online: www.ukla.org/news/story/open_letter_concerning_the_phonics_check_for_six_year_olds_in_english_prima/

Villaume, S.K. and Brabham, E.G. (2001) Guided reading: who is in the driver's seat? *The Reading Teacher,* 55 (3): 260–63.

Vygotsky, L.S. (1978) *Mind in Society*. Cambridge, MA: Harvard University Press.

Walker, M., Bartlett, S., Betts, H., Sainsbury, M. and Worth, J. (2014) *Phonics Screening Check Evaluation*. London: DfE, https://www.gov.uk/government/publications/phonics-screening-check-evaluation, accessed 19 July 2014.

Warner, C. (2013) Learning to comprehend, in D. Waugh and S. Neaum (eds), *Beyond Early Reading*, pp. 53–68. Northwich: Critical Publishing.

Warner, C. (2013) *Talk for Reading*. Leicester: UKLA.

Washtell, A. (2008) Reading routines, in J. Graham and A. Kelly (eds), *Reading Under Control: Teaching Reading in the Primary School*, pp. 55–91. London: David Fulton.

Waterland, L. (1988) *Read with Me: An Apprenticeship Approach to Reading*. Stroud: Thimble Press.

Waugh, D., Neaum, S. and Waugh, R. (2013) *Children's Literature in the Primary School*. London: Learning Matters.

Webb, S. (2004) *Tanka Tanka Skunk*. London: Red Fox.

Wenger, E. (1998) *A Brief Introduction to Communities of Practice*, http://wenger-trayner.com/theory/, accessed 23 July 2014.

Wiesner, D. (1999) *Tuesday*. New York: Clarion Books.

Willems, M. (2003) *Don't Let the Pigeon Drive the Bus!* London: Walker Books.

William, D. (2003) National Curriculum assessment: how to make it better. *Research Papers in Education,* 18 (2): 129–36.

Williams, M. (illustrated by William Nicholson) (1922) *The Velveteen Rabbit*. New York, NY: George H. Doran Company.

Wrigley, S. (2010) 'What Does APP Spell?', *NATE Classroom Summer*. Sheffield: NATE.

Wyse, D. and Goswami, U. (2008) Synthetic phonics and the teaching of reading. *British Educational Research Journal,* 34 (6): 691–710.

Yopp, R.H. and Yopp, H.K. (2006) Informational texts as read-alouds. *Journal of Literacy Research,* 38 (1): 37–51.

INDEX

Figures and Tables are indicated by page numbers in bold. The letters 'bib' after a page number indicate bibliographical information in the 'Further reading' sections.

UNIVERSITY OF WINCHESTER
LIBRARY